CROSS-CULTURAL TRAINING PROGRAMS

Darlene Eleanor York

BERGIN & GARVEY
Westport, Connecticut • London

Library of Congress Cataloging-in-Publication Data

York, Darlene Eleanor.
    Cross-cultural training programs / Darlene Eleanor York.
    p. cm.
    Includes bibliographical references and index.
    ISBN 0–89789–375–1 (alk. paper)
        1. Multiculturalism—United States. 2. Minorities—Employment—
United States. 3. Cross-cultural orientation—United States.
4. Employees—Training of—United States. I. Title.
HF5549.5.M5Y67   1994
658.3′1244—dc20   93–37846

British Library Cataloguing in Publication Data is available.

Copyright © 1994 by Darlene Eleanor York

All rights reserved. No portion of this book may be
reproduced, by any process or technique, without the
express written consent of the publisher.

Library of Congress Catalog Card Number: 93–37846
ISBN: 0–89789–375–1

First published in 1994

Bergin & Garvey, 88 Post Road West, Westport, CT 06881
An imprint of Greenwood Publishing Group, Inc.

Printed in the United States of America

The paper used in this book complies with the
Permanent Paper Standard issued by the National
Information Standards Organization (Z39.48–1984).

10 9 8 7 6 5 4 3 2 1

TO

JACQUELINE JORDAN IRVINE

WITH DEEP RESPECT AND GRATITUDE

Contents

Acknowledgments		ix
Introduction		xi
Chapter 1	Cracks in the Melting Pot	1
Chapter 2	Rigging the Races	13
Chapter 3	The World on a String	25
Chapter 4	Ourselves as Strangers	39
Chapter 5	The Inexact Science of Helping	57
Chapter 6	Deliberate Remedies Carefully Applied	71
Chapter 7	Charting the Routes	101
Chapter 8	Some Suggestions for Building a Better World	131
References		145
Index		183

Acknowledgments

An undertaking of this kind depends on the time, resources, and talent of many people. I wish to acknowledge the following people who have contributed greatly to my understanding of culture and its consequences. Jacqueline Jordan Irvine, my mentor, guide, and friend, made the whole journey with me. Carole Hahn and Vanessa Siddle-Walker provided guidance in the creation and execution of the project. I also wish to thank Mary Jo McGee Brown, George Englehard, James Gustafson, Fraser Harbutt, Bob Jensen, Jim Miller, Don Riechard, and Charles Strickland—all of whom influenced my thinking during the past few years. Thanks also to Bob Denby, Bill Jones, and Don Mocker from the University of Missouri, who first encouraged me to pursue advanced work.

This book could not have been written without a fellowship from the Emory University Graduate School of Arts and Sciences. I wish to thank Lynn Flint and Jude Grant at Greenwood whose enthusiasm and confidence were greatly appreciated throughout. My gratitude also goes to Denise Beltzner and the Frontline Group. Finally, I wish to thank my family and many friends who gave their support, love, and encouragement throughout this process. Their confidence and faith kept me strong.

INTRODUCTION

Last summer I had lunch with a man who is the head of a PBS affiliate in a major city. He is well traveled and well educated, and he carries influence in a media environment sensitive to many current social issues. As the conversation drifted toward areas of my research in culture, I expected his private conversation to mirror his institutional image. Instead, he repeated a litany of racial and cultural explanations I frequently hear: that color barriers are imaginary; that too much has been given to minorities from the government; and that differences in vocational and educational achievement among cultural groups are attributable to deficits in effort, values, and ability. He was sincere and commanding.

He said these freely—as do many people—because I am white. At the office where he must work with people of color, he tells me, he publicly accepts the idea of multiculturalism and cultural diversity. When politically necessary, he champions it.

He is astute enough to know that the cultural landscape of his professional world is changing. He has learned the rhetoric of change, but he has not changed. He has gone through the motions of change, but his perspective on cultural diversity remains unchanged. He can unhesitatingly accept a minority middle manager on his staff who "works as hard as the white execs." He cannot accept minorities whose work ethics or priorities or management styles deviate from his own.

His thinking underscores three difficulties present in American social discourse about cultural and racial equality. The first difficulty is that the legislation of the 1960s mandated changes in areas of public discrimination, but left unattended areas of private confusion. We are not sure how to build cultural bridges. Following the lead of the federal government, we continue to institutionalize cultural contact. Our places of work now have bulletin boards honoring Black History Month and Native American Awareness Week. We've created Japanese-style work teams. We've learned a few phrases in Spanish. In the rush to create new programs and policies for equality, we have almost completely overlooked powerful dimensions of culture that must be addressed on the human level in the workplace and must be addressed one employee at a time. Policies of acceptance and appreciation are useless when they exist only in institutional language and have no real meaning for employees. A new way of thinking about cultural change is needed.

The second difficulty is that levels of racial tension and ambiguity within the workplace have resisted efforts to decrease them. We are unclear about what causes the tensions, how to remedy them, and how to measure subsequent levels of racial cooperation and cross-cultural competence. Our schools and streets have once again become areas where our racial tensions are displayed, yet we frequently view the workplace as insulated from racism and bigotry. It is as though the camaraderie we establish with ethnically diverse co-workers is unattached to our broader cultural and social troubles. If our coffee breaks and corporate cafeterias are divided by color, we accept the racial divisions as a natural, normal part of working in America. Yet tensions are close to the surface. When promotions are given, when salaries are raised, when layoffs are announced, our sensitivities to color and culture are heightened. A way to evaluate the impact of cultural change is needed, as are intervention strategies to encourage positive cross-cultural cooperation at work.

Finally, the third difficulty is our current view of the value of culture in the workplace. In the drive to increase profit margins and to strengthen our competitive edge globally, we are learning that no institution can achieve its potential when employees operate within a system of confusing and sometimes contradictory cultural codes. A new atmosphere of communication and cooperation is needed, as are the effective means to create that atmosphere.

This is a study of culture in the workplace. It is not a study of corporate culture—the idiosyncratic values and rituals peculiar to specific companies. Instead, it is a study of the ways in which our broader cultural identities—our language, race, dress, patterns of thought, values, and behaviors—function within the American workplace, the school, the hospital. Important to the discussion is an examination of the personal changes, cultural changes, and institutional changes that occur when people from different cultural backgrounds work together.

More specifically, this is a study of the remedies that are being tested to cure racial and cultural tension at work. Cross-cultural training—once used to prepare missionaries, members of the Diplomatic Corps, and Peace Corps volunteers—is now being used to train people in education, business, health care, and a broad range of social service fields. This study examines who is doing what, and how well it is being done. It attempts to elucidate the most effective procedures for training employees to work in culturally diverse environments. More than 500 cross-cultural programs are analyzed, spanning some four decades in more than a dozen different occupations.

Finally, this study offers suggestions on ways to make places of work more culturally responsive. It is hoped that this study will draw attention to the ways that cultural diversity can operate positively in culturally diverse places of work, so that the talents and creativity of all types of professionals and artisans from many different cultural backgrounds can be effectively shared.

PURPOSE OF THE STUDY

To ease workplace tension, to lower failure rates, and to increase effectiveness among workers in cross-cultural environments, cross-cultural training has been implemented in many organizations, with varying results. Cross-cultural training begins with the assumption that people in one culture have difficulty when they enter another culture, and that cognitive, affective, or behavioral training (or some combination of the three) can ease the difficulty (Landis & Brislin, 1983). Thus, the goals of cross-cultural training programs are to achieve changes in the ways trainees think, feel, and behave, and to make them more effective in culturally different work environments.

The chapters that follow examine cross-cultural training from a variety of theoretical, research, and application perspectives. Theories of cultural anthropology, cross-cultural psychology, intercultural communication, social psychology, and behavioral psychology have all contributed to our understanding of cross-cultural contact and its potentially deleterious effects. Pertinent research that examines how cross-cultural trainees are selected, trained, tested, and evaluated is also examined. Finally, recommendations for cross-cultural training are included.

QUALITATIVE ETHNOLOGY

This study borrows from the traditions and research framework of ethnology—a type of research that systematically compares qualitative studies in order to interpret meaning, to clarify research foci, and to resolve existing substantive, methodological, or interpretive problems (Adams & Schvaneveldt, 1985; Noblit & Hare, 1988). Essentially, the work of the qualitative ethnologist is to define, synthesize, and interpret. The idea is to create an environment of interpretation that allows for a "reciprocal translation of studies into each other" (Noblit & Hare, 1988, p. 26). The purpose of this research is to "seek out new insights, ask questions, and assess phenomena in a different perspective" (Adams & Schvaneveldt, 1985, p. 103).

Knowledge in the social sciences does not exist in a vacuum; it is used to improve practice in the field. Thus, it becomes important, when large bodies of complementary research exist, to examine how research constructs are conceptualized, how variables are selected and defined, how explanations and evaluations are generated, and how interpretations are made.

The purpose of qualitative ethnology is to provide an adequate interpretive explanation of these research concerns relevant to the specific studies selected, despite the potential lack of generalizability of the findings to other fields of research (Geertz, 1973). Thus, the aim of qualitative ethnology is twofold: first, to develop adequate, appropriate methods of analysis specific to the research examined; and second, to generate meaningful interpretations of the synthesized research. From these, further research directions can be identified and more appropriate implementation in the field can be achieved.

Of the two major paradigms used by social scientists—that is, positivist and interpretivist—qualitative ethnology originates from within the interpretivist paradigm. Rather than using experimental data, the ethnologist relies on ethnographic study and seeks explanations for social and cultural events in the context observed (Bogdan & Biklen, 1982). Significance does not arise from statistical analyses of selected variables, but from meaning understood within the society under examination, from the "webs of significance" (Geertz, 1973) that communities use to order their lives. When, as in qualitative ethnology, a great many ethnographic studies are synthesized, the aim is to place the studies within a larger framework of examination in order to generate more holistic meaning and "to draw cross-case conclusions" (Noblit & Hare, 1988, p. 13).

The synthesis of knowledge exists in both the positivist and interpretivist paradigms. Qualitative ethnology, which arises from within the interpretivist school, has its counterpart in the positivist school: meta-analysis. Meta-analysis allows many small-scale studies to be examined simultaneously in order to "integrate numerous and diverse findings and to apply the full power of statistical methods to the task" (Glass, McGraw & Smith, 1981, p. 21). Meta-analysis, then, provides a means of synthesizing knowledge within the positivist paradigm. However, although both qualitative ethnology and meta-analysis share a common goal—that of synthesizing knowledge—the similarity extends no further.

Qualitative ethnology contains four distinct characteristics not congruent with the process of meta-analysis. First, the knowledge base in qualitative ethnology is emic; that is, meaning is understood from within the community examined, not imposed by the researcher. Second, the understanding of meaning is holistic; that is, an effort is made to describe multiple perspectives rather than to isolate pure variables for manipulation. Third, the examination is historical in nature: events are placed within a context that includes some understanding of their antecedents and consequences within the community. Fourth, the explanations are inclusive; that is, meaning is derived from a variety of perspectives rather than from statistical significance (Spicer, 1976). In short, meta-analysis extracts observation and quantifies it; qualitative ethnology studies meaning and interprets it. Thus, the knowledge yielded from qualitative ethnology is different from that gained through meta-analysis.

Noblit and Hare (1988) define three types of qualitative ethnologies, which may be applied separately or in concert. They are the reciprocal translation synthesis, the refutational synthesis, and the lines-of-argument synthesis. The reciprocal translation is essentially additive; that is, each separate study is assumed to complement the others and to contain some similarity to the whole. Each study provides new information that allows for a constant comparative method of analysis. By contrast, the refutational synthesis assumes that, rather than being complementary, each study is contradictory to the others. Studies are examined to unearth competing theories, paradoxical assumptions, and incongruent findings. Finally, the lines-of-argument synthesis assumes that studies are neither complementary nor contradictory; they are cumulative. In other words, each study provides some clue to a larger design: complementary and contradictory findings are considered clues to new meanings and new explanations. Each study represents one line of a broad but essentially consistent argument.

In this study, the lines-of-argument approach was used because, first, the reciprocal translation approach required sufficient similarity among the studies to allow for a comparison of like entities, and cross-cultural training literature did not provide such a similarity; and, second, the refutational synthesis required an inherent dissimilarity among studies—which restricted the interpretive power of a cross-cultural training research synthesis. The lines-of-argument approach demanded that both complementary and contradictory results be specified without diminishing the potential interpretation of results. Because many academic fields are included in the examination and many occupations are described in the training programs, this method both restricted generalizations and encouraged new interpretations of research findings.

In interpretivist study, two different researchers may generate different findings from observation of the same context. This happens because each brings different experiences and values to the study. Furthermore, each brings a unique constellation of analytical preferences to the data (Atkinson, 1990; Coustas, 1992; Feleppa, 1988; Hammersley, 1992). These different findings, however, would both be considered reliable and valid if they did not yield "contradictory or incompatible results" (Bogdan & Biklen, 1982, p. 44). The sole criterion for determining reliability and validity within the interpretivist paradigm is that of establishing the closeness of the relationship between context observed and findings generated.

Turner's (1980) understanding of social science was based on three broad premises: (1) that all social science is inherently comparative; (2) that the comparison is essentially interpretive; and (3) that new explanations derived from broad comparisons must be inductive. As a logical consequence of such inductive comparison, an interpretation of multiple studies must necessarily lose some degree of specificity in order to gain a needed abstraction of the data as a whole. In qualitative ethnology, material from each study is compared to all other studies, and new interpretations are generated (Naroll, 1968; Naroll, Michik & Naroll, 1976).

In one sense, findings from such a method of analysis constitute an interpretation of interpretations (Noblit & Hare, 1988). The new interpretation is at once analogical, metaphoric, and idiomatic. It must explain and interpret; it must invite complexity rather than closure. The aim of this study was to be as inclusive as possible. The research selected for examination spans almost four decades of cross-cultural training research. Several fields of study are represented: education, theology, health care, business, and counseling, as well as research generated in several organizations, including the U.S. military, the Peace Corps, and Teacher Corps.

Cross-cultural training program literature meets few standardized research criteria. Opinion papers, recommendations, information analyses, theoretical arguments, course and program descriptions, as well as quantitative and qualitative studies take on an ill-defined shape. Thus, not all studies consciously or consistently adhere to a single theoretical base, a clearly defined set of variables, or a particular method of training. In many cases, the inclusion of a control group and statistical verification are lacking. Discerning which training effects are fully linked to which causes is often difficult.

Furthermore, this study is limited by the treatment of cross-cultural training as a generalizable construct, regardless of the field or vocation to which it is applied. Real differences in job task—not directly considered in this study—may influence cross-cultural training outcomes. Finally, this study does not include training literature pertaining to programs outside North America (specifically the United States) although several countries have examined cross-cultural training in a variety of occupations. These were eliminated for the sake of brevity. Also, almost all of the training programs in the United States are offered for middle-class whites. Because of the preponderance of this research perspective and in order to maintain design consistency, historical perspectives from other cultures were not specifically addressed.

Although this study encompasses many organizations and academic disciplines working in the area of cross-cultural training and research, not all groups are represented equally. The largest proportion of published research is in the area of education; the smallest, from the military. Hence, this study reflects, to some degree, the levels of available research from each field. This is not to imply that most cross-cultural training is done in education. However, educators are striving to find immediate solutions to difficult cultural problems that impact the lives both of teachers and children in classrooms. Furthermore, public education enjoys wide public interest. If at no other level of involvement, all American taxpayers support schools. Hence, the attention and interest generated in this field are understandable. Nevertheless, many programs are used in other organizations. However, not all are published and, of those that are, some—as in the case with the military—are not accessible without government clearance.

GENERAL CONTENT OF CHAPTERS

Chapter 1 explores dimensions of cultural change in the United States. An examination of demographic changes is included that illustrates ways these changes influence how we educate children in our schools, the ways we construct our neighborhoods and communities, and the ways we conduct business in the workplace. These data suggest that our abilities to train people to enjoy working with culturally different people and to be effective in their work are lacking. Given the influx of new cultures and languages, our chances of creating a productive culturally diverse workforce seem to be diminishing.

Chapter 2 is an examination of relations between ethnic groups in the United States. The chapter explores theories of ethnic conflict and examines research that suggests minority status may shape the personalities and world views of minority group members. A central concern in this chapter is whether or not it is defensible to consider domestic subcultures and foreign cultures in the study of cross-cultural training, or whether a psychic history of racism and discrimination weakens the effectiveness of training between ethnic groups in the United States.

Chapter 3 is an examination of several culture theories and the implications these theories have for cross-cultural training. The chapter also considers the research surrounding the difficulties of cross-cultural contact. The research examining aggregate contact between cultures is reviewed, emphasizing those elements of contact that seem least and most resistant to the impact of cross-cultural training.

Chapter 4 explores the problems sojourners experience when they travel between cultures. The concept of culture, the theory and research surrounding culture shock, cultural adaptation, and cross-cultural contact are examined. Unlike Chapter 3, which addressed the difficulties of cross-cultural contact among groups, the examination of cross-cultural contact in this chapter narrows to a focus on individuals.

Chapter 5 is a description of the history of cross-cultural training in the United States. The political and social agendas that surrounded the training at various times are examined in some detail. Current cross-cultural philosophies and goals are discussed from within this historical context.

Chapter 6 is a survey of organizations that have used cross-cultural training. Many of the experiments that were attempted through the years and subsequent modifications in training are examined. Different organizations pursue cross-cultural training to achieve different results in employees. Whether these stated goals alter the process of training, or whether crossing cultures carries its own pattern of difficulties that transcend job descriptions, is explored.

Chapter 7 discusses the results of the training, emphasizing methods of selection, training, testing, and evaluation. A synthesis of the research findings across organizations is used to explore several aspects of training so that a more holistic view of training can be gained.

Finally, Chapter 8 suggests ways cross-cultural training might be better used to create culturally sensitive and highly effective places of work. The chapter includes a discussion of the special difficulties of such training as well as specific recommendations for implementing cross-cultural training in different organizations. Some of these recommendations are applicable despite vocational differences; some will be better fitted to occupations that incorporate other kinds of intensive employee training. Finally, a model for cross-cultural training is proposed.

In some cross-cultural work environments, the nature of the task rather than the cultural climate of the workplace may prove to be the best way to explain differences in employee outcomes. At other times, task and culture may be so intertwined that distinguishing between them may add little to our understanding. Whatever the relationships between and among people-as-workers and people-as-culture-bearers, there is sufficient evidence that our places of work and our work itself can be influenced by our cultural differences. These differences are not viewed as undifferentiated and irreconcilable; rather, culturally different employees are the complex products of our collective and distinct cultural histories.

CROSS-CULTURAL TRAINING PROGRAMS

1

CRACKS IN THE MELTING POT

> I can show you what is left. After the pride, passion, agony, and bemused aspiration, what is left is in our hands.
> —Robert Penn Warren
> *World Enough and Time*

On the evening of March 3, 1991, after a high-speed police chase, a black man was forced out of his car and surrounded by police. The man was Rodney King, and in the next eighty-one seconds, King—lying defenseless and unarmed on the pavement—was struck fifty-six times by uniformed white police officers using nightsticks. Yet in Simi Valley, the North Los Angeles suburb where charges against police in the arrest of King were heard by a jury composed of ten whites, one Asian and one Hispanic, the police were acquitted on all but one count.

Within three hours after the jury's decision, South Central Los Angeles—a forty-six-square mile area filled with poverty, drugs, and gangs—erupted into riots. In the next two days, more than 3,700 fires were set, more than forty people were killed, and media coverage of white passersby dragged from their cars and beaten by angry blacks mirrored the Rodney King beating in intensity and fury (Ellis, 1992).

In the weeks that followed, as the fires were extinguished and the streets grew calm, observers of race relations suggested that there were lessons Americans did not learn during the Civil Rights Movement of the 1960s. We did not learn to get along. More importantly, we did not acknowledge the strength of cultural differences between groups, and the ways in which those differences are complicated by poverty, unequal educational opportunities, unequal economic attainment, and a tradition of racism. The growing polarization of American society along racial, educational, and economic lines makes it difficult to understand, accept, and cooperate with those unlike ourselves.

Yet the Rodney King incident was not an aberration, an isolated remnant left over from the turbulent 1960s. Excessive police force against minority groups has a long history in the United States. In 1983, when a police officer was killed by members of a black religious cult, the Memphis, Tennessee, tactical police squad descended on the seven cultists (who were armed with two .38 revolvers) and killed them all. Three cultists were shot in the back or in the back of the head (Kovel, 1984). It is estimated that more than half of all police-caused deaths are to nonwhite people (Kovel, 1984). Dennis (1987) outlined a recent record of excessive police force used against blacks:

- In 1983, a thirty-five-year-old black man died at the hands of the New York transit police.

- In 1984, a twenty-year-old black male was shot to death by white police officers as he walked down a New York street.

- In 1985, a black honors graduate of a leading prep school was shot to death on the street in New York City by white plainclothes officers.

There is further evidence of police treatment of blacks that is not violent, but humiliating. Wainwright (1987), for example, points to the black man in California accused by a white mounted police officer of walking his dog without a license. The officer arrested the man, tied him to the saddle with a rope, and had him walk behind the horse to jail.

RACIAL TENSION IN THE AMERICAN SOCIAL LANDSCAPE

In addition to discriminatory police treatment, street violence among the races is escalating and is moving in all directions—white against black, black against white, black against Asian, white against Asian, and so on:

- In 1982, a thirty-four-year-old white man was chased onto a major highway and killed by a gang of black youths in Brooklyn, New York (Dennis, 1987).

- In 1989, a black youth, Yusuf Hawkins, was killed by a white gang in the Brooklyn neighborhood of Bensonhurst (Stone, 1989).

- In 1986, a forty-four-year-old black woman and her two daughters were subjected to taunts, broken windows, graffiti, and bottle rockets when they rented a house in an all-white area of Cleveland. One night the family shot a rifle into a crowd of whites, wounding eight. In another all-white Cleveland area, a black woman was killed when her house was firebombed (Klein, 1990; *Time* Staff, 1986).

- In 1990, a black gang cornered three Vietnamese men on the street, fracturing the skull of one of the Vietnamese with a claw hammer (Klein, 1990).

- In 1988, two Detroit white men chased and killed an Asian man with a baseball bat after the Asian, who was attending his bachelor party, gave a white dancer a tip (Moore, 1988).

This litany of racial animosity is not limited to lonely streets in dangerous neighborhoods. Racism seeps into American institutions and into the social fabric of everyday life. Unchecked, it takes on a life of its own, and it gains status. It becomes part of the vernacular, part of our social currency, part of the way things are.

Racism has become part of American sports. In an interview about major league baseball, Al Campanis, then vice-president of the Los Angeles Dodgers, said that, while blacks made fine players, they lacked the "necessities" to be major league managers (Jackson, 1987). The notion that minority athletes (primarily blacks) are body oriented while coaching belongs to whites—who are command oriented—is part of sports tradition. For example, the National Basketball Association, whose players are almost all black, employs only two black coaches on its twenty-three teams (Kovel, 1984). Television ads of black athletes selling sneakers or soft drinks encourage many black youths to practice for major league sports in deteriorating inner-city neighborhoods, where the odds are more than 20,000 to 1 against success (Kovel, 1984).

Racial and ethnic divisions in American society have become institutionalized, and the divisions surface at all levels of social exchange. For example, in a rather recent issue of *Life* (Tiny cuts and constant pressure, 1988), blacks reported being refused admission into swanky nightclubs, and they reported having tips automatically added to restaurant checks. In St. Louis, white merchants requested and were granted the right to block a footbridge leading from black East St. Louis, Illinois, to downtown St. Louis, Missouri, during a street fair (Tiny cuts and constant pressure, 1988). Finally, a KKK television program, White Aryan Resistance (WAR), now appears on cable channels in fifteen major cities (Miller, 1987).

CULTURE AND THE CLASSROOM

Perhaps most surprising is the degree to which racism has recently flared on the American college campus. The period of university education—traditionally a time when scholarship took precedence over group identity—has become a time for using group identity as a personal and political weapon (Stafford, 1992). The Justice Department reports a growing number of racist episodes on campuses across the country—nearly 300 in 1988 alone (Corn & Morley, 1988). In the San Francisco Bay Area, for example, the Justice Department reported a 62 percent rise in "hate crimes" against Asian-Americans, prompting the University of California at Berkeley to limit its Asian enrollment (Moore, 1988).

Since 1982, racial animosity and vandalism have made national news at Dartmouth, where the Dartmouth Review published a satire of black students on campus titled "Dis Sho' Ain't No Jive, Bro." At the University of Michigan at Ann Arbor a campus radio station gave air time for listeners to call in anti-black jokes, and at Indiana University at Bloomington a black student's dormitory door was defaced with "Nigger" and "KKK" and then burned. At the prestigious University of Pennsylvania an all-white fraternity hired two black strippers and shouted racial epithets. At the University of Mississippi a recently established all-black fraternity house was gutted by arsonists (Randolph, 1988), and at the Citadel—a predominantly all-white military college—a black cadet awoke to find five of his classmates dressed as Klansmen leaving a burning cross in his room (Howard, 1987).

Not only at the university level, but at every level of education there exists mounting evidence that minority children are being systematically excluded from social participation and academic attainment (Carnegie Foundation for the Advancement of Teaching, 1988; College Board, 1988). A recent study showed that, as early as age two, both black and white preschoolers select positive qualities to describe whites, and negative to describe blacks (Perry & Bussey, 1984). By age six, children form ingroups and outgroups. Children not only label but also frequently mistreat outsiders (Ostow, 1991). This perceptual and behavioral discrimination becomes problematic as children enter schools. In a study of a racially integrated secondary school, Collins (1979), for example, found that white students participated in student government and the yearbook; black students tended to join the school chorus or a sports team. Collins concluded that the discrepancies of participation in school activities by race indicated that students of different races, when given the opportunity to interact, avoid cross-race contact. Instead, racial resegregation creates schools-within-schools: a black school and a white school that function separately but are housed in the same facility.

Institutional practices create further difficulties. Methods of school financing that discriminate against poor children and children of color have a long history

(Kozol, 1991). Additionally, other institutional practices and policies—such as ability tracking (Oakes, 1988), student resegregation (Schofield, 1986), minimum-competency curricula, and student discipline policies that punish a disproportionate number of minority students—have led Irvine (1990) and other educational researchers to conclude that the processes and products of public educational institutions are not synchronized with the culture, learning styles, and aspirations of minority children.

These institutional policies are complicated by teachers who are not trained to understand or accept cultural differences. Monocultural teachers may try to propose solutions for cultural "problems" they do not understand. Grubis (1985) tells of new teachers in the Alaskan bush who visited the homes of their native students and were horrified to discover that food cupboards in all the houses were bare. Fearing the approaching winter and mass starvation, the teachers demanded the federal government provide food for the natives. The government complied, airlifting thousands of pounds of canned meat into the village. The natives opened the cans and promptly fed the meat to the village dogs. Alaskans eat only fresh or smoked meat; they consider canned meat unsuitable for humans. A few days later, when the herds came close to the village, the Alaskans killed enough caribou to last the year.

A more recent study of teachers was conducted by Law and Lane (1987). The Bogardus Social Distance Scale (Bogardus, 1959)—an instrument that asks respondents to rank various social groups on levels of preferred social intimacy (e.g., "would accept in marriage" to "would exclude from my country")—was given to 141 student teachers at the end of their training. All the teachers were white. These newly trained teachers exhibited less tolerant attitudes toward minorities of any mainstream group tested in the six previous decades. Furthermore, the teachers ranked as almost wholly unacceptable a purely fictitious group, the "Pyreviarians."

THE COLORS OF AMERICA

If racism, and the attendant social, educational, and economic distance it creates, have been historically legitimized and reinforced by the weight of white numerical superiority, demographic data indicate that the scales are tipping. By the year 2050, there will be more minorities than whites in the United States (Abbasi & Hollman, 1991). In fact, by the year 2000, blacks will be the majority population in fifty-three major U.S. cities (Coates & Jarratt, 1987). In terms of speed of growth, the Native American population leads all other minorities, quadrupling within the last two decades (Rosenberg, 1991). However, in terms of proportionate population size, Abbasi and Hollman (1991) suggest the following probabilities for minority population growth by the year 2000:

- Asian-Americans will increase by 22 percent.

- Hispanic Americans will increase by 21 percent.

- Black Americans will increase by 12 percent.

- White Americans will increase by 2 percent.

- By the year 2015, Hispanics will outnumber blacks in the United States.

Not all changes in demographic composition will stem from shifts in native populations, however. Immigration will continue to account for a high percentage of U.S. net population growth (approximately 25 percent per year in recent years); furthermore, many of the new immigrants are not from traditional countries of immigration—such as Britain and Western Europe—but from Mexico, Eastern Europe, South and East Asia, Latin America, and Africa (Coates & Jarratt, 1987). More than 66 percent of the world's total immigration is to the United States (Hodgkinson, 1986), and some demographers estimate that the combination of legal and illegal immigrants per year entering the United States is equal to 1 million (Coates & Jarratt, 1987). The United States accepts more refugees for permanent resettlement than any other country in the world (Haines, 1985a, 1985b, 1985c).

THE CHANGING AMERICAN WORKFORCE

Both internal and external pressures have worked against stabilizing American society during this period of cultural change. Externally, newly industrialized countries, such as Brazil, and Pacific Rim countries have captured a growing percentage of the world trade. The United States—suffering from a staggering trade deficit, high unemployment, increased foreign ownership and management of formerly U.S. owned companies (Coates & Jarratt, 1987; Ronen, 1986), and a workforce in which one out of every five workers reads at or below a fifth grade level (Wagel, 1990)—continues to lose a competitive edge in the global marketplace. Abbasi and Hollman (1991) estimate that U.S. businesses now lose $20 billion of global trade annually because of rising rates of illiteracy, and that nearly

3 million functional illiterates enter the U.S. workforce every year. Ironically, the cost of maintaining the Equal Employment Opportunity Commission—charged with ending discriminatory practices in the workplace—now exceeds $550 million annually (Glazer, 1983), making it one of the most costly government agencies.

Internally, economic and employment difficulties mount. The U.S. workforce is growing more quickly than the country's job pool (Rosenberg, 1991). Although it is estimated that 75 percent of all new jobs in the next two decades will require postsecondary education (Hankin, 1990), 5 million of the nearly 8 million jobs created since 1982 have been low-skill and minimum-wage work (Coates & Jarratt, 1987).

Many of these new jobs will be taken by women and minorities. In 1985, almost half of all workers entering the American workforce were white males; however, between 1985 and 2000, fewer than 15 percent of the total number of workers entering the U.S. workforce during this period will be white males (Abbasi & Hollman, 1991). Nevertheless, despite Equal Employment Opportunity and Affirmative Action guidelines, black unemployment rates are double those of whites (Coates & Jarratt, 1987), and more than 30 percent of all Hispanic families—many of them employed full-time—live at or below the poverty line (Reusswig, 1981). In fact, more than 4 million full-time workers in 1988 were eligible for poverty benefits (Hodgkinson, 1989). Recently, the percentage of white employment—traditionally the highest in the United States—was surpassed by the influx of older and more highly educated Cuban refugees (Haines, 1985c). The American workforce is changing, and the rise of women and minorities has forced many companies to search for new, culturally responsive styles of leadership (Banach, 1990; Crump, 1989; Edwards, 1991; Gemson, 1991; Hankin, 1990; Hui, 1990; Rubin, 1991).

NEW LANGUAGES, NEW CHALLENGES

The increase of languages other than English in the school and business communities has created further problems. Buchanan (1990) estimates that more than 30 million Americans speak a language other than English at home. As early as 1979, Reusswig (1981) estimated that almost 4 million children in U.S. public schools needed some form of English training to aid them in understanding the regular school curriculum. More recently, Haberman and Post (1990) conducted a language census among schoolchildren in Los Angeles and found that more than 184 different languages are represented among the children enrolled in public schools.

Telephone operators at the Southern California Gas and Power Company, for example, speak Cantonese, Mandarin, Spanish, Vietnamese, and English (Hodgkinson, 1986). Under Title VII of the Elementary and Secondary Education Act of 1974, parents of children who speak a variety of languages—including Cherokee, Menominee, and Vietnamese—have successfully demanded that American schools educate their children in their native language instead of English, despite the lack of qualified teachers and the lack of additional funding necessary to pay them (Glazer, 1983; Williams, 1981).

THE COLOR OF POWER

Cultural diversity, argues Dorotich and Stephan (1984), "is a political fact and social fact and economic fact and cultural fact and psychological fact" (p. 96). Nonetheless, the educational and economic disparities between whites and non-whites in the United States have created a condition in which people of color encounter few other people of color in positions of leadership or influence in the American workplace. For example, within the academy, American professors are predominantly white: only 4 percent of full-time faculty at four-year state universities and colleges are black, and the number appears to be dropping (Collins, 1990). Between 1982 and 1986, the number of black males receiving doctoral degrees decreased by more than 40 percent (Collins, 1990); and between 1980 and 1990, the total number of black doctorates dropped by nearly one-third (Stephan, 1991). Although the percentage of international students in higher education is expanding (Grubbs, 1985), most college students in the United States are educated by white professors. Furthermore, pressure to desegregate colleges and universities may significantly lessen—or even eliminate—federal funding to historically black colleges and universities (Stephan, 1991). Minority students in higher education encounter few minority professors.

The same trend is apparent among schoolchildren of color. The number of minority candidates for teaching certificates is steadily eroding. By the turn of the century, more than 95 percent of U.S. teachers will be white (Banks, 1991). In less than one decade, from 1975 to 1982, the number of newly certified black teachers dropped 73 percent (Murnane, Singer, Willett, Kemple & Olsen, 1991). However, the seventeen largest school systems already have minority student populations in excess of 60 percent (Hodgkinson, 1986); and in twenty-five of the fifty largest school systems, minority students are the majority (Banks, 1991). By the year 2010, nearly 40 percent of all schoolchildren will be minority members, most of them in classrooms with white teachers whose racial, cultural, and, in many cases, linguistic backgrounds are monocultural (Hodgkinson, 1986; National Education Association, 1987). Minority children encounter few minority teachers.

There is evidence that minority children encounter few mainstream children. In a review of research addressing children in desegregated schools, Stephan (1991) found that relatively few students—despite the efforts of the Commission on Civil Rights—attend desegregated schools. By 1980, for example, 69 percent of white students attended schools that were less than 5 percent black. Of those students who attend desegregated schools, Stephan (1991) found that, in 4 percent of the cases, the self-esteem of black children increased; however, in 25 percent of the cases, the self-esteem of black children dropped. This phenomenon may exist for a variety of reasons, including the psychological harm that may be inflicted because the proportion of minority children is so distorted in schools.

This pattern of racial distortion is much the same in American business. In a survey by Livingston (1991) of twelve major firms in the United States that "do the right thing" by supporting increased minority representation, an inverse relationship between minority presence and level of management is apparent. For example, at Avon, DuPont, and Hewlett-Packard, the total number of minority employees at each firm is approximately 20 percent. However, the number of minorities at executive management levels is only 5, 3, and 2 percent, respectively. Minority employees encounter few minority executives.

In major league sports and in the U.S. military, the pattern repeats again. The racial distortions in basketball and baseball, mentioned earlier, show that minority players and fans encounter few minority owners or coaches. The U.S. military, after the creation of an all-volunteer army in the years following the Vietnam War, became almost 30 percent black, partly in response to soaring unemployment rates. Most blacks were placed in combat units. This means that, if prolonged combat were necessary, 30–50 percent of the total casualties would be black. However, as of 1984, fewer than 6 percent of military officers were black (Kovel, 1984). Few minority members of the military, particularly in the army, encounter minority officers.

INCREASING CROSS-CULTURAL CONTACT AND CROSS-CULTURAL FAILURE RATES

There is evidence that cross-cultural contact is increasing in the United States. Contact between majority culture members and domestic subculture members continues to grow. Furthermore, the shrinking global business community, the political demise of the Soviet Bloc countries, and the strength of the European Economic Community have increased contact with international cultures (Rubin, 1991). The American Field Service, Boy Scouts, Girl Scouts, Rotary, YMCA, and more than 4,000 communities in the United States now sponsor international youth exchanges, and more American college students study abroad than ever before (Rhinesmith, 1985). It is estimated that almost 2 million Americans live and work overseas in a variety of diplomatic, military, religious, business, volunteer, and professional roles (Fontaine, 1986).

Increased contact between different cultural groups does not seem to eradicate cross-cultural conflict in domestic or international cross-cultural environments. In many cases, workplace conflict seems to increase when members of different cultural groups must work together. Evidence of this conflict can be measured in the rates of failure of cross-cultural workers.

Failure rate can be defined as the percentage of total cross-cultural workers who leave an existing job for reasons other than compassionate or medical emergencies (Guthrie & Zektick, 1967). Failure rates among cross-cultural workers are high, ranging from 20 percent for Peace Corps volunteers (Thompson & English, 1964) to more than 50 percent for missionaries (Lindquist, 1982) and teachers in predominantly minority schools (LeCompte, 1985). Schools on Native American reservations have teacher turnover rates exceeding 90 percent (Kincheloe & Staley, 1983), and teachers in Alaskan bush schools stay an average of two years before leaving teaching altogether or finding teaching posts elsewhere (Mayne, 1980). Despite an arduous application process, half of all Fulbright scholars leave before completing a full term (Hansen & Hansen-Krening, 1988).

In the corporate sector, approximately 68 percent of American business people sent to Saudi Arabia fail to complete the work they are sent to do. Failure rates of multinational personnel stationed in Third World countries exceed 70 percent (Hall, 1989). In fact, a placement firm specializing in career hospital administrators reported a 100 percent attrition rate for workers stationed anywhere in the Middle East (Storti, 1989). Furthermore, despite the seemingly close cultural alignment of the United States and Britain, a recent business survey showed that one out of every five Americans assigned there returned before the end of the contract (Brooks, 1987; Ojile, 1984).

On average, the chances of finding a satisfying life abroad in another culture are only one in seven; for those who cross domestic subcultures, the chances are slimmer still (Storti, 1989). Furthermore, the fiscal costs of failure can be high, ranging from approximately $11,000 for a Peace Corps volunteer to $43,000 for a failed missionary (Schipper, 1988) to more than $200,000 for a family of four abandoning a corporate position overseas (Storti, 1989). The costs in terms of personal emotional stress, career and professional sacrifice, and lowered organizational goodwill are nearly incalculable.

Cross-cultural training is not designed to solve the social or religious problems faced by any society. It is a tool used to aid people who work—particularly people who work with people from other cultures. Because it cannot correct social inequalities, its power and importance are limited. However, cross-cultural training is a step toward cultural harmony. Its effectiveness really lies in the fact that, when the training is done well, "sojourners"—that is, those who live or work among those culturally unlike themselves—simply feel better about who they are, where they are, and what they do. Given the rapidly expanding cultural mixture through which we move, and the shrinking global village in which we live, even a small step toward cultural harmony seems a step worth taking.

2

RIGGING THE RACES

> Judging Western civilization is a kind of baying at the moon; it does no more than relieve inner tension and allow one to feel morally superior. If I rail against certain fundamental horrors which have characterized our history, it is only to draw them into focus for the purpose of practical struggles in the here and now. And it is also a way of reminding us that racism takes place because things are distorted and lost sight of in the mystifying light of "progress."
>
> —Joel Kovel
> *White Racism: A Psychohistory*

In Chapter 1, many of the social mores that have sustained cycles of individual, institutional, and structural racism were discussed. The evidence suggests that America is changing rapidly, and that the nation is unprepared for many of the economic and political changes ahead. Driving these changes are profound and swift movements within American culture. New languages, new minority groups, newly arriving immigrants, and the pressure of a weakening domestic economy are challenging our financial and human resources. Furthermore, a resurgence of racial tension and violence has complicated our efforts to cooperate with each other across cultural boundaries. In this chapter, a theoretical examination of cultural conflict is presented. If cross-cultural training exists to solve a cultural "problem," then an exact specification of the problem is needed. This chapter attempts to delineate further the problems associated with cross-cultural contact and conflict by examining American culture more closely.

THE IMPORTANCE AND MEANING OF ETHNIC IDENTITY

Since the 1960s, America has witnessed a growing interest in multiculturalism, cultural pluralism, and ethnic pride among many diverse groups. This renewal of interest in ethnic identity and in the desire to retain ethnic differences is a departure from the nineteenth-century push for full assimilation. Today, a new awareness of distinctive ethnic cultures has made America more a "salad bowl" than a "melting pot" (D'Innocenzo & Sirefman, 1992).

Various explanations of this change have been offered. Some scholars believe that a drive for assimilation underscores a belief in the superiority of the nation and its values. Hence, the resurgence of ethnic identity is evidence of a public disenchantment with American life and ideals (Gouldner, 1977). Similarly, Horowitz (1976) suggests that increasing ethnic identification represents social regression, a movement away from the modern demands of American society toward an Old World system of clans and kinsfolk who built relationships of trust and loyalty with those who shared the same cultural heritage.

In contrast, Glazer and Moynihan (1975) and Glazer (1983) suggest that high rates of unemployment and demographic change have caused ethnic identity to eclipse traditional social identification systems such as occupation and religious affiliation. For example, people may believe there is a greater social dignity in identifying themselves as Irish-Americans rather than as plumbers or Presbyterians. Furthermore, particular ethnic groups—especially Hispanics, Native Americans, and blacks—have used ethnic identity as a vehicle for economic, political, and cultural power. This increased power has created higher levels of interethnic tension: cultural relationships have become political relationships with status and power agendas.

Not all ethnic groups have equal access to social power or to the channels of power. Some groups cannot simply "choose" to be fully incorporated into American society. They either pull away from the mainstream or are pushed out of it. They are not granted equal access to "the formal institutions, official language, social values" or other aspects of the macroculture (Bennett, 1990, p. 42). For example, Hispanics, Native Americans, and blacks are part of what Novak (1973) refers to as the "unmeltable ethnics"—groups that cannot assimilate fully into mainstream American life. They are special minorities because, unlike many Asian-Americans, these groups continue to be excluded from educational, economic, and status privileges within society. Furthermore, these three groups have a distinct history that separates them from all other American ethnic groups (Levine & Havighurst, 1989). They are involuntary immigrant groups (Ogbu, 1988). Many did not choose—either individually or corporately—to live in America; they were forcibly brought to American shores, or their land was forcibly taken from them.

All other ethnic groups—including groups such as Jews and Asians, both of whom have been targets of discriminatory treatment—were voluntary American immigrants.

Hispanics have been the victims of discriminatory treatment since the early nineteenth century when, to protect its political and territorial interests, Mexico allowed a flood of European immigrants into its northernmost territory—an area that is now Texas. Within a decade, Anglos outnumbered Hispanics six to one; and within another decade, Texas was annexed by the United States. Even though Hispanics were full citizens of the United States, they were denied access to channels of upward social mobility (Alvirez, Bean & Williams, 1981).

Native Americans, who have lived on American soil for more than 30,000 years, were the nineteenth century targets of genocide as Europeans pushed westward for land. Native Americans are the only ethnic group systematically forced to live for generations on government property, and they are also the only ethnic group without an ancestral homeland apart from America (Weyler, 1992).

Billingsley (1968) distinguishes blacks from all other ethnic groups because, first, the norms and values of Africa were dissimilar from those of America; second, various African tribes, each with its own culture, language, and traditions, were forcefully combined; third, in the beginning, only African males were brought to America; and fourth, Africans were brought as slaves. The tradition of racism in America that keeps blacks out of the mainstream is amply documented (Kovel, 1984).

MINORITY GROUPS AND THE RESPONSE OF A DOMINANT SOCIETY

These unmeltable ethnics are not only ethnic groups; they are minority groups. The term minority is a sociological—not a statistical—term. All minority group members are also ethnic group members, but not all ethnic group members are members of minority groups. All ethnic groups exhibit certain aspects that distinguish them from all other groups. These include verbal patterns (grammar, semantics, conversation structures, etc.), nonverbal patterns (kinesics, proxemics, haptics, etc.), orientation patterns (attention and time modes, body positions, etc.), social value patterns (behaviors, goals, values), and intellectual modes (ways of learning, bodies of valued knowledge, and valued skills) (Longstreet, 1978).

Although an ethnic group is distinguishable within the larger society by language, race, ancestral homeland, or other cultural characteristics (Bennett, 1990; Yinger, 1976), a minority group is singled out for differential and unfair treatment by a dominant group that enjoys higher social status and privilege. Minority group members know they are targets of discrimination, racism, and prejudice; they know they are denied full participation in the dominant society (Simpson & Yinger, 1987). Hence, the size of a minority group can be of any proportion to the dominant group; a minority need not be, by numerical measure, a "minority." South African blacks, for example, overwhelmingly outnumber South African whites; yet, to date, whites have continued an almost unbroken grip on the power, wealth, and resources of the area. Although numerically superior, South African blacks are a minority group. Americans with British, German, Irish, or other Western or Eastern European ancestry are members of ethnic groups; however, they are not minorities (Bennett, 1990). American minorities, as Banks (1984) metaphorically quipped, "stuck to the bottom of the melting pot" (p. 71).

Minority groups, as social phenomena, have been extensively studied. The responses of a dominant group to a minority group has been one area of examination. Wirth (1945) proposed a categorization of minority aims and argued that all minority groups desire, at different times and to different degrees, one of the following:

- Pluralism, characterized by a peaceful coexistence with the dominant group and other minorities;

- Assimilation, characterized by absorption into the larger society with loss of ethnic identification;

- Secession, characterized by cultural and political independence from the dominant group; or

- Militancy, characterized by a desire for domination of the dominant group and a reversal of statuses.

These minority group aims may spark a variety of responses from the dominant group, including forced or permitted assimilation, pluralism, legal protection of minorities, forced or peaceful population transfer to another geographic area, continued subjugation, or extermination (Simpson & Yinger, 1987). To achieve these aims, the dominant group may also employ various forms of institutional or administrative discrimination, such as withholding goods and services from minority group members as a matter of policy. The dominant group may employ legal or sociological sanctions, such as residential and educational segregation. Such practices may be viewed as necessary, by the dominant group, to support its beliefs that minority members are socially backward, morally unfit, or mentally deficient. These forces exert pressure on minority groups to conform to the aims of the dominant group (Simpson & Yinger, 1987).

There is evidence that subtle forms of prejudicial thinking exist in the United States regarding minorities. Dovidio and Gaertner (1981), for example, report that pollsters have found a significant reduction in racism among the general public in recent years. However, when whites are attached to lie detectors and given the same poll, their responses toward blacks are significantly more negative. There is further evidence that whites may exhibit paradoxical thinking on many race-related issues. For example, polls indicate that whites do not support laws banning interracial marriage, but 60 percent of whites disapprove of such marriages (Dovidio & Gaertner, 1981). Furthermore, 90 percent of whites believe in integrated schooling, but only 25 percent believe the federal government should intervene to ensure integration (Dovidio & Gaertner, 1981). Thus, despite gains on interpersonal levels, America as a society, in the words of Goldsmith, "has a dark side" (1989, p. 222).

Minority groups, as opposed to other ethnic groups in America, have been the victims of generations of ongoing ethnic conflict. This struggle and strife is a conflict between ethnic groups as ethnic groups; it is not merely social competition (Gest, 1987; Milburn, 1979). "Ethnic conflict is a struggle in which the aim is to gain objectives and simultaneously to neutralize, injure, or eliminate rivals" (Horowitz, 1985, p. 95). The primary condition necessary for such conflict is widespread minority dissatisfaction. Minority groups such as the "untouchables" in India—that accept or tolerate their subjugation—are not engaged in ethnic conflict with the dominant group (Horowitz, 1985). However, ethnic conflict exists in America. Simpson and Yinger (1987) maintain that ethnic group conflict is more likely to occur in mobile open societies, such as American society, where "the suppressed groups have some hope of improving their status and the dominant group has some fear that the minorities may advance" (p. 24).

THE CAUSES OF ETHNIC CONFLICT

Several social theorists have attempted to explain the cause of ethnic conflict. Kovel (1984), for example, takes a Marxist view and argues that the dominant economic class uses minority group labor to weaken the demands of the white working class. He explains the increase in ethnic conflict as a function of the current job supply. As the American economy becomes more highly technological, the labor of undereducated and underutilized minorities is becoming irrelevant. Hence, although the number of jobs may remain fairly steady or even grow, there is an overall loss of higher paying jobs. Unskilled or semi-skilled jobs that commanded fairly high wages for minorities a few years ago are now being replaced by fast-food jobs and other menial labor (Kovel, 1984).

A similar view, called the "split–labor market theory," is that competing economic groups work to keep certain groups at the bottom. This creates, in effect, an internal colony within a society. Dominance over the colony is maintained by a cultural division of labor superimposed over class lines (Arrow, 1971; Becker, 1971; Clark, 1965; Reich, 1981). This hypothesis is similar to one proposed by Myrdal (1944), who argued that the lower economic classes (composed largely of minority group members) subdue each other to keep any from gaining an advantage. The dominant group thus maintains power without using overt action to protect its status.

Adorno, Frendel-Bruswick, Levinson, and Sanford (1950) take a psychoanalytic view. They argue that dark-skinned minorities trigger suppressed images of sensuality, irrationality, and evil in lighter-skinned dominant group members. Dominant members, seeking to control the sensual and irrational parts of their own psyches, act out the subjugation socially by subduing, controlling, or even, in the case of slaves, owning darker-skinned minorities (Dovidio & Gaertner, 1981).

Horowitz (1985) suggests a more sociological perspective, arguing that ethnic conflict is related to modernization. Ethnic conflict, for example, may be a social relic of an Old World past that will fade as more ethnic members gain power. It may be a by-product of modernization, symbolizing the resistance of some social groups to relinquish traditional identities and roles. As society becomes more mobile and people become more detached from extended families, ethnic identity may serve as a means of creating a broader, less individualistic social identity. Finally, the desire to retain ethnic identity may be a consequence of modernization since, in a growing economy, not every ethnic group will gain equally. Groups that experience lowered economic achievement may feel a stronger sense of kinship.

A social psychology explanation is proposed by Kanter (1977), who studied societies in which the number of women was quite small in proportion to men. Kanter argues that the structural inequalities in population size polarize the dominant and minority groups. Because there are relatively few minority group members, they are accorded a special social status. Minority group members stand out in the crowd, and they are targets of distorted stereotypes the dominant group creates. To escape the unwanted attention, minority members try to reduce their visibility. In response, the dominant group increases pressure on the minority, forcing minority members into false social roles. These false roles are taken by minority members in the presence of majority members as a means of meeting, confusing, or resisting majority social expectations. Structural discrimination implies that majority and minority groups face tremendous obstacles in creating genuine interaction and trust.

Finally, there is the belief in the natural superiority of the dominant group. If the minority group is perceived as intellectually, biologically, or morally inferior, then the conviction that minority groups should be subjugated becomes morally defensible (Simpson & Yinger, 1987). This kind of ethnocentrism can be so deeply rooted that, even when the dominant group's economic or political interests are injured by it, hostility and discrimination may persist. Tajfel (1970) argues that the prejudice can be socialized so completely into cultural norms that it exists even when it is not sustained by individual or group needs.

Not all theorists, however, have concentrated on such broad cultural explanations of minority presence. Some have explored the impact of minority group status not in economic, political, or sociological terms, but in terms of human personality. This view is not individualistic; that is, it does not address unique parenting experiences, individual educational or income levels, age, gender, or any of several factors that influence the personal development of a single individual. Instead, these theorists, who have written predominantly on the experiences of black Americans, suggest that social traditions of discrimination and subjugation create a kind of "group personality" that seeps into individual personalities within minority groups.

Ogbu (1988), for example, suggests that American blacks have developed an "oppositional social identity" (p. 23). His theory is that less dominant groups within society develop interactional skills, perceptions, and norms that are designed to function within the minority culture. Minority parents socialize their children into minority norms, and they rarely change the social competencies they establish for their children. By maintaining a status quo, minority parents socialize their children for the cultural enclave, rather than the cultural mainstream. Because minorities are discouraged from crossing boundaries, minority members perceive of their identities as acquired and maintained in opposition to white identity.

In an early study, Elkins (1959) suggested that slavery has warped the personalities of African blacks in the United States. He argued that the experience of complete subjugation, in which the white slaveowner was the center of all authority and power, created a group of black people who assumed a childlike status. Blacks became totally dependent on white society to provide food, money, clothing, and shelter. The stereotype of blacks as docile, shiftless, and lazy—an image wholly contradictory to the energetic culture of West Africa—was created by white adults who made black adults into children.

Others have disagreed with Elkins's conclusions, but not his premise. For example, Stampp (1965) agreed that blacks became childlike and dependent, but he suggested that these behaviors disguised resentment against white slaveowners.

More recently, Genovese (1974) argued that docility and pretence were the only effective means of resistance, survival, and adaptation open to black slaves. Gutman (1976), in a similar vein, pointed to the strength and resilience of the slave community as evidence of the resistance of blacks to internalize submission. Although each argues toward a different conclusion, all of these writers suggest that the experience of slavery had a profound impact on the personalities of blacks as a group, and that the strains of the impact are both observable and operational today.

In a related vein, Adorno, Frendel-Bruswick, Levinson, and Sanford (1950) have suggested that majority group members may possess independent traits or total personality patterns that create "prejudiced" personality types. Authoritarian or prejudiced persons exhibit a rigidity of outlook, an intolerance of ambiguity, pseudo- or anti-scientific views, suggestibility and gullibility, and unrealistic goals (Heider, 1958). Ball-Rokeach (1973) and Rokeach (1960) have suggested that dogmatism, rather than authoritarianism, is a stronger determinant of personality. They argue that people tend to reject outgroup members on the basis of conflicting beliefs more readily than on the basis of race or culture. In other words, a black and a white who are Christians are less likely to reject each other than are two whites when one is a Christian and the other is an atheist. Core values supersede racial and cultural distinctions (Kluckhohn & Strodbeck, 1961).

Another investigative arm has traced the impact of poverty on personality. There has been a recent emphasis on the "culture of poverty" as an element in personality development. This examination is not as cleanly racial as the examination of slavery, since not all majority members are rich and not all minority members are poor.

When researchers such as Lewis (1966) and more recently Wilson (1978) (although Wilson's argument that the significance of race was declining in American institutional life met with strong opposition among many sociologists) allude to the culture of poverty, they are referring not simply to poor people, but to a culture that "in the traditional anthropological sense . . . provides human beings with a design for living, with a ready made set of solutions to human problems . . . [and] so serves a significant adaptive function" (Lewis, 1966, p. 19). Some support for seeing poverty as an internalized pattern of response was made by Abell and Lyon (1979), who analyzed a national survey sample and found that there is no significant difference in work ethic and in locus of control among poor and nonpoor people.

This seems to indicate that poverty exists quite separately from personal aspirations and power. Poverty, hence, may be maintained in the same way a culture is maintained—by socializing its members into the behaviors, attitudes, and perceptions designed to perpetuate the group. If poverty operates within a closed social system—quite distinct from endless social programs to eradicate it—then the people caught in its cycle and the social conditions that surround it mutually reinforce the structure. Core personality traits may differ little between poor and nonpoor, but the poor may have internalized behaviors and responses that sustain poverty.

Thus, middle-class society may continue to invite the poor—particularly minority poor—into full social participation (via welfare and job training programs) without risking economic revolution. The culture of poverty creates a frustrated, disillusioned personality. The poor are socialized to fail, to encounter restricted economic and educational opportunities, and to see little connection between aspiration and opportunity, or effort and reward (Simpson & Yinger, 1987).

An extensive literature dealing with the concept of marginalization offers further insights into minority group personality characteristics. To be marginalized is to be restricted from enjoying one's interests and displaying one's talents within constricted social contexts. Marginalization is a kind of social inconsistency; it occurs when one's credentials, abilities, and interests are disregarded or ignored by the culture. For example, a highly educated person who must work at a menial task is marginalized; that is, his or her individual knowledge is not welcomed or valued by the surrounding society. In short, income and status are not commensurate with education.

Membership in a minority culture complicates marginality. For example, minority members may feel forced to choose between attachment to the dominant group (where full acceptance is limited) and identity within the minority group. Ogbu (1988) suggests these identities may be mutually exclusive; gaining status in mainstream culture may necessarily produce a loss of status in minority culture. His studies suggest that many African-Americans may fear that adopting mainstream behavioral norms will make them "white." Similarly, Wiley (1967) argues that advancement in the society of an adolescent minority gang—by the acquisition of weapons, drugs, and violence—blocks advancement in mainstream society. Only by losing ethnic gang identity can mainstream identity be gained. Minority group members are socialized to gain acceptance by inculcating the norms of the cultural enclave. However, according to these theorists, upward social mobility may demand that minorities move away from acceptance in their own culture in order to gain acceptance in mainstream culture. Hence, as long as the acquisition and maintenance of minority identity requires anti-mainstream behavior, marginality persists.

CROSSING CULTURES AND THE CREATION OF CONFLICT

It seems obvious that the structural and individual consequences of minority status affect cross-cultural contact between and within minority and majority groups. Minority group members in the United States are subject to social, political, and economic marginalization and are excluded from the channels of change. Given the special case of U.S. minorities—particularly Hispanics, Native Americans, and blacks—is cross-cultural training useful and effective domestically? Should training be reserved for international cultures only? If cross-cultural training is used domestically, should the emphasis be placed more on lessening prejudice rather than on understanding, accepting, and enjoying another culture?

There seems to be strong evidence indicating that crossing cultures triggers essentially the same difficulties among minority members who are permanent members of a society as among temporary sojourners in a society. For example, Bochner (1982; Furnham & Bochner, 1986) points out that the dimensions of cross-cultural contact are universal. Contact can be analyzed by territory on which contact occurs, time-span, purpose, type of involvement, frequency of contact, degrees of intimacy between groups, relative status, numerical balance, and by distinguishing physical characteristics between groups. Although minorities are permanent members of a society and must live out their lives in that social setting, all of the dimensions of cross-cultural contact can be as variable for them as for international sojourners. This is especially true in areas where minority groups develop specialized work roles (Bochner, 1982) and form a self-sustaining, separate culture.

Whenever people from different cultures interact, the differences between them become salient. Historically, skin color, language, and other physical characteristics activate the sense of separateness (Klineberg, 1971). Minority members within a culture are as subject to separation as are sojourners. In fact, the added sense of isolation and exile associated with "stranger" status among international people living in the United States may be more problematic and cause greater anxiety than minority status among domestic citizens (Heiss & Nash, 1967). Nonetheless, the sense of separateness impacts both international people and minorities when they interact with mainstream culture members (Spradley & Phillips, 1972).

How and why human cultures define and defend the exclusion of some and the inclusion of others has been the subject of a great deal of scholarly interest. Sherif's (1970) hypothesis that intergroup conflict is caused by the competition for scarce resources—resources so scarce that only one group can attain them—is one explanation of the ways in which different group boundaries are created and maintained. Sherif (1970) argues that social competition creates an "us" and "them" perspective, or ingroups and outgroups. Other theorists, supporting the ingroup/outgroup distinction, argue that forces other than economic competition cause the separation. Tajfel (1970), for example, suggests that merely dividing people into random groups produces similar levels of hostility and separation.

People may create a psychological "us" in opposition to a "them" unsupported by tangible benefits, as implied in Allport's (1954) theory of scapegoat prejudice. Zimbardo (1969) lends further support to this perspective, by arguing that members of outgroups are "deindividuated"; that is, that they do not emerge as distinct persons, but are treated as outgroup objects.

Harm done to anonymous outgroup members has been shown in several studies. Best known, perhaps, is the Milgram (1974) study in which ordinary persons were instructed to administer electric shocks to others. Those administering the shocks were less willing to harm victims they could see; but when the anonymity of the victim was total, far greater jolts were given. In a similar study, Haney, Banks, and Zimbardo (1973) found that ordinary persons were capable of behaving brutally toward others who had been randomly labeled as prisoners.

Not all research supports this theory. Some researchers have found that ingroup members are more willing to "forgive" an outgroup member who makes a mistake, such as a foreigner who mispronounces a word (Feldman, 1968). Likewise, a few studies of reverse discrimination (Bochner & Cairns, 1976) seem to suggest that, in some cases, ingroup members treat outgroup members far more favorably than their own ingroup peers. Furthermore, Zurcher (1977) argues that ingroup and outgroup distinctions become blurred in complex societies, and that definitions of the "other" become mutable.

One difficulty with studies that explore the impact of random assignment to an ingroup or outgroup is that such assignments cannot adequately or perhaps completely unearth ingrained psychological reactions. Random assignment to an ingroup creates prejudice that is fresh, discrimination that is new. Neither the prejudice nor the discrimination have been embedded in the cognitive structures of the mind or in the patterns of ordinary behavior. Although random assignment to an ingroup or outgroup may trigger hostility, the hostility is not deeply rooted or long-standing and is apparently subject to repeated and capricious change. College students who are told, as part of a class activity, that a group of peers are inferior in some way may sustain their prejudice for the duration of a class period, but probably no longer.

It is difficult to tell white Americans that black Americans are part of a new ingroup, and then have both groups behave accordingly. The cultural distance between the groups is greater and more complex. Furthermore, Brislin and Pedersen (1976) suggest that a phenomenon they call the "Lena Horne-Harry Belafonte" response can complicate ingroup/outgroup relations. This phenomenon exists when people interact with handsome, well-educated, articulate outgroup members and are attracted to them. The attraction is real, but it is not generalizable. Ingroup members do not transfer their positive feelings to average outgroup members.

Thus, difficulties experienced by members of foreign cultures are similar both in kind and in intensity to the difficulties faced by domestic minority members. In contact with mainstream society, both become outgroup members. The universality of ethnocentrism and the persistence of ingroup/outgroup distinctions seem to indicate that the elements of cross-cultural training are likely to be as effective with domestic subcultures as with international foreign cultures. In both cases, the intricacies of language, ritual, etiquette, and behavior—as well as myriad other elements of culture—must be identified, understood, and respected. These aspects of culture and their salience during intercultural contact will be more closely examined in Chapter 3.

3

THE WORLD ON A STRING

"Gracious!" exclaimed Mrs. Snip, "and is there a place where people venture to live above ground?" "I never heard of people living *under* ground," replied Tim, "before I came to Giant-Land." "Came to Giant-Land!" cried Mrs. Snip, "why, isn't everywhere Giant-Land?"
—Roland Quig
Giant-Land

Definitions of culture abound. Even a superficial survey of the literature of cultural anthropology reveals repeated efforts to draw distinctions between groups of people. Early attempts to explain culture seem simplistic by modern standards. One popular method of defining culture was to emphasize ways in which humans differed from other animals. For example, salamanders can blend in with almost any salamander community, but humans in one culture cannot easily blend in with humans in another culture. Comparisons with the animal kingdom are limited, however, despite the efforts of sociobiologists and others who make a strong case for the biological basis of personality and culture (Konner, 1982). Mere observation will almost universally confirm that birds who are not of the same feather, do not flock together.

In the fifth century Before the Common Era, the Greek historian Herodotus explained culture by comparing non-Greeks with Greeks. Although many of his comparisons were fanciful and overtly disparaging of non-Greeks, Herodotus established an important precedent: his definition of culture served both a scholarly and political purpose (Klineberg, 1982). Although the nature of cultural study has undergone substantial revision (particularly since the beginning of the twentieth century), the political component of culture study persists. In a very real sense, the scholarly community continues to struggle for construct clarity and definitional objectivity because political agendas can be so closely interwoven with cultural perspectives.

For example, if one believes that all cultures are good, or at least benign, the kinds of changes appropriate in cross-cultural training differ widely from the kinds of training given when the new culture is believed to be a superior or inferior one. Such distinctions have both methodological and practical consequences. The conceptualization and design of a study, and the results that accrue from it, will be distorted proportionate to the theoretical bias and political outlook of the researcher (Geertz, 1973).

THE CONCEPT OF CULTURE

Until Franz Boas began his appointment at Columbia University, the academic world largely held to the view of culture proposed by Benjamin Tylor. Tylor, who began the modern discipline of anthropology, was not an academician, but an ailing man instructed by his doctor to live a life of leisure. Tylor complied, living comfortably on an allowance from his father, a businessman who owned a brass foundry in London. Tylor traveled throughout the world. His descriptions of his travels are the first systematic and scholarly accounts of cultural differences ever published. Although he never received an academic degree, the importance of Tylor's works was recognized by the academic community. He was eventually offered and accepted a position on the faculty of Oxford University (Hatch, 1973).

Tylor grappled with differences between cultures, and he sought to explain them. Undoubtedly influenced by the popularity of Darwin's theory of biological evolution, Tylor believed that evolutionary theory could adequately account for what were seemingly mystifying differences in culture among members of the human species. If Darwin could argue that humans evolved from monkeys (implying that humans had achieved a higher form of life), Tylor believed he could build a case that Western Europeans had achieved a higher form of culture than primitive tribes. According to this argument, cultures were hierarchical; some cultures were more developed than others. Furthermore, the slow grand march of evolution explained dynamic aspects of cultural change. Cultures—particularly those Tylor considered savage—changed because they were beginning the climb toward European civilization (Radin, 1987; Tylor, 1958/1871).

One of Tylor's most important theoretical contributions—and one that distinguishes him from anthropologists who followed him—was his belief in the intellectual underpinnings of culture (Hatch, 1983). Tylor believed that cultural development was a rational process, that social rituals and institutions proceeded from a careful consideration of cultural alternatives. Cultures improved, and they improved by a kind of collective thought process that led to the creation of better societies.

The idea that cultural change occurred within a developmental, intellectual context is different from the views of more modern anthropologists such as Franz Boas, Ruth Benedict, and Margaret Mead (Klineberg, 1980) and sociologists such as Emile Durkheim (Hatch, 1973). These later scholars believed that culture was created by emotion and feeling, not by cool rational thought. They believed the passions and habits of a people—both of which were unattached to and unsustained by reason—created culture.

Boas, Benedict, and Mead gave rise to what some have called the "snowflake theory" of culture. Each believed that, like snowflakes, cultures are unique, orderly, emic, balanced, and, in a sense, beautiful. Boas (1940), for example, believed that cultural differences were not signs of inferiority or superiority, but unique adaptational methods operational within a particular social context. Benedict (1946) saw culture as a series of interrelated wholes, a *gestalt* of human life acted in various personal and institutional dimensions. Mead (1955), whose 1928 study of the culture of Samoa and of cultural maturation are seminal, believed that one's individual character is created by growing and passing through the filter of one's unique culture. Some recent educational researchers also argue that culture is a filter for learning (Irvine, 1990; Wolcott, 1987).

Another view of culture is open systems theory which unifies all global life and culture in a hierarchical but nonjudgmental pattern. According to this theory, the tiniest cells are connected to form anatomies, anatomies to form cultures, cultures to form global life. Thus, all formal academic disciplines are united in focus and, essentially, in purpose, though not in level of abstraction. Furthermore, all life is interrelated and interdependent (Bochner, 1982). A young child studying the impact of pollution in a stream is connected in a large organic open system to the study of the global consequences of the loss of the rain forest.

These later theories of culture—in contrast to Tylor's developmental theory of cultural change—share a different philosophical premise. Boas, Benedict, and later anthropologists believed that cultures were not hierarchical, but equal. Measuring cultures against the standards of Western civilization was not intellectually defensible; hence began what Hatch (1983) calls a "call for tolerance" against all claims of intellectual, moral, or ethnical superiority.

CULTURAL RELATIVISM

This new tolerance for and acceptance of cultural differences—that is, the theory of cultural relativism—was ushered in during the early years of the twentieth century. The emergence of this theory marked nothing less than an intellectual revolution. It provided an entirely new way of understanding human life. No longer would one's own cultural standards be universally applied; no longer would differences in culture be explained as deficiencies in intellect or morality; no longer would the assumption that all cultures were moving by slow degrees toward the pinnacle of Western society be touted. Since then, the theory of cultural relativity has remained at the heart of anthropology and all related cross-cultural inquiries, despite stiff philosophical resistance from some quarters. The argument for cultural relativism rests on four fundamental assumptions. The first is that socialization patterns—rather than intelligence—determine the shape and style of social behavior (acculturation processes). The second is that unconscious patterns influence the things cultures will accept and will not accept from each other (selective diffusion). The third assumption is that unique geographic, cognitive, and linguistic environments explain differences in what people think and in how they think and act (componential analysis). Finally, the fourth assumption is that no cultural hierarchy exists. Cultures are simply different from—not better than—each other (Hatch, 1983).

Although it holds some attractions, the theory of cultural relativity is not without serious philosophical difficulties that strike at the heart of cross-cultural contact and training. For example, are the ways in which people experience the world and act on it, the ways in which they understand reality, and the ways in which they interpret life dependent on ways of knowing that are specific to cultures? We know that Indian and European conceptions of time are different, and that people who speak different languages understand the world differently (Stocking, 1968). If our ways of knowing are culture-bound, then there is no way of understanding what is ultimately true, since to determine truth we can invoke nothing except our own cultural standards. The tribesman who explains disease as the work of demons appeals to the same relative standard for truth as the biochemist who explains disease as cell dysfunction (Hatch, 1983; Phillips, 1984). Ways of interpreting, of knowing which is the truer explanation, are not merely inappropriate; they are impossible, for there exists no standard by which validity can be established. Thus, one difficulty with cultural relativism is the *relativity of knowledge*, particularly when culturally different children in classrooms may know very different "truths."

If what is true cannot be established under the tenets of cultural relativism, then neither can what is good. Yet moral injunctions are endemic in all human societies. Each culture values and rewards certain beliefs and behaviors, and it censures and punishes others. These are not privately held opinions about the nature of right; these operate as public sanctions within communities. A difficulty arises when the ethical systems of cultures clash, since none can appeal to an absolute moral standard. Thus, a second tenet of cultural relativity is the *relativity of values*. In classrooms—where the teacher serves as moral mediator—even the call for a tolerance of cultural diversity may impose a moral standard that is antithetical to a child's native culture (Howell, 1981).

Finally, cultural relativism invites another criticism. If cultures are wholly relative and wholly unique, then generalizations about human societies cannot be made. Each culture and each institution within it must be studied in isolation from other cultures and institutions. A historical relativism prevails which—if true, "means that anthropology can never be a theoretical discipline and will always be limited to purely descriptive studies" (Hatch, 1983, p. 9). It also means that neither can generalizing principles that are drawn from cultural studies be utilized across cultures, nor, presumably, can models for cross-cultural interaction be generated.

DEFINITIONS OF CULTURE

While these theories provide ways of understanding culture, they fail to give a clear definition of exactly what culture is. The absence of a shared concept of culture is apparent in two ways. First, the extant definitions of culture tend to be too long, too short, or too simple. Second, few definitions exist to specify what culture is not. The recent focus on institutional "cultures" (e.g., school culture or corporate culture) leads almost inescapably to the conclusion that any people who form a group must also be forming a culture.

Hence, the multiplicity of culture theories addresses an ever-widening circle of scholarly concerns. For example, the definition of culture now stretches to include the creation of culture, the elements of culture, and the operations of culture. Some current definitions attempt to reflect this inclusiveness (Hoopes, 1977). For example, Hoopes and Pusch (1981, p. 3) describe culture as "the sum total of ways of living." Haughton (1982) describes culture as a "constant, ever-growing exchange among physical, intellectual, and spiritual layers" (p. 21). More expansively, Cere (1985) defines culture as almost a personified being, a god of culture who "determines which values, meanings, hierarchies, timing, roles, spatial relationships and concepts...members will adopt and follow, and . . . decides what structure they will give to their physical realm and social reality" (p. 317).

Some scholars take a more simplified—even reductionistic—view. Hofstede (1980), author of *Culture's Consequences*, defines culture as the collective mental programming of people in a particular environment. Brislin (1990), in a similarly succinct manner, defines culture as simply "the recurring patterns of behavior" exhibited by people in a particular environment (p. 10). Although definitions of culture are legion, four components in varying degrees of emphasis—inclusiveness, historicity, moral codes, and the division of observable and unobservable aspects of culture—are ubiquitous throughout the literature.

SOME DIFFICULTIES WITH CULTURE RESEARCH

The conceptual fuzziness surrounding culture has methodological and practical consequences. For example, in general, the specification and containment of culture as a moderating variable in culture research is largely inadequate. Researchers often fail to stipulate in advance the precise role of culture, thus undermining the validity of *post hoc* explanations drawn from culture studies. Furthermore, because culture is unquestionably a multidimensional variable, it becomes important that cultural subcomponents be particularized in both quantitative and qualitative research so that the significant effects, no effects, intervening effects, or interactive effects can be clearly substantiated.

Beyond the difficult process of defining culture as a moderating variable, the specific cultural dimensions under examination must be operationalized if explicit relationships (and variations within relationships) are to be measured. Otherwise, although culture may be specified as an independent variable, poor conceptualization and measurement techniques may reduce culture to a residual variable. Lastly, the problems that trouble the cultural relativist pursue the researcher as well, particularly as the researcher interprets findings. For example, there is the question of how the researcher defines and interprets change. Defining "benefit" through a myopic cultural lens is clearly unacceptable, yet some standard for measuring success must be established. Furthermore, if the harmonious blending of cultures requires the relinquishment of specific cultural norms and values, then how can a researcher determine whether specific cultures or subcultures appropriately or inappropriately yielded norms and values to accommodate the standards of success?

ADDITIONAL DIFFICULTIES IN CROSS-CULTURAL RESEARCH

The difficulties of studying cultures become magnified in cross-cultural study. Again, the research constructs, their measurement, and selected criteria for change are difficult to specify. Furthermore, cross-cultural study demands an "adequacy of translation" across cultures; in other words, the meanings of concepts in one culture must be matched interculturally, or cross-cultural analysis is of little benefit (Feleppa, 1988, p. 2). In recent years, several cross-cultural theories have been advanced.

One important school of cross-culture theory was begun by Sapir. Sapir argued that all human thought originates in the language of one's culture. A study of language, then, reveals the limits of human thought and aids in the interpretation of thought. Later, Whorf expanded Sapir's thesis by suggesting that people cannot share a world view (Bennett, 1990) unless they also share a similar language. What became known as the "Sapir–Whorf hypothesis" has been tested in a variety of ways, most interestingly perhaps with measurements of cross-cultural color perception (Klineberg, 1971). People in one culture may use the same word for what English speakers call "blue" and "green," and another single word for the colors "yellow" and "red." Sapir and Whorf maintain that having only one word for two colors indicates the perception of only one color. Language, in a sense, creates color; and by extension, language creates culture.

The Sapir-Whorf hypothesis rests on the assumption that the difficulty of contact between cultures rests on the fluency of the foreigner in the foreign language and in the perceptions, gestures, and postures that derive from it. Contact among cultures is problem-free to the extent that the sojourner understands the meaning and nuances of meaning salient in intercultural communication and can respond appropriately within the new linguistic and cultural context. All language-based cross-cultural theories stem from this assumption (Giffin, 1970; Martin & Hammer, 1989).

Another cross-culture school of theory ties culture to Piagetian cognitive developmental theory. Ogbu (1988), for example, suggests that culture guides human development and ensures the acquisition of increasingly more complex cultural coping mechanisms such as language, motivation, and skills. People within cultures determine and formulate a set of competencies that they acquire and transmit. Not all cultures value the same kinds or levels of learning, or teach multiple learning styles to their children. Difficulties in cross-cultural contact stem from the acquisition of different and, in some cases, oppositional cultural competencies.

A related theory is proposed by Bandura (1977) and others (Bochner, 1982; Perry & Bussey, 1984). Bandura believes that social learning—rather than cognitive development—explains cultural differences. As children grow, they form relationships and negotiate social transactions that equip them with competencies for life in a particular culture. These competencies include such things as conformity to behavioral codes, creativity, an internal locus of control, an understanding of morality, and self-esteem. These competencies are taught to children, suggest Rollins and Thomas (1979), through control, monitoring, induction, coercion, support, and reinforcement. Different cultures teach their children different social skills. The difficulty in cross-cultural contact, then, stems from an inadequate knowledge of which behaviors the new culture values. Once learned, cross-cultural transition becomes easier.

These theories give way to a search for dimensions and variables. The effort to find the points at which cultures vary most significantly has prompted scholars to test several broad measures of comparison—ways of summing up whole cultures in bipolar terms. For example, cultures have been classified as "high" or "low" (Hall, 1976), as "tight" or "loose" (Pelto, 1968), and as "simple" or "complex" (Freeman & Winch, 1957).

Other comparative schemes exist as well. Riesman, Glazer, and Denney (1955), authors of *The Lonely Crowd*, divide cultures into three dimensions: cultures that are tradition-directed; those that are inner-directed; and those that are other-directed. Malinowski (1962) developed a list of "basic needs" and "derived needs" within human societies. From these needs come seven "cultural imperatives," which include an economic system, an educational system, and a system of social order. Triandis (1977) differentiated between "objective" culture (that which is observable) and "subjective" culture (the thoughts, feelings, beliefs, and values of a people). Murdock (1949) created a list of what he considered seventy-three cultural universals—human regularities found in all cultures. These universals include biological similarities such as the relative strength and size of men and women, similarities in patterns of breathing, eating, and sleeping, and common methods of burial. Similarly, some psychologists (Lonner, 1980) suggest that culture arises out of four psychological universals: behaviorism (such as acting on emotion, aggression, etc.), functional universals (such as goal-setting), systemic behavioral universals (such as human consciousness, sex drives, ego, etc.), and interpersonal structures (such as status and role). Aberle (1960) created a list of nine "functional prerequisites" of cultural survival. They form the basis of what might be considered a "culture," and include: the formulation of shared goals, the assignment of social roles, the formation of shared cognitive orientations, a system to socialize new members into the culture, and a means of controlling behavior that is disruptive to society.

The study of cultures reflects the diversity of definitions and dimensions. Elements common to cultures are frequently sorted and compared across two or more cultures. For example, how people learn, what they consider to be reliable knowledge, and ways that knowledge is prioritized and shared among cultural familiars are all unique within cultures. Some cultural anthropologists study the ways in which geography and ecology impact cultural formation. As discussed in Chapter 2, some scholars examine socialization patterns and try to determine whether "personality types" are created or conditioned by cultures (Price-Williams, 1972).

What happens when people of different cultures interact? Cross-cultural contact, as evidenced in countless studies, is not easy. It raises difficulties on the group level as well as the individual level. To move away from one's ingroup—to become an outgroup member—is to leave one's cultural moorings. The loss of an anchor into the herd of cultural familiars can create international tension and individual strain (Byrnes, 1966).

THE CONSEQUENCES OF CROSS-CULTURAL CONTACT

Simpson and Yinger (1987) and Bochner (1982) discuss several consequences of cross-cultural contact between large groups. As discussed in Chapter 2, a group that maintains its dominance by numerical superiority or tradition may respond in any of several ways to the appearance of a cultural minority. These responses include genocide, assimilation, forcible deportation, forced or voluntary segregation, or pluralism. These responses most frequently occur on the national level, either among competing groups within one country or between two or more countries.

Cross-cultural contact between large groups can stimulate wide-scale social change—sometimes unwanted or unsought change. For example, missionaries in the nineteenth century believed they had been commissioned to save souls and to change social practices they deemed immoral, distasteful, or unethical. Kane (1982) describes these religious crusaders as people who "attacked child marriage, the immolation of widows, temple prostitution, and untouchability in India; footbinding, opium addiction, and the abandoning of babies in China; polygamy, the slave trade, and the destruction of twins in Africa" (p. 159).

On the individual level, one persistent problem resulting from cross-cultural contact is that all people are, to varying degrees, ethnocentric (Brewer & Campbell, 1976). That is, membership in a culture seems to require a fundamental belief that one's own culture is superior to all others. To some extent, "every culture believes its system of morality is the best" (Howell, 1981, p. 2). Although a culture may view itself as religiously and morally neutral (Ferrell, 1984), full membership within a culture demands not merely allegiance to but also belief in the core values of that culture.

The strength of individual and group cultural commitment aids in the survival of the community. While survival is necessary, the persistence of ethnocentrism eventually dilutes the freedom of members of a culture by restricting social choices and eliminating the drive for social change (Banks, 1992). Furthermore, the difficulties ethnocentrism may create can cause moral and ethical problems. Individuals thoroughly and exclusively immersed in their native culture are, in one sense, blind to it. They live life as they know it; they may be unable to see cultural alternatives (Banks, 1984). When these culturally encapsulated individuals cross cultures, they may suffer. For example, they may negatively judge the behaviors and beliefs of the culturally different. This judgment can "lead to inappropriate racist, sexist, and ethnocentric attitudes and behaviors" (Adler, 1986, p. 230), which, in turn, may further isolate them within the new culture.

On the other hand, cultural sojourners may discover a new set of appealing values and beliefs that contradicts the values of their native culture. As a result, cultural sojourners can form allegiances to inherently contradictory moral values without fully recognizing the contradiction. Howell (1981) describes these individuals as "not only culture *bound* . . . [but] culture *blind*" (p. 6).

Several scholars (Banks, 1977, 1992; Bochner, 1982) have proposed stage models to identify phases of cultural growth among sojourners. Bochner (1982), for example, outlines the following four steps to cross-cultural growth:

1. *Passing.* In this stage, sojourners relinquish their own cultural identity and adopt the norms of the new culture.

2. *Chauvinistic.* In this stage, the new culture is rejected, and the norms and values of the native culture are exaggerated.

3. *Marginal.* In this stage, the norms and values of both cultures are accepted, but sojourners vacillate between the two cultures. The two cultures are perceived to be mutually incompatible.

4. *Mediating.* In this stage, sojourners are able to synthesize the culture differences, appreciate them, and act to preserve them.

Banks (1988) views cultural growth as a six-step process beginning with ethnic psychological captivity, characterized by blindness to one's own ethnocentrism and to life within other cultures. Successive stages include ethnic identity clarification, bi-ethnicity, and globalism. Like Bochner (1982), Banks's (1988) stages are not inherent aspects of human social maturation. People who live in richly diverse societies may stop cultural development at one stage and never progress beyond it. However, these stage models do provide a general measure of cross-cultural perspective and growth.

INSTRUMENTS DESIGNED TO MEASURE CROSS-CULTURAL CONTACT

Many researchers have selected a variety of dependent variables to measure the impact of cross-cultural contact and to operationalize theories and models of cross-cultural contact (Neimeyer & Fukuyama, 1984). In this way, what happens to people who cross cultures can be measured more precisely. One area of examination has been *sojourner attitudes*. Many instruments exist to measure attitudes, and several have been adapted to measure cross-cultural attitudes. Four of the most frequently used are the following:

1. *Kahl's Achievement Orientation Scale.* Designed to measure the extent to which the subject is motivated to excel, it contains four subsets that address whether doing well carry priority over other alternatives; whether one trusts others and believes in the stability of life; whether one is planning for the future; and whether one feels a greater loyalty to oneself and career or to one's parents and family (Kahl, 1968). Cross-culturally, the test has been used in the United States, Mexico, and Brazil to compare achievement orientation with social class.

2. *Langer 22 Mental Health Index.* Originally developed for community-wide surveys of psychological disorders, the test was found to discriminate between mental hospital patients and the psychologically healthy (Langer, 1962). Cross-culturally, the test has been used to measure the severity of culture shock.

3. *Miller's Scale Battery of International Patterns and Norms.* A test designed to measure norms of national cultures, the test consists of twenty rating scales (Miller, 1983). Among the subtests are patterns of social acceptance; family solidarity; class structure; belief in democracy; and levels of civic participation. Cross-culturally, the test has been used to compare the United States with other nations.

4. *Neal and Seeman's Powerlessness Scale.* Designed to measure whether one believes events are controlled by oneself or by others like oneself, the test measures the perception of mastery or powerlessness (Neal & Seeman, 1964). Cross-culturally, the scale has been used with people who work at similar occupations in different countries.

A second area of examination has focused on the *psychosocial perceptions of sojourners*. While several instruments exist to measure individuals' attitudes, there is a shortage of instruments designed to measure social perceptions—the views individuals hold of outgroup members. Two standard social perception scales are listed below:

1. *Bogardus Social Distance Scale.* Designed to measure the level of social acceptance between groups, this scale has been adapted to measure racial and cultural distance (Bogardus, 1959). Typically, an outgroup is listed, and the subject is asked to rank the level of social acceptance in one of seven dimensions from "would accept in marriage" to "would exclude from my country." Cross-culturally, the scale has been used to measure resistance to cross-cultural contact.

2. *Sociometry Scales of Spontaneous Choice and Sociometric Preference.* Designed to measure the degree to which individuals are accepted as members of groups, the subject is asked with whom in the group she or he would prefer to associate for specific activities (Moreno, 1934). Cross-culturally, the test has been used to measure interethnic relationships.

A final area of examination has been the *behavior* of people in cross-cultural situations. Several ingenious studies have been conducted in this area, many of them conducted without the subjects knowing they were being observed and measured. For example, Bryan and Test (1967) found that contributions to a Salvation Army kettle were significantly higher when attended by a white rather than a black woman. In a related study, West, Whitney, and Schnedler (cited in Bochner, 1982) found that, when a car broke down by the roadside, the "victim" was more likely to receive help from same-race members than from those of a different race. Finally, a broadcast of *Prime Time Live* on December 3, 1992 showed marked disparities of treatment received between a black man and a white man in St. Louis, Missouri. The white man was able to buy a car for less, find rental property more easily, and get a job more quickly than the black man. The black man, who dealt with the same merchants and landlords as the white man, was repeatedly turned away or charged higher prices.

Behavioral indexes are important, but they are somewhat limited in their usefulness. They are important because people may express attitudes that their actions contradict. This contradiction may signify that the reported attitudes are false. However, it may also indicate that the attitudes are genuine, but that knowledge of appropriate behavior is lacking. Thus, a triangulated measure of a subject's cross-cultural responses—attitudinal, psychosocial, and behavioral—is more likely to produce an accurate assessment of cross-cultural competence.

In summary, culture is a tangled theoretical construct, and many theories have be~~ 'vanced to capture the creation, survival, growth, maintenance, and conse- ~f culture. Some scholars have reduced culture to a constellation of di- 'hat can be compared across cultures. Some have proposed cultural ~ models to measure cross-cultural acceptance. Others have devised a variety of measures designed to indicate whether the attitudes, perceptions, and behaviors of sojourners are culturally competent. While none of these theories and models fully captures the construct of culture, they do provide a variety of theoretical perspectives for designing research studies. Designing cross-cultural studies, however, is a complex undertaking, since meaning and perspective can vary from culture to culture. Furthermore, the consequences of cross-cultural contact can vary at both the group and individual levels. An examination of these consequences is addressed in Chapter 4.

4

OURSELVES AS STRANGERS

> It was hard to live in a glass cage.
> For that year, I spoke to no one
> of what was in my heart.
> I ate 800 meals alone in a large, empty room.
>
> —M. D. Miller
> *Reflections on Reentry after Teaching in China*

In previous chapters, cross-cultural theory and contact were examined in aggregate terms. Special consideration was given to minority and ethnic cultures in the United States, and their interaction with mainstream society. In this chapter, a different angle of cross-cultural contact is examined: contact between relatively small groups of people within institutions or cultures. Additionally, the impact of cross-cultural contact on individuals is examined.

THE CONTACT HYPOTHESIS

What happens when one person or a small group of persons interact with a new culture? Several prominent theorists have proposed models of interaction. One of the best known is the contact hypothesis. The contact hypothesis is based on "the long and widely held belief that interaction between individuals belonging to different groups will reduce ethnic prejudice and intergroup tension" (Hewstone & Brown, 1986, p. 1). The idea is that, in and of itself, sustained contact between different cultural groups will eventually produce social harmony (Obot, 1988). Bochner (1982) adds that "persons in contact will either undergo or resist changes in their cultural identities . . . making them, in a very real sense, different persons" (p. 23).

This theory is an interesting one for several reasons. First, it seems to require no intervening variables. Mere contact, and contact alone, is expected to change society and people for the better. Second, it changes both the individual and the group. The environment of change is fluid, continuous, and positive. Third, it assumes that attitudes cause behaviors within particular social contexts. In a cross-cultural contact situation, the contact will create a favorable social context, thereby changing individual attitudes, producing culturally sensitive behaviors, and shaping a better, more tolerant society (Stephan & Stephan, 1985; Stephan, 1987).

The contact hypothesis continues to undergo critical examination. Allport (1954), as early as 1954, asserted that contact alone is not enough to create social harmony. He stressed that the status of the group members must be equal before intergroup harmony will occur. Allport (1954) created a taxonomy of contact, including the following descriptors:

- the frequency and duration of contact;

- the number of people in each group;

- the status of the groups;

- the roles of individuals;

- whether the contact is voluntary, forced, or intimate;

- the personality of the members; and

- and the conditions of the contact—occupational, recreational, religious, civic, political, and so forth.

Cook (1978) further expanded the contact hypothesis by attempting to specify what situations favored contact, which representatives from outgroups were received best by ingroups, and what types of interactions were necessary to produce changes in attitudes. Like Allport (1954), he agreed that equal status among participants was crucial, but he also discovered additional conditions necessary for positive contact:

- The characteristics of outgroup members must disconfirm traditional outgroup stereotypes.

- The situation must encourage or require cooperation among groups to achieve a shared goal.

- The situation must have high "acquaintance potential"; that is, it must foster social interaction.

- Finally, the social norms of contact between individuals must favor group equality.

Thus, Cook (1978) added several significant, and somewhat complicating factors to the original formulation of the contact hypothesis. For example, the idea of the "disconfirmed stereotype" continues to receive scholarly attention. In a review of schooling desegregation research, Stephan (1991) found that in schools where minority students were encouraged to respond in ways that contradicted traditional minority stereotypes, racial tensions were significantly lower and achievement measures were higher than in schools where minorities were expected to behave in stereotypical ways. In a study mentioned earlier of an integrated school of black and white students, Collins (1979) found that white students participated in student government and the yearbook; black students tended to join the school chorus or a sports team. This division by color seems to support the idea of the disconfirmed stereotype and to suggest that, when given the opportunity to interact in unfavorable conditions, students of different races avoid cross-race contact.

A second important contribution of Cook's (1978) was the idea that contact is more favorable when groups are encouraged or required to work together to achieve shared goals. In an earlier review of contact hypothesis research, Amir (1969) had suggested that superordinate goals were necessary, and that the goals must be jointly owned and commonly created by the groups. Furthermore, Amir (1969) specified six conditions under which contact increases social tension rather than cultural harmony:

1. when the contact produces group competition;

2. when the contact is unpleasant or involuntary;

3. when the prestige or status of one group is lowered by the contact;

4. when members are in a state of frustration;

   5. when groups have moral or ethical standards in conflict; and

   6. when the minority group has lower status than the majority group.

In 1979, Klineberg and Hull (1979; Hull, 1978) published the results of a study they conducted using foreign students in American universities. They found that contact between groups requires more than mere presence. In other words, the presence of foreign students on campus will not produce good relations. Contact requires interaction between groups. They also found that contact between groups tended to have an additive effect: positive contact created more positive contact. As positive contact increased, so did the positive adjustment of the foreign students. Hence, Klineberg and Hull (1979; Klineberg, 1982) seem to suggest that a further crucial factor in positive contact may be that the social needs of each group are met.

Hewstone and Brown (1986), in a review of contact hypothesis research, specify several theoretical limitations. For example, the direction of causality in individual and social change is unclear. Does group contact change individual attitudes, or do changes in individual attitudes alter group contact? If the causality is mutual and dynamic, then the prediction of overall change becomes extremely complex. Part of the added complexity stems from having to separate and measure the impact of interpersonal versus intergroup contact. Which produces the greatest level of change? To what extent does group identification influence individual behavior? Furthermore, if group identification is strong, then can the researcher assume that positive changes in intergroup contact in one social setting (such as the workplace) will produce more positive attitudes in intergroup contact in other social settings (e.g., the community)? Finally, the contact hypothesis does not address the impact of institutional and political racism, or how racism and prejudice affect intergroup relations, even among very small groups. Hence, Schofield (1986), in a study of black and white contact in schools, concludes that "the precise conditions of contact are crucial in determining what the outcome of contact will be" (p. 80).

OTHER THEORIES OF CROSS-CULTURAL ENCOUNTERS

Two other recent theories suggest that, when members of different groups encounter each other, the personalities of members of one or both groups change. Ogbu (1988) argues that minority group members are socialized to acquire an "oppositional social identity" (p. 23). It can be assumed that, although perhaps not continuous in all contexts, this oppositional identity becomes salient in the presence of majority group members. This oppositional stance is maintained by acting in ways that subvert or resist mainstream injunctions. For instance, when minority children are in schools, the maintenance of minority identity may require them to disregard or resist the demands of white educators.

McDermott and Godpodinoff (1979) suggest that, when two groups encounter each other, the personalities of both groups change. This is called the "collusion theory," and it assumes that differences between cultures are maintained or exaggerated in ordinary social interactions. The differences are preserved to fulfill predetermined social or political roles. Some research seems to support this theory. In a study of Zuni reservation schools, Osborne (1989b) suggested that Native American and white faculty members worked to preserve cultural distances by lessening communication, by withholding cultural information, and by maintaining patterns of non-interaction.

A similar theory is proposed by Boateng (1990), who describes a process called "deculturalization." When culturally distinct individuals meet, one individual may be deprived of his or her culture and subsequently conditioned to accept other cultural norms. Deculturalization is most likely to occur in societies where dominant and minority groups exist. Unlike Ogbu (1988), who seems to suggest that minority cultures are altered by contact with a dominant group, Boateng (1990) suggests that the minority culture remains intact but is devalued and ignored. "Deculturalization does not mean a loss of a group's culture, but rather failure to acknowledge the existence of their culture and the role it plays in their behavior" (Boateng, 1990, p. 73).

In another vein, Meintel (1973) applied Festinger's (1957) theory of cognitive dissonance to cross-cultural contact. Meintel (1973) argues that, during cross-cultural contact, members of both groups experience psychological distress. This distress, or dissonance, is a motivating factor. Both groups will attempt to weaken the dissonance internally by avoiding situations outwardly that increase it. Hofstede's (1980) massive study of more than 116,000 workers in fifty countries may support this theory. Hofstede (1980) studied differences in work patterns along four dimensions: power distance, uncertainty avoidance, individualism-collectivism, and masculinity-femininity. He suggests that the differences in work habits and perceptions can be defined as cultural outcomes, and he adds that cross-cultural business encounters may be avoided if there are dissonant perceptions among members of different cultural groups.

To explain what happens when individuals cross cultures, the fields of anthropology, linguistics, and psychology have produced a combined theory of intercultural communication (Westwood & Borgen, 1988). This theory has been the subject of intense interest in recent years, much of the work headed by Triandis and Brislin (1984), Landis and Brislin (1983), and Gudykunst (1983). Like more traditional communication theories, this view of communication focuses on the abilities of communicators within culturally different groups to interpret the messages each sends. Each communicator is assumed to possess varying degrees of ability in decoding, interpreting, and evaluating the messages of other communicators (Atkinson, 1990; Daley & Labit, 1979). It is further assumed that differences in the cultural backgrounds of different groups complicate communication, thus impeding the flow of shared meaning between communicators.

The variables for study (such as verbal and nonverbal behavior, intent, and interpretation) are drawn largely from standard communication research, with "the level of interculturalness" (Sarbaugh, 1988, p. 37) functioning as an intervening variable between communicators. Brislin (1990) specifies cultural barriers that impede communication, including language differences, gestures, stereotyping, and anxiety. In an attempt to specify further the impact of culture in communication, McGuire and McDermott (1988) have proposed the Alienation, Deviance, Assimilation (ADA) model. This model is based on the theory of Kim (1970), who suggests that certain kinds of communication produce and reinforce cultural alienation. For each of the three psychological states, McGuire and McDermott (1988) describe the kinds of communication patterns they believe produce and maintain these states. For example, communication patterns that lead to assimilation include the host making himself or herself available for communication interactions with the sojourner, or perhaps giving the sojourner an affectionate nickname. Alienation behaviors include avoiding communication contact with the sojourner, and refusing (usually passively) to help the sojourner understand the new culture.

Intercultural communication theory has its weaknesses. A central assumption of the theory is that, while members of the same culture may certainly have problems communicating, the chances of misunderstanding and conflict become greater as the cultural distance between people widens (Stening, 1979). However, in intercultural communication research, only the behavior of the communicators is subject to measurement and interpretation. Therefore, the researcher must specify, as Brislin and Pedersen (1976) and McGuire and McDermott (1988) have tried to do, the cultural distance between communicators and then predict the magnitude and type of communication difficulties. While researchers can specify the kinds of problems culturally different communicators may have, it is difficult to predict the intensity and pattern of the problems based solely on a measure of cultural distance. Hence, intercultural communication is frequently criticized for misidentifying or overgeneralizing cultural identity as a predictor of communication competence (Collier & Thomas, 1988).

Triandis and Brislin (1984) and Berry (1990) have been prominent researchers in the area of cross-cultural psychology theory. This theory assumes that culture is an independent variable in the study of perception, cognition, motivation, social behavior, and group dynamics. Culturally different people operate from mismatched conceptual references. Whether these differences are purely psychological or are biological in nature is the subject of continuing research. Regardless of the source of the difference, cultural dissimilarities are inherently problematic, although status, values, gender, personality attributes, and social class may act as intervening or interacting variables to lessen the impact of culture differences (Kagitcibasi & Berry, 1989).

Cross-cultural training begins by adhering to one or more of these theories to explain dysfunction within an organization or institution. The way in which the organization or institution diagnoses its problems will, in large measure, determine the kind of training offered. Nunes (1987) suggests that cross-cultural training can be analyzed from the assumptions on which it is based. However, few criteria exist to identify or measure cultural tension or cooperation. For example, an American CEO may believe that, at bottom, all people think and feel in much the same way. Thus, the kind of training offered to the company's executives who will be stationed in Taiwan may be exclusively centered around foreign language learning while little or no attention is paid to the emotional changes involved in relocation. In contrast, a white school principal may believe that the difficulties teachers face with Hispanic students are totally centered in the teachers' perceptions of Hispanic culture. This principal may offer teachers sensitivity and cultural awareness training, but leave culturally different communication patterns untouched. A missiologist who believes that mere contact, and contact alone, will produce the desired results may offer missionaries job and Bible training, but give them no cross-cultural training at all.

CULTURE SHOCK

A change in institutional or organizational personnel may cause difficulties with group dynamics or morale problems. However, these problems are not necessarily culturally related. Many personnel problems may be distinct from difficulties that accrue from crossing cultures. However, one of the first signs of dysfunction that signals a culturally based problem is culture shock.

Culture shock is a term first used by Oberg (1960) to describe the anxiety that sojourners feel when they lose all "familiar signs and symbols of social intercourse. These signs or cues include the thousand and one ways we orient ourselves to the situation of daily life" (p. 177). The term has undergone some revision: Guthrie (1975) prefers the term *culture fatigue*; Smalley (1963) uses the term *language shock*; Higbee (1969) coined the term *role shock*; Meintel (1973) uses the term *self-discovery shock*; Coffman and Harris (1980) enlarged the term to *transition shock*; Russell (1978) uses the term *psychosocial shock*; McClenahen (1987) uses the term *commercial shock* to describe changes in business culture for Americans overseas; and Briggs and Harwood (1983) have recently used the term *culture death* to describe the crush of the unfamiliar that sojourners feel in a new cultural environment.

Despite differences in terminology, researchers into culture shock largely agree on its symptoms:

- the inability to "assign a meaningful cause-and-effect relationship or impose a cognitive order to . . . [a] situation" (Adelman, 1988, p. 185);

- the "loneliness and tensions inherent in finding [one's] way in institutions built around an alien culture" (Fiske, 1988, p. 29);

- "a noxious intra-psychic process" (Bochner, 1986, p. 348);

- "an extinction schedule of past reinforcers" (Reinicke, 1986, p. 3);

- "stress, poor self-image, and depression" (Fry, 1984, p. 36);

- a "threat to security, fear, inadequate skills, helplessness, defensiveness, role conflict, loneliness, and frustration" (Mungo, 1983, p. 27);

- "serious mental health problems . . . anxiety and paranoid reactions, somatization, and reactive psychoses" (Aylesworth & Ossorio, 1983, p. 46);

- distress over the memory of unresolved childhood conflicts (Kracke, 1987);

- "depression, anxiety, obsessive-compulsive traits, psychosomatic or hyphochondriacal predispositions, ethnocentric tendencies, authoritarianism . . . the excessive need for privacy or dependency . . . affective instability, identity confusion or other indicators of borderline psychosis" (Locke & Feinsod, 1982, p. 817);

- personality disintegration, fatigue, asthma, hives, headaches, ulcers, decreased resistance to disease, muddled thinking and emotions (Befus, 1988);

- a state of "detachment and ontological confusion" (Wiley, 1987, p. 78);

- an "excessive concern over health or cleanliness, a sense of helplessness, a fear of exploitation, a longing for home and friends, and general irritability . . . frustration over diet, digestion, housing, and transportation . . . excessive washing of hands, an absent-minded faraway stare, excessive fatigue . . . and excessive drinking" (Waltman, 1987, p. 4);

- "reactions of anger and hostility toward the host culture, nostalgia for things back home, difficulty in concentrating, fits of anger over minor pains and frustrations, problems with eating and sleeping, anxiety, depression, loneliness, a despair of ever fitting in, getting along, or understanding the host environment and its people" (Coffman & Harris, 1980, p. 3);

- excessive preoccupation with cleanliness, great concern over minor pains, excessive anger over delays, fixed ideas that people are taking advantage of the situation, reluctance to adapt to the new culture, strong desire to return home, desire to associate with one's cultural familiars, decline in inventiveness and flexibility (Stanojevic, 1989);

- disrupted sleep patterns, stomach trouble, anxiety, nervousness, accidents, emotional reactivity, dissatisfaction with the new and idealization of the old, hostility, withdrawal, depression, shyness, fighting, and crying (Coffman & Harris, 1980).

It seems obvious that culture shock is serious and debilitating to the cross-cultural sojourner. Despite the variety and severity of many of its symptoms, all shock symptomology is rooted in the mind. That is, the new culture may be physically secure and the changes may be positive, but the mental trauma—and the disparate physical maladies it may produce—seems to be an inescapable aspect of cross-cultural experience. As early as 1830, immigrant German Lutherans who had been healthy, hardworking, and deeply religious people became dependent on alcohol, fatigued, angry, ill, and nonreligious when they reached Texas—effects church historians attribute to the shock of changing cultures (Wagner & Lutz, 1985). In 1956, an American missionary trainer—baffled by the early return of his trainees—admitted that "emotional reactions are among the leading problems" (Parsons, 1956, p. 162).

What causes such profound changes? Grove and Torbiorn (1985) take a rather interesting and straightforward look at the cause of shock. They see a healthy person as one who functions in culture by balancing appropriate behavior with mental clarity. That is, "mere adequacy" in a culture combines knowing how and why to act in a given way in a given environment (Grove & Torbiorn, 1985, p. 208). When the environment changes, mere adequacy drops, and culture shock begins. The thoughts and behaviors of the sojourner lack both the internal and external reinforcements of the native culture. Befus (1988) defines this shock as "an adjustment reaction syndrome caused by cumulative, multiple, and interactive stress in the intellectual, behavioral, emotional, and physiological" areas of life, suffered by someone in a culturally unfamiliar environment (p. 387). Reinicke (1986) defines the shock as a form of "learned helplessness"; that is, as sojourners repeatedly encounter the unfamiliar, they gradually cease attempts to master the environment. Instead, they learn to be helpless, and this helplessness complicates their adjustment. In contrast, Bowlby (1969) and Arrendondo-Dowd (1981) view shock as a grieving process that is similar to the patterns of grieving for a loved one's death. The familiar culture must die in the sojourner, and the process of dying is multiphasic. Denial, anger, negotiation, and acceptance form some of the phases of adjustment a sojourner must experience in order to adapt to a new culture.

Undoubtedly, much of the shock originates in the sheer number of difficulties encountered in an unfamiliar culture (David, 1972). Ascher (1985) cites changes in sex roles, work roles, intergenerational roles, language, and social patterns as a few of the many changes faced by a sojourner. Banach (1990) adds that work and sex roles may form a complex matrix of change. For example, a foreign woman in American business may refuse promotions if her husband's status is threatened. Conversely, American women may be ignored by foreign males in business. Thus, both work roles and sexual roles become blurred, confused, and debilitating (Barnes, 1987; Heger, 1989; Larson, 1984).

However, these changes may only brush the surface. An excellent review of many of the variables surrounding cross-cultural adjustment was conducted by Church (1982). Cultures have different levels of aggressiveness, standards for education, emphases on sports and play, levels of affection and demonstrativeness, standards of wealth, and levels of dependency on the family and authority figures, and different heroes (Sung, 1985). Sojourners have different feelings about leaving the home culture, about changes in colleagues, about new or altered job responsibilities (Gardner, 1987). Sojourners bring to the cross-cultural experience different religious backgrounds, understandings about family life, levels of trauma and stress, expectations, educational backgrounds, and different levels of physical health (Furnham, 1988; National Museum of Natural History Staff, 1991).

They bring different degrees of cross-cultural experience and different levels of ethnocentrism (Albert, 1986).

Countless research studies make these difficulties clear (Cochrane, 1983). Studies of immigrants in America have produced a body of research that exposes many of the problems of integration into American life. For example, in a study of Southeast Asians who had lived in the United States for five years, Ascher (1985) found that many of the difficulties of cultural transition still were not resolved. More than 59 percent reported that they were still seriously homesick. However, because of the passage of time and distance away from home, 58 percent reported that they now experienced difficulty communicating with people in their home country. A study of Vietnamese youth produced similar findings. Fry (1984) interviewed 150 Vietnamese immigrants between the ages of twenty-five and thirty-five. The interviews were coded on levels of helplessness, low self-esteem, social isolation, and general anxiety. Fry points out that, although their families believed they had adjusted well, all of the youth showed significantly high scores on all measures. In a study of sixty Indochinese who settled in the Rocky Mountains, Aylesworth and Ossorio (1983) found a disproportionately high level of mental health problems, which Western treatment methods had failed to alleviate. Likewise, in a study of European immigrants in Australia, Weissman and Furnham (1987) found a higher than average rate of mental illness among the immigrants. Finally, in a cross-national analysis of immigration, Stack (1981) found that "immigrants to the United States have higher suicide rates than both the native American population and the population of the nations of which the immigrants were natives" (p. 207).

In the United States, minorities who must interact in mainstream institutions fare little better. In a recent study of black graduate students in higher education, Faison (1993) found that a variety of social, emotional, and institutional factors impeded full transition for many minorities into a predominantly white private university. In a similar study of Hispanic college students, Fiske (1988) found that Hispanics struggle with issues of identity and behavior inside white institutions. Many feared becoming "coconuts"—brown outside, white inside. Many reported stress and tension in the dual irresponsibilities of living up to white academic expectations without losing contact with Hispanic social and cultural norms.

Recent studies of corporate executives stationed in foreign countries have provided some insight into specific ways in which culture shock is devastating and long term for some sojourners, but mild and temporary for others (Howard, 1980; Keys & Wolfe, 1988; Lee & Larwood, 1983; O'Reilly, 1988; Popham, 1991). In a study of "expats" (American business executives working abroad) assigned to Singapore, Armes and Ward (1988) found some rather surprising information about culture shock. Their results showed that expats who had the most extroverted personalities had the greatest difficulties with depression, poor physical health, frustration, and boredom. Introverted expats had significantly lower levels of culture shock. This is particularly interesting because extroverts in all fields—business, industry, and education—are frequently considered successful in American culture, but they may make the poorest choices for cross-cultural work. Women tended to have more problems adjusting than did men, although this may have been linked to differences in sex roles in Singapore (where this research was conducted). Most surprising was the finding that neither prior knowledge about Singapore nor prior cross-cultural experience affected the duration or intensity of culture shock. Furthermore, relatively high levels of cultural knowledge and experience did not ensure adjustment.

Sieveking, Anchor, and Marston (1981) examined expat marriages and found that, during cross-cultural contact, marital strain increases. Furthermore, the strain on spouse and children is frequently more severe than on the expat employee. Their results suggest "it is desirable to select somewhat introspective individuals with relatively stable marriages" (Sieveking, Anchor & Marston, 1981, p. 197). In a similar study of German wives whose husbands were expats assigned in the Philippines, Koehler (1980) found that the wives who believed they needed to make a significant life change had the lowest levels of general dissatisfaction and culture shock. Of all the changes inherent in such a move, these wives reported they were least satisfied with the environment and with their children. Koehler (1980) suggests these results indicate that people who have the richest and healthiest private lives suffer the least from culture shock.

Some researchers have suggested that the concept of culture shock needs additional definition. For example, many researchers have turned their attention to the phenomenon of "reverse culture shock," the shock of re-entry into one's native culture. Reverse culture shock seems to be as strong—sometimes stronger— than the original culture shock. Furthermore, both culture shock and reverse culture shock repeat with each cross-cultural experience and, according to many, strike with equal levels of intensity despite repeated experience. If this is so, then something other than an unfamiliar culture must be triggering the original shock. Meintel (1973) suggests that culture shock is not really cultural at all, but the shock of self-discovery. He argues that, "when stresses are attributed to the strangeness of the culture to which the individual must adapt, the intensity of so-called reverse culture shock becomes difficult to explain" (Meintel, 1973, p. 49).

In a study of remigrated individuals, Hertz (1984) suggests that culture shock and reverse culture shock are influenced by age and growth phases associated with certain periods of life. People who are going through major life transitions (raising adolescent children, divorce, parent's death, etc.) make poor risks for cross-cultural experience, regardless of whether they are entering a new culture or returning to a known culture. In a study of American students returning from study abroad, Westwood, Lawrence and Paul (1986) found that "demands for conformity to family, friends, political, and professional groups, spiritual or religious authority . . . may conflict with newly developed concepts of the self" (p. 225). This seems to imply that students—of whatever age—whose concepts of themselves are malleable may do quite well adjusting to a new culture, but not readjusting to the old (Morris, 1960; Sewell & Davidsen, 1961; Spaulding & Flack, 1976).

For these students and others in similar life-changing phases, gains in intercultural experience may signal losses within the native culture: "colleagues with whom one has shared a common professional code may no longer be available" (Westwood, Lawrence & Paul, 1986, p. 226). A similar study of returning American students by Uehara (1986) found that, of fifty-eight students who had been abroad for up to four years, their levels of flexibility with respect to personal values regarding old friends, male-female relationships, clothing, achievement, and individualism all correlated positively with re-entry adjustment. Brein and David (1972) conclude that people who respond to life analytically and rationally rather than emotionally and spontaneously will sustain the longest periods of culture and reentry shock. This, too, may be related to age and growth experiences.

Not all researchers view culture shock in a negative light. Some, such as Adler (1972), believe culture shock offers a unique channel for learning. Culture shock demands introspection and provocative self-examination; it forces a re-evaluation of all personal relationships. Furthermore, it allows for experimentation with new attitudes and behaviors, and it allows for comparative learning in an environment unavailable to culturally encapsulated individuals. Wilson (1985), using national social survey data, found that people who move from rural to urban environments experience culture shock, but that they also develop a greater tolerance for different people and unexpected experiences. Moving from urban to rural, however, produced little shock and no additional tolerance. Finally, Irving (1984) suggests that culture shock should be welcomed and positively viewed as an experience "which can pave the way to deeper cultural awareness" (Irving, 1984, p. 140).

MODELS OF CROSS-CULTURAL ADJUSTMENT

Many researchers have formulated stage and curve models to track the path of culture shock. However, few criteria exist to identify and measure different patterns of cross-cultural adjustment (Benson, 1978; Hawes & Kealey, 1981; Ruben

& Kealey, 1979). One of the best-known of the curve models was proposed by Lysgaard (1955), who studied 200 Norwegian Fulbright scholars who spent varying amounts of time at American universities. Lysgaard divided the time periods into three levels: 0–6 months; 6–18 months; and over 18 months. Using several instruments to assess personal, social, and educational adjustment levels, Lysgaard found that those in the shortest and longest time groups scored best; those in the middle group were less well adjusted. Lysgaard proposed that cultural adjustment is shaped like a U-curve. In other words, sojourners experience an early stage of discovery and elation, a middle trough of despair and shock, and a final stage of adjustment and productivity.

In a recent review of U-curve hypothesis research, Black and Mendenhall (1991) find little support for the hypothesis. They review several qualitative studies that describe—rather than statistically measure—the adjustment patterns of sojourners. These studies suggest J-curves (Davis, 1963), W-curves (Gullahorn & Gullahorn, 1963), and other patterns of adjustment (Menninger, 1988). The shape of the curve indicates the level of adjustment in the sojourner. For example, the J-curve model suggests that sojourners may experience a somewhat difficult period of adjustment during the initial phase of cross-cultural contact. The difficulty deepens into a low trough of dysfunction until the sojourner begins to move back into a positive period of adjustment. Eventually, the sojourner surpasses the initial coping level and enters a highly productive and positive period. Similarly, the W-curve model implies that sojourners begin the cross- cultural contact with a high level of positive energy, but that two distinct low periods—interrupted by a time of increased coping—are evident. Again, as the sojourner adjusts over time, the high level of functioning is regained. One complicating factor in these time-analyzed studies is that age, time, and culture are variable across the research spectrum. For example, Davis (1963) studied 286 Turkish students in the United States, and found that the J-curve best described their adjustment pattern. However, their perceptions about Turkish culture and U.S. culture are unaddressed. Perhaps these students came to the United States believing that life in America would be better than in Turkey. Such an expectation might significantly influence the speed and smoothness of adjustment.

Hughes-Weiner (1986) suggests that adjustment moves in a circular pattern, rather than in a curve. The spiral begins with concrete experience, which leads to reflective observation. From reflective observation comes analytical conceptualization or understanding. This is followed by active experimentation with additional concrete experience. Grove and Torbiorn (1985), who believe that sojourners must go through shock to achieve full adjustment, propose four stages: euphoria, shock, progressive recovery, and full adjustment. Wapner (1981) proposes four different global changes: changes in self-world relationships, isolation, conflict, and integration. Maretzki (1969) and Menninger (1988)—in a study of Peace Corps volunteers—take the view that all movement in and out of cultures provokes a sense of crisis, and they propose four adjustment periods of crisis: the crisis of arrival, the crisis of engagement, the crisis of acceptance, and the crisis of re-entry.

Stewart (1986) proposes only three stages: cultural survival, intercultural comparisons, and cross-cultural contrasts. Szapoczik, Santisteban, Kurtines, Perez-Vidal, and Hervic (1983) also suggest three stages, but theirs are more communally, less individually centered. They are, first, a period of family development during which a changing world view is being formulated; second, a time of family stress and conflict as new relational styles are explored; and third, the establishment of a family world view that is transcultural.

Adler (1975) suggests five stages rather than three. These are contact, disintegration (during which the native culture is rejected), reintegration (during which the new culture is rejected), autonomy, and independence. Adler adds that "Americans are particularly prone to 'being shocked by culture' because they view themselves as culture-free" (Adler, 1975, p. 21). Yoshikawa (1988) also proposes a five-stage model of adjustment:

1. Contact—the sojourner fails to recognize any real cultural differences;

2. Disintegration—the sojourner sees clearly discrepant world views;

3. Reintegration—the sojourner begins to solve problems and to strive to belong;

4. Autonomy—the sojourner becomes flexible and accepts differences and similarities of culture; and

5. "Double swing"—both realities are complementary and are in constant interaction within the sojourner.

Finally, in a study of Chinese immigrants who formed a Mandarin-speaking Christian church in San Diego, California, Palinkas (1982) suggests an altogether different pattern of adjustment. The Chinese immigrants experienced the full range of cultural shock symptomology, but Palinkas found that the church—as a healing community—alleviated culture shock and provided a necessary channel for adjustment. The church could provide, in some sense, a mental health system; that is, people within the church could provide active listening, clarification, interpretation, suggestion, and accountability. However, the mental health system alone did not provide the greatest magnitude of change. Rather, the provision of a kinship network and support system seemed most effective. The church was filled with people at all stages of adjustment. These elements operated within the church—making it, in one sense, a transitional community where traditional Chinese identity could be joined to modern Chinese-American identity within a supportive social framework.

Other treatments designed to alleviate or eliminate the deleterious effects of culture shock have been suggested in recent years (Adler, 1976). One of the most popular is based on a social-skill—or second-culture—learning model (Black & Mendenhall, 1989; Bochner, 1973). This treatment involves teaching the sojourner the precise skills necessary for interaction with the host culture. There is no emphasis on personal growth, cultural awareness, or cultivating an openness to new experience. Rather, appropriate behaviors are taught to sojourners for a variety of specific situations (such as negotiating contracts or eating breakfast) that they are expected to encounter.

Befus (1988) takes a radically different view. She proposes a combination of physical and emotional remedies. For example, deep breathing, relaxation exercises, positive thinking, and social analysis are used in concert to aid the sojourner through the period of shock. In a study of fifty-three U.S. and Canadian citizens who went to Costa Rica to learn Spanish, Befus (1988) found that her treatment method produced far fewer "symptoms of psychological distress characteristic of sojourners experiencing culture shock" (p. 397).

In contrast, Adelman (1988) suggests that a careful analysis of sojourners' systems of support is the key to lessening the impact of culture shock. Adelman (1988) suggests that sojourners analyze their history of adapting to new situations: "helping them to identify their individual and relational strategies for coping, and enabling them to see patterns as well as unique sources of social support can be empowering" (p. 196). Additionally, Adelman advocates the use of "weak-tie" social support systems—relationships with landlords, shopkeepers, and neighbors—to strengthen the sense of belonging.

In a similar vein, Serrie (1984) also emphasizes the importance of social support, suggesting that flexible, sensitive, kind, and cautious sojourners are in the best position to make cross-cultural friends. Serrie further suggests that sojourners cultivate friends who are the same sex, roughly the same age, and with whom they share no language or other communication barriers. In friendship, the loneliness and isolation of the culture shock is eased. Interestingly, Serrie (1984) adds that some time should be taken before overtures of friendship are made: "sometimes the first person to befriend a newly arrived stranger is someone who is marginal in his own culture" (p. 57). Similarly, Waltman (1987) suggests that an empathetic perspective is a cure for shock. Sojourners must try to see life as the hosts see it.

Others, such as Locke and Feinsod (1982), suggest a more straightforward approach to culture shock. They believe that defining clearly one's purpose in the host culture, and interacting heavily with other sojourners, provide the best methods of culture shock treatment.

Taken as a whole, this research suggests that interacting in an unfamiliar culture is not easy. Several theories have been advanced to explain the interaction of individuals from distinct cultural groups. These theories include the contact hypothesis, the collusion theory, intercultural communication theory, and cross-cultural psychology theory. Each of these theories attempts to provide an explanation of the underlying interaction when culturally different groups encounter each other. On the individual level, researchers have examined culture shock. Culture shock includes a range of symptoms, from stomach trouble to borderline psychosis. Several researchers have studied the impact of the shock and have suggested ways to alleviate or eliminate it.

In Chapter 5, the history of cross-cultural training is examined as an antidote to cross-cultural shock. Cross-cultural training does not claim to eradicate shock, but to ameliorate it. Of particular interest are the goals, methods, and anticipated outcomes of cross-cultural training.

5

THE INEXACT SCIENCE OF HELPING

> People like to know where they stand. They read about buried loot and maidens in distress, water rising in the cellar, and they are thoroughly familiar with them—so that when they experience these things for themselves they really know they have had an adventure. Put them through something too unfamiliar—they merely have a disagreeable experience they would rather forget. Life should imitate fiction wherever possible.
>
> —Agatha Christie
> "The Case of the Discontented Soldier"

The history of cross-cultural training in the United States is less than fifty years old. It began at the end of World War II, and it is impossible to understand the purpose of this early training without placing it in a political context. The recently reported horrors of the Holocaust and of Hiroshima had generated a global outcry; and the study of prejudice, discrimination, and cultural imperialism became popular among cultural anthropologists, psychologists, and sociologists (Ostow, 1991). Furthermore, the United States was weary of war, and international peace was a top priority.

In the days before the official beginning of the Cold War, cross-cultural training grew out of the needs of the post-World War II Diplomatic Corps (Leeds-Hurwitz, 1990). Training seemed to promise the advancement of global peace without sacrificing American culture in the process. During these early days, the training was brief, atheoretical, practically oriented, and non-philosophical. It was designed to provide the sojourner with the means to navigate through a new culture.

The training did not address the sojourner's motivation or purpose, nor did it emphasize an appreciation of other cultures. The absence of any emphasis on training the corps members to appreciate and value cultural differences is understandable. The United States had destroyed Germany, bombed Japan, and herded her own Japanese citizens into detention camps. Legal and social sanctions against blacks and Native Americans had created a separatist American society. Furthermore, tensions with the Soviet countries were increasing, and cross-cultural training was used with political caution. Despite somewhat blatant inequalities at home, it was not at all clear to the American political leadership that any global culture was equal or superior to the culture of the United States.

In 1946, Congress passed the Foreign Service Act, which reorganized the foreign service and altered the fundamental purpose of it (Leeds-Hurwitz, 1990). Gradually, anthropological study became incorporated into cross-cultural training, and many of the concepts of culture, language, social organization, and political autonomy were applied wholesale into cross-cultural training. This is not to imply that the training went smoothly. It did not. Although more than 15,000 military officers had been assigned to foreign language training during the war—and these same military training materials were used by missionaries in the years that followed (Smalley, 1953)—there was little agreement in the academic or training community (the two frequently overlapped) as to what constituted culture (Leeds-Hurwitz, 1990).

This confusion about culture led to many of the classification schemes and theoretical models discussed in the previous chapters. One fundamental problem was that the disciplines of cross-cultural psychology, social psychology, and intercultural communication were in their infancy, and the reliance on anthropology to address the issues of cross-cultural training was, in one sense, inappropriate. In large measure, the task of anthropologists was to examine and compare cultures as independently functioning wholes; cross-cultural training demanded a structure that could ease the dynamics of cultural contact and conflict.

A particularly compelling example of the dichotomy between pure research and practical training can be seen in the interactions of the federal government and research anthropologists during World War II and immediately after it. During the war, the federal government sought advice and information from anthropologists. New information was needed about Japanese and German culture; a Native American language was needed as a military code. This information was supplied by anthropologists. Toward the end of the war, American anthropologists advised that different surrender terms be drawn for Germany and Japan. If the American military deposed the Japanese emperor and occupied Japan, the anthropologists predicted that widespread Japanese resistance would break out. Owing largely to the counsel of anthropologists, the Japanese emperor was not deposed, but he was allowed to present the terms of surrender to the Japanese people (Partridge & Eddy, 1987). Clearly, the methods, substance, and process of anthropological thought were valued and applied during the war.

After the war, however, the American anthropological community retreated from government activity to the university. The tenor of anthropological study became decidedly apolitical; it regained a focus on culture as ritual, symbol, and action. By the 1960s, when the federal government asked American anthropologists to train new Peace Corps volunteers headed for Nigeria, the anthropologists responded with lectures on initiation ceremonies and primitive rites among tribes. Nigerian students who were studying in America protested the courses and picketed the lectures. The Nigerian students believed little could be learned about the political and social climate of Nigeria by the examination of kinship systems or burial practices. Anthropologists, in the words of Mead (1975) "were absolutely myopic and did not take anything into account except nice little bits of ethnology" (p. 15).

STAGES OF CROSS-CULTURAL TRAINING HISTORY

The Laboratory of Comparative Human Cognition [LCHC] (1986), cites three developmental stages in cross-cultural training since the end of World War II. The first of these was a technology transfer. After the war, U.S. diplomats, scientists, and businesses began to share technological knowledge with global allies at an unprecedented pace. Along with technological knowledge came the transfer of other kinds of knowledge as well. For example, American educational standards and curricula were placed in foreign countries as a kind of foreign "aid." However, the textbooks transmitted not merely knowledge, but American values. One of the core values was peace with the United States and her allies, and American cross-cultural training was initially directed toward "the exportation of modes of social organization" (LCHC, 1986, p. 1050) that would imitate or complement life in the United States.

The second stage, which began in the 1960s, was an adaptation to local conditions. The drive to transfer American life abroad was coupled with a recognition that meaningful cultural change could only be accomplished in an arena of mutual understanding. During this period, the Peace Corps was formed to help initiate cultural change abroad, and the Head Start and Volunteers in Service to America (VISTA) program were formed to accomplish much the same at home. The same philosophical current ran through both programs (LCHC, 1986). Both were designed to help unfortunates; both required the helper to enter the environment of the needy; both were massive programs under federal control. Importantly, both programs were based on the assumptions that certain cultural outcomes and styles were inadequate for survival in the modern world and that these outcomes could be remedied by the infusion of middle-class, white, American culture.

Attention began to turn to the idea of a universal human mind; and for the first time, experimental quantitative culture indexes developed by prominent anthropologists were compared to psychological indexes, such as intelligence measures. It was hoped that "cultural profiles" would emerge that would explain, in part, differences in development, industry, and economic attainment worldwide. Cultural interdisciplinary study thus began on a small scale, and training was merged with education and psychology. The mood had changed from the postwar years: understanding the local culture, rather than immediately substituting American culture in its place, was paramount.

Glazer (1983) marks this period as a time when American thinking about culture became paradoxical. The Civil Rights Act of 1964 had ended discrimination based on race and color, but its larger purpose had not been realized. Glazer believes the purpose of the legislation had been to make America "color-blind." However, because the Equal Employment Opportunity Commission forced the systematic tracking of every minority person in every institution in the United States, America had become more "color-conscious" than ever before.

The seeds of this ethnic perceptual confusion were planted during World War II. During those years, a battle had been fought on not only national but ethnic grounds, and the ethnic conscience of America had been aroused and somewhat distorted. Americans excoriated the practices of German treatment of Jews in concentration camps, yet concentration camps for Japanese citizens of the United States existed throughout the war as well. National identities became blurred with ethnic identity. This bifurcated perspective was politically maintained, but philosophical and ethical difficulties arose. How could a clear, consistent view of human life and culture arise from two contradictory beliefs? How could America equalize color and culture in her social practices and simultaneously institute a massive identification system for people of color?

This confusion ushered in the third stage of cross-cultural training evolution (LCHC, 1986). In this stage, which began in the late 1970s and is current in the early 1990s, the emphasis is not on exporting American culture, or adapting to the local culture, but on finding a "match" between cultures. In other words, the drive today is to identify and train sojourners in a type of "interactional etiquette" that allows them to switch cultural skills and norms without lessening the integrity of either culture (Barnlund, 1982).

MODERN CROSS-CULTURAL TRAINING

By 1981, more than 20,000 cross-cultural training programs existed in more than seventy-three countries (Pusch, 1979; Pusch, Patico, Renwick & Saltzman,

1981), and the number is growing. These programs employ a variety of training techniques, ranging from sensitivity group encounters to the study of catalogs of cultural patterns (English, 1981). Still, the confusion over culture persists; and despite the presence of several academic disciplines addressing cross-cultural training, little interdisciplinary research is done. "Investigators from diverse disciplines...[have studied cross-cultural training] without being aware of the work of their colleagues in other disciplines" (Adler, 1983, p. 3). Several current cross-cultural scholars and trainers complain that this academic factionalism continues to mitigate against real expertise in the field (Salas, 1984).

Current definitions of cross-cultural training reflect the emphasis on cultural switching and on the discovery and application of proper forms of interactional etiquette. For example, Hannigan (1990) defines the well-adjusted sojourner as one whose changes have been "cognitive, attitudinal, behavioral, and psychological" and who has experienced in the new culture a "movement away from uncomfortableness to feeling at home" (p. 92). Hannigan visualizes this at-home feeling as a product of social harmony and increased personal satisfaction.

Similarly, Hughes-Wiener (1988) divides culture training into three kinds of education: global, cultural, and intercultural. From these flow several dimensions, including "cultural understanding" and "intercultural sensitivity," both of which emphasize developing the skills, knowledge, and attitudes necessary to interact within the new culture. Finally, LeCompte (1985) recognizes "substantial difficulties in interaction" among domestic and international groups, and suggests that cross-cultural workers—particularly teachers—should learn "alternative modes of response" (p. 112). Importantly, none of these definitions of training and adjustment includes rejecting the native or new culture, forcing one's culture to replace the new culture, or retreating from the new culture to avoid further cross-cultural contact.

MODERN TRAINING, MODERN PROBLEMS

While there is some agreement in definition, the ethical and philosophical tangles of training reflect problems not only with the construct of culture—discussed earlier—but with the myriad etiology of culture shock and the vast complexity of modern cultures. For example, Orem (1991) rightly concludes that "the need for cross-cultural training stems from our inability to recognize easily how our values and behaviors differentiate us from others" (p. 8). However, undertaking even the initial process of recognizing the multitude of culturally conditioned human behaviors is a herculean task.

Learning a culture is a symbolic, polyphasic, complex, and limitless process.

Hence, teaching sojourners even a few "cultural basics" is not easy. Human society has tried "repeatedly to accomplish in their members a completely predictable response system" (Henry, 1960, p. 268). Societies cannot condition all of their own members into socially acceptable behaviors; the idea that training will enable sojourners to fit in a new cultural milieu seems almost ludicrous.

Additionally, there is the question of whether the responsibility of adjustment lies solely with the sojourner, or with the host, or with both. The answer to this question may determine not only who receives training in "cultural switching," but whether cultures that prefer encapsulation are allowed to retain that preference. Will cultures that socialize their members in ethnocentric, isolationist, even violent behaviors remain untouched while the rest of the world learns tolerance, acceptance, and cross-cultural interactional etiquette? Should we try to aid sojourner adjustment to the norms of "sick" societies (Lefley, 1981; Littlewood & Lipsedge, 1982)? Furthermore, if cross-cultural training should support the hosts' "perceptual framework," as Wigglesworth (1983) suggests, then what levels of cross-cultural interaction, if any, are acceptable without interfering with the dynamics of the existing culture?

Missionaries, for example, have traditionally been trained to alter the cultures they enter. This active form of cultural change was foundational within the Protestant missionary movement. Missionaries were trained to spread both the Biblical and social gospels. Although the training of missionaries has undergone some philosophical revision in recent years, many missiologists still argue that social change is part of the missionary call. Ferrell (1984), for example, explains that "the Christian knows that all practices in all cultures, including his own, will ultimately be measured against the moral absolutes found in God's Word" (p. 280).

While scholars in many fields would undoubtedly express reservations about applying Scriptural acid tests to cultural norms, Palmer (1984) and Shenk (1980) warn that all cross-cultural research and training are forms of cultural change and that all outcomes are political. There is evidence to suggest that many in the field of cross-cultural research and training possess a predetermined perspective they impose on the study. In other words, many scholars possess ethical and moral codes that they apply with the same conviction as do the missionaries. For example, Banks (1992) treats the "Western democratic ideals of equality and justice" as cultural absolutes, and he concludes that cross-cultural training and education exist to close the gaps between these ideals and the social practices that contradict them (p. 32). Hilliard (1992) advocates the acquisition of a "critical orientation" for all cultures and groups, but he does not specify the criteria used in cultural evaluation. Such criteria form a type of absolutist moral and ethical code by which Hilliard would measure all cultures. Finally, Ravitch (1983) argues for the identification and transmission of a national culture to "forge a national identity." (p. 10). Although her code diametrically opposes Banks's and Hilliard's, the same invocation of a moral (or at least social) absolute is evident. Ravitch contends that whatever does not contribute to a national culture will strengthen factionalism and separatist policies, leading eventually to cultural disintegration.

This is not to suggest that tolerance, openness, acceptance, and mutuality are not right and good. It is to suggest that our conviction that they are right and good may be a culturally conditioned response that other cultures may ignore or resist. Under the tenets of cultural relativism, their right to resist (in fact, the responsibility of other cultures to support resistance in the name of "cultural tolerance") forms the greatest problem in the field of cross-cultural training. Even the fundamental issues of training—such as behavior, attitudes, attributions, values, social support, role expectations, and the meaning of effectiveness—carry culturally based philosophical assumptions about what cross-cultural interactions should be like (Albert, 1986; Patico, Renwich & Saltzman, 1981).

THE GOALS OF CROSS-CULTURAL TRAINING

Not surprisingly, the goals of training reflect the specific outcomes pertinent to the field in which the training occurs. For example, Stipe (1956), a missionary trainer, views the training as a transformational experience that produces missionaries whose lives "will be altered beyond the imagination of the uninitiated" (p. 22). Others (Latourette, 1957; Long, 1984)—observing the "caught and taught" phenomenon among missionaries who both baptize and socialize their converts—believe that missionaries should be trained to live a life-style that will be attractive to all cultures, including their own.

Kohls (1987), a cross-cultural business trainer, views training as the development of competencies in specific skills that will produce cost-effective functioning in a new corporate environment. Likewise, Grove and Torbiorn (1985), also involved in business, are interested in training as a means to increase the rate of speed at which the trainee can learn appropriate business behaviors.

Other disciplines reflect other concerns. For example, Ruben (1989), an intercultural communication specialist, believes training should involve "relational building and maintenance" and "information transfer" (p. 233). Similarly, Brislin and Pedersen (1976), cross-cultural psychologists, view training as a means to increase personal stability "with minimal interpersonal misunderstanding in another culture" (p. 1). Foust, Fieg, Koester, Sarbaugh, and Wendinger (1981) likewise suggest that the goals of training include developing in sojourners the capacity to deal with changing patterns of self-adjustment.

The goals of cross-cultural training in education are complex. This complexity stems, in part, from a traditional focus on changing children, not teachers. Head Start, Chapter I, and a host of other programs were aimed at resocializing minority children into mainstream schools, rather than at training teachers to interact with minority cultures. In fact, some scholars suggest one anticipated outcome of desegregation was that, by interacting with whites, black children would use whites as role models (Schofield, 1986). Singer (1980) notes that early attempts to combine cultures in schools were conducted with the expectation that minority children would change; they would become more like white children. A "blaming the victim" perspective dominated: that is, something was wrong with minority children, and majority schools could cure it. Success, then, came to be measured by how quickly and how well minority children became invisible in white schools. As Schofield (1986) argues, many in education believed "the best approach to desegregation [was] to proceed with business as usual and to take no special notice of the fact" that schools were culturally mixed; "in this view, success [could] be judged by the extent to which the school's status quo [was] maintained" (Schofield, 1986, p. 87).

In recent years, the focus has shifted away from cultural treatment for children to cultural training for teachers. Mitchell (1987), in a recent survey of fifty offices of state superintendents of public school instruction, found that the greatest "need was deemed to be appropriate [multicultural] teacher preparation" (p. 11). The prestigious Holmes Group (1986) echoes the newly recognized need for culturally trained teachers. Citing a need for more than 200,000 new teachers in the years ahead, the Holmes Group is calling for a restructuring of teacher training. Nevertheless, disagreements persist. Whether all kinds of disadvantaged groups (homosexuals, disabled, poor, etc.) should be included under the cultural umbrella (Bullard, 1992), whether culturally specific curricula should be developed for each group or whether such a plan would lead to resegregation (Jones, 1985), whether teachers should interact with minority culture or change the social environment (Banks, 1977, 1984), and whether teachers must undergo perceptual and psychological change (Darity, 1985) are all subjects of ongoing debate.

WHO CAN (OR SHOULD) CROSS CULTURES?

The selection of appropriate candidates for cross-cultural experience and work has received increasing attention as researchers seek to distinguish those who seem most likely to succeed in a different cultural environment from those who do not. Job performance or task ability is usually considered a necessary prerequisite for selection, although some have suggested other kinds of background criteria (Kealey & Ruben, 1983). For example, Greenway (1983) suggests that region of origin should be considered in candidates for cross-cultural work. Speaking specifically of missionaries to the Third World, Greenway (1983) complains that "the problem is that the city, any city, is foreign turf to most evangelical white Christians. The majority of missionary recruits come from small towns and suburbia" (p. 88). Greenway suggests that stronger candidates might be drawn from urban areas.

Brislin and Pedersen (1976) offer a generalized list of characteristics of potentially competent candidates. The candidates must:

- be technically competent;

- adjust to different, even primitive, technology;

- determine the effects of such work on their families;

- determine if they have the necessary physical stamina to undergo such a change;

- understand why they have chosen this work; and

- try to select areas of work best suited to them.

In a more recent review of research on personality traits that contribute to cross-cultural effectiveness, Hannigan (1990) found that the possession of a high level of social skills plays an important part in cross-cultural success. Nonjudgmental, bicultural, tolerant, patient, empathetic people seemed best equipped emotionally to undertake cross-cultural work, as well as those who are flexible and can deal with stress. Finally, sojourners with realistic pre-departure expectations exhibited an increase in ease of interaction, more positive attitudes, a higher regard for the host culture, and greater job competence (Hannigan, 1990). Hannigan (1990) and Brislin and Pedersen (1976) underscore the importance of the support of family and friends in cross-cultural success. This support may be critical. Fendrich (1967), for example, in a study of American students abroad, found that the readiness to participate in interracial activity was more closely related to the student's perceptions of family and friends' support than to the subject's own attitudes.

TRAINING PROGRAM CONTENT AND CHARACTERISTICS

Many generalized suggestions regarding appropriate training content have been advanced in recent years (Kohls, 1979). One of the most comprehensive was created by Brislin (1986), who believes that eighteen broad areas of cultural difference should form the base of all cross-cultural training. Among these areas are included: belonging, anxiety, disconfirmed expectancies, rituals and superstitions, ambiguity, and time and space differences. Other scholars suggest fewer areas. Wendt (1984), for example, teaches the Describe, Interpret, Evaluate (DIE) method of cross-cultural communication; similarly, Gay (1977) suggests that training is composed of acquisition of cultural information, development of cultural perspectives, and involvement in cultural change.

Some training seems to emphasize the candidate's feelings, thoughts, or attitudes; other training, the cultural environment. For example, Belbin and Belbin (1972) and Adelman (1988) underscore the importance of reducing tension in candidates, creating systems of social support, instilling individual confidence, providing a congenial atmosphere, and using the trainer as a coach, ally, and facilitator. In contrast, Tallman (1984) suggests that candidates be trained in more than one occupation and that they acquire a textbook knowledge of poverty, injustice, materialism, and ethnicity. Similarly, Kinsler (1989)—discussing changes in seminary training for all ministers—emphasizes the importance of giving candidates a changed world view, a changed curriculum, a changed pedagogy, a changed theology and hermeneutics, changed goals, and a changed methodology. On a more individual level, Triandis, Brislin, and Hui (1988) advocate training that is centered on the acquisition of self-knowledge through activities and values clarification exercises.

In the field of education, Banks (1991) suggests that teachers need cultural knowledge, knowledge of teaching styles potentially useful in teaching children from different cultures, and knowledge of subject matter. Grant and Secada (1990)—discussing multicultural education applicable to teacher training—developed a typology of five training concerns that range from teaching the different child (stressing appropriate pedagogy and curriculum) to social reconstruction.

Some suggest intensive language training. Schneller (1989), for example, believes that cross-cultural tension can only be overcome when candidates acquire the linguistic, paralinguistic, and kinesic codes of the new culture. Likewise, Machida (1986) suggests that women may make better cross-cultural candidates than men, since women seem better able to decipher verbal and nonverbal communication cues than men.

Regardless of the content of training, all cross-cultural training is united by five core characteristics (Pusch, Patico, Renwick & Saltzman, 1981). First, training occurs within a limited time. Second, the goals and outcomes of training are tied to events people find distressing and confusing in a new culture. Third, the training is trainee-centered. Fourth, the motivations that propel trainees into programs, and their intentions for success, vary greatly. Fifth, the training may be addressed to all cultures (culture-general) or to one culture in particular (culture-specific).

All training should provide transition from training into the real culture (Argyle & Kendon, 1967; Brislin & Pedersen, 1976). Bennett (1986a) provides an excellent developmental model of training programs, viewing them in six stages:

1. *Denial.* Real or difficult differences between cultures are ignored. Characterized by a training emphasis on foods, music, dance, and costumes.

2. *Defense.* The similarity of all cultures is emphasized. Characterized by a training emphasis on the environment and the similarities of all peoples and cultures.

3. *Minimization.* All cultures are different, and not all cultures can live harmoniously. Characterized by a training emphasis on the ways cultures function to preserve themselves.

4. *Acceptance.* Cultures are different, but people can learn to function in them. Characterized by a training emphasis on acquiring communication and behavior skills for cross-cultural effectiveness.

5. *Adaptation.* Cultures are different, and people can learn to feel at home in them. Characterized by a training emphasis on developing a bicultural, integrative perspective.

6. *Integration.* Cultures are different, but their differences can be appreciated and valued. Characterized by a training emphasis on developing an individual social and cultural ethic that transcends one's native culture.

EVALUATING TRAINING EFFECTIVENESS

The search for measures of cross-cultural success for trainees has been somewhat elusive. Are successful trainees those who complete training? Or is there a criterion of success within the new culture that must be met before we can say that a trainee is successful? If there is a criterion, is it centered in job performance or emotional stability or some combination of skills, attitudes, and behaviors? When should the field evaluation occur? Culture shock theorists suggest that, if the measure is taken in the first six months, the novelty of the experience may not yet have worn off. The measure, therefore, may be artificially high. If the measure is taken between six and eighteen months, the most difficult period of adjustment is underway. The measure may be artificially low. However, if the measure is not taken until after eighteen months, is it really possible to establish causality between training and subsequent adjustment?

Argyle (1982) suggests that four indicators of adjustment should be measured intermittently. These are, first, levels of personal satisfaction and happiness (Gudykunst, Hammer & Wiseman, 1977); second, ratings of levels of acceptance of the trainee by hosts; third, ratings of levels of job performance by supervisors; and fourth, performance in specific observed intercultural tasks. Argyle's (1982) dimensions are accepted as standard, but they are underutilized. It is often not possible for successive and multidimensional measures to be taken. Self-reports—and more frequently, retrospective self-reports—form the basis for most post-training measures of long-term effectiveness.

McCaffrey (1986; McCaffrey & Hafner, 1985) suggests that a neglected area of cross-cultural training lies in the failure to measure the unintended outcomes of training. McCaffrey (1986) suggests first, that—because training is often short, superficial, ignored by top management, and easy—trainees learn that the training is unimportant. Hence, because trainees undervalue the importance of cross-cultural training, they leave ill-prepared. Second, because training relies on generalized statements about other cultural groups, trainees learn to reinforce racial and cultural stereotypes. Third, because training often makes claims about subsequent adjustment levels and ease of cultural entry, trainees learn to expect that crossing cultures will be easy. Fourth, because trainers are "experts" on the new culture, trainees learn to depend on trainers to solve cultural problems, rather than learning to solve problems themselves. Finally, because words like *shock*, *survival*, and *coping* are frequently used to describe the experience for trainees, trainees develop negative and resistant attitudes toward training.

Starosta (1990) addresses a different—and potentially serious—unintended outcome. In some cross-cultural training, participants are asked to assume roles and act out assigned parts in a cross-cultural situation. At times, the roles may be confrontational and explosive. Furthermore, some trainers use psychodrama as a role-playing exercise. These methods can unearth highly sensitive feelings and deeply held convictions about race, culture, and self. Starosta (1990) complains that undertrained trainers who dabble with these explosive techniques may anger their trainees and may have to "attempt to reassemble the pieces of their trainees' psyches" (p. 2). Since training is designed to produce better adjusted and more competent people, such outcomes are clearly inappropriate.

According to Ruben, Askling, and Kealey (1979) the lack of clear and consistent criteria to measure cross-cultural success shows that the indications of success come from another quarter. They maintain that the goal of changing behaviors and attitudes, in any real sense, is naive wishful thinking. Even personal readiness to change does not guarantee change. Instead, Ruben, Askling, and Kealey (1979) suggest that a far heavier reliance on a variety of situational and cultural factors is necessary. They believe that, in a successful and supportive culturally different environment, all trainees can succeed. Gemson (1991) agrees that environmental factors may be the key to success, and suggests that multiple styles of leadership (including cooperative, visionary, authoritarian)—when appropriately applied in different contexts—contribute to high levels of adjustment in sojourners. In a related vein, McGuire and McDermott (1988) suggest that full cultural adjustment occurs only when the sojourner receives consistently positive reinforcement from hosts. This seems to suggest that sojourners will continue to adjust as long as they believe they are successful in the new culture.

In conclusion, cross-cultural training seems to offer great potential for cross-cultural adjustment, although many of the variables for successful programs have yet to be specified, operationalized, and measured. Despite its brief history, cross-cultural training has enjoyed an increasing popularity since World War II. Although many of the problems that surround the study of culture influence cross-cultural training, the values of concern, respect, tolerance, and openness seem to be the current ethical cornerstones of training.

Disagreements persist about the selection standards, training content, and outcomes of cross-cultural training. Some suggest that successful cross-cultural adjustment occurs when the sojourner is trained to understand the external or environmental reinforcements of success, rather than relying on the presence of positive feelings or the passage of time. Exactly what produces healthy sojourners remains unclear. Some researchers seek a constellation of personal traits in potential candidates. Others advocate the identification and transmission of culturally sensitive behaviors. Still others seem to suggest that sojourners succeed only when they are placed in a supportive environment, leading to the conclusion that cross-cultural training may need to be instituted among both sojourners and hosts. Organizations that have attempted cross-cultural training and the results they have produced are examined in Chapter 6.

6

Deliberate Remedies Carefully Applied

> There is an internal landscape, a geography of the soul; we search for its outlines all our lives. Those who are lucky enough to find it ease like water over a stone, onto its fluid contours, and are home.
>
> —Josephine Hart
> *Damage*

In an article criticizing traditional approaches to cross-cultural adjustment, Bochner (1986) claims that three solutions to the problems of culture contact have been tested. The first solution is to eradicate the people who are different. This occurs when one culture is targeted for genocide by another culture. The second solution is to eradicate the contact between different cultures. This takes the form of segregation. The third solution is to eradicate the differences between people. This suggests assimilation or acculturation, wherein difficulties between people are relieved by eliminating the troublesome distinctions between them. It is important, in a discussion of cross-cultural training, to distinguish the ways in which training differs from these three approaches and to establish its philosophical perspective.

A PHILOSOPHICAL FRAMEWORK FOR TRAINING

Cross-cultural training begins with the assumption that people from different cultures are different (Landis & Brislin, 1983). As we have seen in earlier chapters, theorists disagree on the origins, intensity, type, and outcomes of the differences. However, modern theorists are largely united in the belief that cultures are different, that morals and ethics and knowledge are relative to cultures, and that no culture can be considered better than any other. Cross-cultural training, then, does not opt for genocide as a means to eradicate different people; instead, the training exists to aid sojourners in respecting and supporting the culturally different.

Cross-cultural training assumes that people who are given some form of cognitive, affective, or behavioral training can live happy and productive lives interacting within another culture (Landis & Brislin, 1983; Olson & Tucker, 1974). The training does not ignore cross-cultural conflict, but neither does it propose to settle aggregate economic, political, or social differences. Although it may involve whole institutions such as schools and businesses, cross-cultural training exists to train one sojourner at a time. The primary purpose of training is to change people, and to change institutions only secondarily or incidentally. This does not negate, of course, powerful contextual variables in organizations that can impede or encourage cultural harmony. However, cross-cultural training does not advocate segregation as a means to eliminate difficulties in cross-cultural contact; rather, training exists to prepare individuals for meaningful, enriching, and peaceful integration.

Finally, cross-cultural training is not a form of cultural imperialism. That is, it does not assume that, in order to do business in Japan, American businesses must train their executives to "become Japanese." It does not assume that, to succeed in schools, black children have to "become white." Cross-cultural training does not require that individuals become acculturated or assimilated within a new culture. Instead, using a combination of cognitive, affective, and behavioral methods, cross-cultural training strives to create bicultural or multicultural persons. The goal is to create people who can be at home anywhere—people who can move between cultures fluidly and easily and who possess an awareness and appreciation of all cultures.

CROSS-CULTURAL TRAINING FOR MISSIONARIES

Several organizations and institutions have attempted to train their members for cross-cultural effectiveness. One of the oldest and largest is the Christian church. Since the time of the first century Common Era, the church set about sending some of its members on evangelistic missions throughout the world. These missionaries have been Roman Catholic (such as St. Patrick, who converted all of Ireland), Protestant (such as the Yale graduates who carried the church—and much of Western culture—to Hawaii), and a variety of other strains, such as Mennonite and Mormon. Until the beginning of the twentieth century, missionaries were by and large united by a threefold mission: to convert the unchurched; to liberate the socially oppressed, and to deepen individual religious commitment.

In the early twentieth century, the Salvation Army, the YMCA and YWCA, and new Protestant missions were begun under the auspices of leaders such as Dwight L. Moody (Brereton, 1981). Because many of the zealous new missionaries were women, the Protestant churches reached an impasse: the new mission zeal had to be directed by and under the leadership of the church, but the ordination of women was out of the question. Because of the need for trained but non-ordained church workers, the American missionary training school was born. Brereton (1981), in a study of early Methodist women training schools, notes that less than two years of academic preparation were required, and that women were more likely to be turned away for inadequate zeal rather than deficient knowledge. Nonetheless, these women were determined. They lived in settlement houses in urban areas and in remote foreign countries, and they tended to the physical and religious needs of the poor. Medical missions flourished during this time as well, and many nurses and doctors worked as missionary teams. In fact, by 1925, medical missionaries had established more than 850 hospitals throughout the world (Grundmann, 1985). As time passed however, and the women's movement became more absorbed with political and educational issues rather than religious opportunities, these training schools closed (Brereton, 1981; Dougherty, 1981). The missionary movement within the Protestant community as a whole is a story of waxing and waning enthusiasm, prompting some to tie renewal movements in the home church to the flux of missionary movements abroad (Pierson, 1989).

After the end of World War II, new missionary movements seemed to mushroom in America. Within a few years, more than 170 new mission agencies were established in the United States, and more than 20,000 new missionaries were sent abroad (Kane, 1982). During the post-war era, cross-cultural training for missionaries within the Protestant church has been increasingly influenced by the Roman Catholic church. Catholic missions—traditionally staffed with highly educated clergy—have preached the gospel of contextualization to Protestant missiologists (Luzbetak, 1988). The process of contextualization involves making the message of the Bible more congruent with the culture in which it is being taught, translating the Gospel into "the local symbolic system" (Luzbetak, 1988, p. 49). More formalized training in cultural anthropology and cross-cultural psychology have recently come into fashion in Protestant training, making the new missionary challenge "to care, communicate, convert, counsel, and cure across the cultural barriers" (Hesselgrave, 1983, p. 79).

This new missionary thrust has had profound impact not only on missionary training, but on seminary training as well. Seminaries now employ the rhetoric of globalization; they seek a "new ecumenical theology . . . that arises from a variety of perspectives rooted in the social, historical, and geographical variety of the human race itself" (Shriver, 1986, p. 11). Webb (1989) notes that current ministry must be sensitive to a "J-curve generation," one in which population growth, urban growth, and changing family and gender roles will change rapidly and will significantly alter the work of the church at home and abroad.

More important perhaps than the demographic and geographic challenges of the twenty-first-century church is the current confusion of Christianity and culture (Anderson, 1984). The mission of missionaries is unclear. At one time, it seemed evident that missionaries were to export both faith and culture; they were to "Christianize" the converts. A Christian society was to be constructed by missionaries in any country in which colonization, intimidation, or invitation granted them access to the people. The cross, it was said, followed the flag (Kane, 1982). However, in many cultures, individual conversion—much less wide-scale social change—proved to be an almost insurmountable challenge. For example, according to Bible society historical data, missionaries in India and China labored for seven years before winning their first convert; in Rhodesia, for thirteen years; and in Thailand, for more than nineteen years (Deer, 1978; Kane, 1982). Whether modern missionaries are sent to relieve social and political injustice, or whether they should focus on the spiritual lives of the unchurched, constitutes a menacing dilemma. Insufficient funding, few staff members, and maintenance of good public relations with home congregations often militate against simultaneously incorporating both elements—social and spiritual—into the mission work of the church.

Today, the Protestant church in the Western world spends $1.3 billion annually to support approximately 67,000 missionaries (Schipper, 1988). However, the surge of missionary zeal in America is waning. Many missionaries sent in the post-World War II years are nearing retirement; and according to one study, between 1980 and 1995, some 15,000-25,000 missionaries will retire (Winter, 1984). Furthermore, the American churchgoer is aging. Many missionary supporters will retire as well (Winter, 1984). Additionally, the composition of the mission force worldwide is changing. Almost 25 percent of all missionaries across the world are non-Western, and the number of non-Western missionaries is growing (Schipper, 1988). The rate of missionary recruitment in Asia and Africa far outdistances the U.S. rate; in fact, in Latin America, the mission force is growing five times more quickly than in the United States—prompting speculations that, by the year 2000, there will be more non-Western than Western missionaries (Schipper, 1988).

Although the combined missionary force of Christian missions (Catholic, Protestant, Mormon, etc.) far outnumbers any other single agency or organization, missionaries have one of the highest cross-cultural failure rates. More than half of all missionaries leave during their first term or fail to enter a second term (Lindquist, 1982). These failures are costly: of the total mission budget, some $13 million are spent annually on lost training, time, and travel (Lindquist, 1982).

Furthermore, problems with disgruntled missionary failures have become serious in recent years. A mission team serving in Papua New Guinea resigned in the late 1980s and sued their mission board for nearly $100,000 because the missionaries had picked up ringworm during their fieldwork (Cummings, 1987).

These changes have prompted many in the mission community to search for explanations of the apparent failure of missionaries and mission boards in the past few decades. Their explanations are instructive to other organizations facing the same mystifying and somewhat dismal cross-cultural results. These explanations can be grouped into four broad categories.

First, several theologians (Bonk, 1984, 1991; Kane, 1982; Reyburn, 1956) have argued that the ineffectualness of Western missionaries stems from the vast disparities of wealth and privilege between the missionaries themselves and the people stricken with poverty and disease with whom the missionaries work. Bonk (1991) asserts that the strategies and outcomes of the Western missionary movement in America "are impossible to understand apart from the massive economic and material superiority enjoyed by the missionaries" (p. 4). Discrepancies of wealth, status, power, values, and economy have isolated the missionary and, more importantly, have blinded mission teams to the world views of the people they serve (Kane, 1982; Reyburn, 1956). Missionaries are unable to bridge a great social gulf in the societies in which they live; they sustain an illusion of personal superiority; and they create mistrust, envy, and hostility in the new culture (Kane, 1982).

Second, some argue that mission boards have failed to provide enough career options for missionaries (Badgero, 1986; Kane, 1982; Ward, 1987). Believing that, like Catholic clergy, Protestant missionaries would forever abandon all claims to career, family, and finances, modern mission boards still operate under a nineteenth-century model of mission work. Children continue to be separated from their parents in many mission areas; women continue to outnumber men by more than one-third; salaries tend to be the same for all missionaries, regardless of time in the field (Kane, 1982). Furthermore, few career options exist for returning missionaries, and little is done to prepare them for retirement and re-entry into the home culture (Dayton, 1984; Kane, 1982; Ward, 1987).

As an antidote to the nineteenth century model, some churches have experimented with the Short Term Abroad (STA) concept for mission work. Begun in the 1960s, the STA is a program lasting from a few weeks to a few months that encourages short-term mission work for students, lay adults, and potential missionaries within a local church. In many instances, the church mission board will offer a "project" (such as building renovation) to an American church. The American church then raises the money, recruits workers—many of whom may use vacation time—with the skills and willingness to go abroad for a specified time, provides materials, and completes the project. The STA program has many advantages, including a short time commitment that need not interfere with other career goals and job responsibilities, a positive public relations function, and the satisfaction of having quickly completed a needed project in partnership with a foreign church (Kane, 1982; Schipper, 1988). Additionally, churches have found that the STA provides a good recruitment function for long-term missionaries; more than half of all current missionaries in the field are STA program missionaries. Furthermore, between 50 and 66 percent of all current full-time missionaries began as STA missionaries (Kane, 1982).

There are problems with the STA program, however. Because of the frequency of personnel turnover, the costs of getting an STA mission team out into the field are higher than staffing career missionary positions (Kane, 1982). Furthermore, the shortness of the stay makes the missionaries more like tourists than real sojourners. There is only time for minimal interaction with hosts and minimal contact outside the American team of workers who are there to accomplish a specified project on a tight schedule (Aagaard, 1985). The STA program usually offers little or no cross-cultural training.

Third, despite the extensive training of Catholic clergy in anthropology and linguistics, many within the Protestant mission community still view too much education of any kind as one of the chief contributing causes of missionary failure. Describing the kind of missionary considered likely to succeed, Walls (1981) writes: "His formal education was not high, and, if an Anglican, his social and educational attainments were not such as would have brought him ordination in the home ministry" (p. 341). Part of the fear of too much education has been that the missionary would be "converted" to the norms and beliefs of the new culture. An educated person would have an open mind, would explore the new culture with an analytical rather than a critical eye, and might forsake the old faith and the traditional ways (Kane, 1982; Stuntz, 1949).

Fourth and finally, as in other fields, some in missiological research and study seem to "blame the victim." Citing personal financial debt, parental objections, lack of clear personal direction, lack of Bible training, and an assortment of other trainee-centered ills, Kane (1982) places much of the responsibility for failure on the missionaries themselves, rather than on the training they received or the social milieu in which they worked.

Others have claimed that the mere presence of Western missionaries disrupts the social fabric of cultures: the missionaries bring strange technology and science as well as religious and ecclesiastical agendas to a new and perhaps unwelcoming environment (Horner, 1953; Newbigin, 1950, 1978). For example, it is not uncommon to find Catholic and Protestant missionaries waging battle for the souls of native people. In the Belgian Congo, newly arriving Protestant missionaries were chagrined to find that the Catholic church provided a school system for native youth. In response, the Protestants—competing with the Catholics—built and maintained a vast school system of their own (Levine, 1979; Samarin, 1959).

Such competition existed on American soil as well. Cremin (1988), among others, notes that Catholic mission schools in the American South (built as an alternative to racially segregated public schools) strongly resembled the Catholic mission schools of Africa. Today the IIMO (Interuniversity Institute for Missiological and Ecumenical Research)—located in the Netherlands—attempts to keep alive a healthy dialogue between Catholic and Protestant missionaries and encourages a balanced concern between theological and practical mission work (Verstraelen, 1985). Not surprisingly, a new emphasis on training local missionaries is gaining popularity. Kuntzer (1986) tells of missionaries in Kenya who trained local people to conduct evangelism. After the Western missionaries left, conversions jumped from 100 to almost 9,000 per year.

Whatever the causes of failure, there is general agreement that American culture itself may be the biggest obstacle to missionary training. Americans are too highly educated, too wealthy, too individualistic, too legalistic, too isolated from nature, and too concerned with their legal and moral rights to be able to succeed in a culture where priorities are different (Atkins, 1990; Ellison, 1978). Gangel (1989) offers a more precise description of the problem, arguing that missionaries are chosen based on three faulty criteria. The first is an availability bias: mission boards tend to accept whomever is available, rather than carefully selecting and recruiting candidates. The second is an association bias: mission boards tend to believe that previous success in the United States will ensure future success abroad, rather than selecting people most likely to succeed in cultures different from U.S. culture. The third is an agreement bias: mission boards tend to send those candidates who are most like them, or who agree with them—rather than candidates whose outlook is most congruent with the new culture.

While most of the more than 700 U.S. mission agencies function under the direction of a particular denomination, some are parachurch agencies. Best known of the "faith missions" are the Moody Bible Institute, Campus Crusade, and the Wycliffe Bible Translators. These groups are interdenominational, drawing recruits from within and without mainline Protestant churches. Some of these groups (and some within mainline churches) have planted training centers in areas where the mission work is to be undertaken (Turner, 1985). Each center trains and evaluates candidates independently. For example, the Indian Evangelical Mission Fellowship requires one year of Bible training and a six-month apprenticeship, while the Indonesian Mission Fellowship requires a full five years of training (Baba, 1981). One of the foremost United States–based interdenominational mission schools is the Overseas Missions Study Center (OMSC) in New Haven, Connecticut. Begun in 1922 as a guest house for missionaries who were home on furlough, the center now contains apartments, tennis courts, gym, and library. More than 800 registrants from around the world come to the center annually for training in cross-cultural and international ministries (Harnden, 1986).

Some interdenominational groups are attempting to break with Western ways. The World Evangelical Fellowship, for example, emphasizes not only the training of non-Western missionaries, but the budgeting of non-Western money (Taber, 1984). Pierson (1987) contends that the Friends Missionary Band in India may find it necessary to refuse North American money in order to preserve an authentic ethnic ministry, and that the Presbyterian church in Brazil has been ruined by too many U.S. dollars. Similarly, World Vision—a major Christian relief agency—now trains its missionaries to be facilitators for local problem-solving efforts rather than to be problem solvers themselves. In other words, World Vision workers are there to assist the native people. The local people define the needs, determine the resources, implement the program, and evaluate its effectiveness while the missionary assists and advises local efforts (Hiebert, 1989).

Many mainline churches actively support mission work. One of the most visible of these is the Southern Baptist Conference. Of every dollar in the denomination's cooperative program budget, almost half goes to foreign missions (Honeycutt, 1989). However, many of the American work values of efficiency and productivity tend to impede mission work, despite the large financial support (Fernando, 1988). For example, 80 percent of all Southern Baptist missionaries work in only eight countries. Why are their efforts so concentrated? It is not because Baptists are not welcomed in other countries; instead, it is because Southern Baptists in the United States require numerical growth in exchange for continuing financial support. Hence, Baptist missionaries are sent to places where they are most likely to attract large numbers of converts (Barnabas, 1983). Furthermore, many Baptist mission boards will accept only "church planters"—who go out into the field primarily to create an institution, and somewhat secondarily to convert the individual. The Southern Baptist Conference, for example, will not send missionaries to North Africa, where missionaries average one convert for a lifetime of service (Barnabas, 1983). These geographic inequities create financial inequities. The performance-based system of support among Baptists means that missionaries who are "called" to areas where the rate of conversion is high may receive salaries as much as five times that of missionaries who work in less "successful" areas (Barnabas, 1983).

Pressures on missionaries to succeed exist in the Mormon church as well. Mormon missionaries—typically college-age boys who wear white shirts and ride bicycles—are among the most performance oriented of all missionaries.

Mormon cross-cultural training consists of an eight-week session: three weeks of language training and five weeks of memorizing the "discussions"—scripts of objections to Mormonism and church-sanctioned answers (Bergera, 1988). Many of the missionaries are not volunteers; they resent being forced into a two-year "friendship" with a stranger, and they resist the regimentation of the work, which allows them no social life and very little free time. These Mormon youth must adhere to a strict set of rules, which, if broken, must be confessed. These confessions are tallied; and depending on the number of infractions and the seriousness of them, letters may be sent home to parents (Bergera, 1988).

The challenges to Protestant mission work have contributed to changes in Protestant seminaries. For example, the Committee on Global Theological Education—a consortium of 110 theological schools—is now pressing for a more globally sensitive theological education that can "aid students in understanding and appreciating . . . social and cultural perspectives as they influence and are influenced by religious communities" (Schuller, 1986, p. 20). A few of the committee recommendations are that Spanish and Korean be substituted for Greek and Hebrew as seminary language requirements and that separate entrance criteria be developed for foreign and minority students (Schuller, 1986).

Seminary perspectives on missions cover a broad range of concerns. For example, Rommen (1985), a professor of missions for the Federation of Evangelical Free Churches, advocates using other international agencies to work in concert with mission efforts. The Fuller Theological Seminary is experimenting with incorporating mission work with degree requirements for a doctorate in missiology (Clinton, 1984; Pierson, 1986). Others focus on ways of translating the Biblical message into culturally relevant language and images (Hoke, 1985; Newbigin, 1978) or on changing and directing cultural awareness (Conn, 1985). At Seattle Pacific University, seminarians are required to spend ten hours in Seattle's international district (Hoke, 1985). In contrast, at Trinity Evangelical Divinity School, the cross-cultural curriculum is designed to "help missionaries understand the reality of demons in the world today" (Warner, 1986, p. 66).

The Catholic church, which has a long history of mission work, takes a decidedly different approach to missionary training. The two largest missionary orders—the Society of Jesus and the Society of the Divine Word—each require seven years of training: four years in anthropology and three years in linguistics (Parsons, 1956). The emphasis on anthropology and linguistics is combined with a style of ministry that incorporates a deep inner spiritual life. Some Catholics call for "a mystical theology, a contemplative wondering articulated with a critical analysis of reality" coupled with an emphasis on communal growth (Coyle, 1989, p. 118). Unlike Protestants who strive to introduce God to the unchurched, modern Catholic missionaries seek to reveal God to people in whom God is "already present and active" (Luzbetak, 1989, p. 73). Catholic missionaries believe that God is operational in cultures without churches, and they strive to reveal God's existing print in the culture. Thus, Catholic theologians and missionaries develop different patterns of listening to native peoples, and approach them with a different—and perhaps more tolerant—cultural perspective than do Protestants (Davidson, Hansford, & Moriarty, 1983).

CROSS-CULTURAL TRAINING FOR PEACE CORPS VOLUNTEERS

The Peace Corps, which began in the 1960s under the Kennedy administration, shares one major commonality with the missionary movement of the church: both are concerned with improving social and environmental conditions in the areas where they are located. Within the church, as we have seen, the social improvement emphasis sometimes follows behind the emphasis on personal salvation; but both organizations are cognizant of social responsibilities. Unlike the church, the Peace Corps is composed primarily of young people who have graduated with degrees in diverse fields; the Peace Corps is not interested in individual edification or religious belief, but in social reform (Harris, 1975; Hautaluoma & Kaman, 1975; Snyder, 1973). The organization is relatively small by church standards: at its peak, the Peace Corps had only 15,000 volunteers in the field (Harris, 1975). Perhaps because it is a federally funded program, the Peace Corps "has invested more in the development of training programs than any other agency, company, or university" (McCaffrey, 1986, p. 161). The Peace Corps, then, can provide important information about the processes and outcomes of training pertinent to other organizations involved in finding the right candidate for cross-cultural experience.

The job of the Peace Corps volunteer is to initiate community projects, to plan games and recreation for area children, to open his or her house to native people, and to develop—insofar as possible—a sense of shared life within the community (Maretzki, 1969). Only 30 percent of applicants to the Peace Corps are invited to train; of those, 50 percent accept. Of those who enter training, approximately 75 percent will go abroad; once abroad, about 15 percent will come home early. Of those who come home early, approximately 4 percent do so because of selection errors, rather than medical or compassion emergencies (Guthrie & Zektick, 1967). When application standards are most stringent, the number of potential candidates falls and the number of failures during training decreases. However, when self-selection procedures are used or the training is "easier," training success rates among larger numbers of candidates increases, but in-the-field failure rates also increase (Harris, 1973): "Total attrition has increased steadily . . .

regardless of the adequacy or inadequacy of the initial screening, selection, placement and retention processes" (p. 236).

Until 1967, when an article published by Harrison and Hopkins (1967) criticized Peace Corps training, most pre-departure training consisted of university-style lectures on major college campuses. After the publication of the article, volunteer training became more situational, more on-site, more experiential (Wight & Hammons, 1970). Although training varies from country to country, an average Peace Corps training sequence begins with pre-invitational staging. This staging sequence lasts about one week. Medical and dental exams are administered during this time. Peace Corps policy, military policy, and political issues are explained to the volunteer in detail (Harris, 1970). Preservice training then commences, a ten to fourteen-week session in the host country led by American trainers and host country nationals. The training lasts five to six days a week, or forty to fifty hours per week. The training is intensive, and it includes language and technical training, skills for survival, and a required course in small engine repair. Following preservice training, inservice training—which lasts from six to twelve months—begins. This training is conducted within the culture and involves far less supervision. No other formal training occurs until the end of service, when the Peace Corps provides a two-day seminar for returning volunteers to aid them in résumé preparation (Barnes, 1985).

By any standard, the U.S. Peace Corps training program has been successful. Unlike the Japanese Overseas Cooperation Volunteers (the world's second largest government-supported volunteer agency—the U.S. Peace Corps being larger), the U.S. volunteers did not enter other countries so that volunteers could demonstrate cultural and political superiority (Skinner, 1988). Nonetheless, the training given by the Peace Corps has undergone substantial revision over time. One significant unintended outcome has been that, the more rigorous and demanding the training, the more dependent the volunteers became by the end of training (McCaffrey, 1986). Trainers were faced with providing a delicate balance between necessary training and cultivation of a sense of independence among volunteers.

From its inception, Peace Corps administrators could ask trainees to leave at any time during training. Furthermore, because the volunteer is a volunteer, quitting at any time for any reason was permitted. Peace Corps trainers had to find candidates who would be both committed and successful. Through the years, a veritable army of psychologists and trainers converged to determine which volunteers would succeed in the field and which would not. More than thirty psychological instruments were either created or employed to determine candidate suitability; a board composed of trainers and professors was asked to make final recommendations; peers were used as selection filters; and, at one point, psychological interviews were conducted to make the final decision (Harris, 1975). However, none of these proved sufficient (Abe & Wiseman, 1983; Chaffee, 1978). In the end, all the psychological tests, board recommendations, and peer review processes were abandoned in favor of self-selection.

One difficulty predicting cross-cultural success was that the Peace Corps volunteer was expected to "tolerate transcultural experiences, but to stop short of the crucial transition where cultural identity—and with it personal identity—became confused or altered" (Maretzki, 1969, p. 208). Selecting volunteers meant finding people who could be predicted to be permeable to cross-cultural contact—but not too permeable. The search for the right candidate became a massive undertaking: a list of the personal attributes expected in candidates is provided in Chapter 7.

A second more obvious difficulty was that—unlike the church, which could measure success by conversion rates—the Peace Corps itself was unclear as to what success in the field might look like. One researcher, bemoaning the strategies for political power and the agendas for social change that were ingrained in the Peace Corps philosophy, suggested that a suitable measure of success might be to count how many latrines the volunteers built (Meyers, 1975). Some researchers suggested that volunteers who were successful were those lucky enough to be in supportive cultural climates (Guthrie & Zektick, 1967); others suggested that success among Peace Corps volunteers rested in the degree to which host nationals perceived of Americans as "unusual" (Popper & Jones, 1972). Like the church, the Peace Corps had to consider the compatibility between American culture and the foreign culture as a factor in program success and in individual success.

CROSS-CULTURAL TRAINING FOR TEACHER CORPS MEMBERS

Between 1963 and 1968—as it was being generally recognized that "traditional means of training teachers, especially for those entering urban classrooms, had failed conspicuously"—returning Peace Corps volunteers were recruited to teach in Cardoza Senior High School in Washington, D.C. (Daly, 1975, p. 386). The returning Peace Corps volunteer received no formal teacher training; instead, an apprenticeship was constructed, giving the returnee time to observe teaching before taking responsibility for a classroom. In a special arrangement with Howard University, the program allowed the returnee to teach at Cardoza during the day and work part-time on a master's degree at night (Organization for Economic Cooperation and Development [OECD], 1981). This experiment was called the "Cardozo Project," and became the topic of a John Kenneth Galbraith article published in *Harpers* in 1964. The project gained national attention; and in 1965, the Teacher Corps was created as part of the Higher Education Act (Bosco & Harring, 1983). The program lasted until 1982 when it was cut from the federal budget by President Ronald Reagan.

During its heyday, the Teacher Corps was one of the most evaluated and best supported programs in history. More than half a billion dollars were allocated from the federal government to 663 projects in fifty states, and more than 245 institutions of higher education—representing 40 percent of the nation's schools that offered graduate programs in teacher education—were involved in the administration of the program (Bosco & Harring, 1983). By 1978, more than 9,000 Teacher Corps teachers had been trained (OECD, 1981). Prior to Teacher Corps funding, the only federal funding that existed for teacher training went for teachers of handicapped children and, after Sputnik, for existing mathematics, science, and language teachers (OECD, 1981).

The single goal of Teacher Corps was to strengthen the educational opportunities for economically disadvantaged students (Rosenblum & Jastrzab, 1980). Although that goal seems fairly simple, the targets for change became increasingly complicated as time passed. By 1976, the program had lost ground: schools that had been placement sites for an average of thirty Teacher Corps team members shrank to an average of four team members (Rosenblum & Jastrzab, 1980). The administration of the program lost ground as well: originally, the program had been run by federal agents and university professors; by 1976, local school districts—with different goals and needs—were administering the program. Furthermore, returning Peace Corps volunteers no longer formed the bulk of Teacher Corps members. As the program expanded under federal funding, Teacher Corps training became almost the exclusive domain of student teachers enrolled in traditional education programs (Jones, 1975).

Candidates for the Teacher Corps were selected based on interviews that probed into the candidate's background and personal attitudes. Once accepted, the candidate was sent to a one-month training institute called Corps Members Training Institute (CMTI), which was attended by all other new Teacher Corps interns and supervisors (Berman, 1980). CMTI was held at various universities around the country. Training at the CMTI was intensive and varied. As time passed, the training content became heavily centered on cultural and social issues, and a sizable body of research testifies to the short- and long-term increases in cultural learning among Teacher Corps members (Andrews, Houston, & Bryant, 1978; Berman, 1980; Bryant & Houston, 1979; Burry, 1978; Houston, Andrews & Bryant, 1977; Fox, Grant, Lufler, Melnick, Mitchell & Thompson, 1978; Hainsworth, 1978; Joyce, 1980; Schroeder & Hainsworth, 1977). In a particularly interesting study of 226 interns from thirty-one states who attended the August 1977 CMTI in San Diego, California, Houston (1979) found that the most positive training results were in white candidates from rural areas. However, training results and field performance are not necessarily related; in other words, white rural candidates may have made the best trainees, but not necessarily the best teachers.

One of the contributing factors to the ending of the Teacher Corps was the contradictory tangle of purposes that surrounded it. While the ostensible goal was to improve the education of poor children, Teacher Corps was designed originally as an agent of change, a catalyst "intended to facilitate improvements in three institutions—the university, the schools, and the community" (Olivarez, 1975, p. 1). This dream was largely unrealized. Corps members were trained and supervised by people within the existing educational machinery (Brooks & Weber, 1975; Hershman, 1974). Candidates who did not "fit" were cut from the program. Hence, the competencies for acceptable performance were created and sustained by an educational establishment that resisted change (Berman, 1980). Additionally, Teacher Corps members were trained in schools that economically disadvantaged children attended, and many of these schools were ineffective, poorly staffed, and poorly funded (Popkewitz, 1975). Corps interns may have been able to diagnose social conditions that contributed to educational difficulties; it is not clear that they were able to generate teaching styles and curriculum to overcome the difficulties. In one longitudinal study of corps interns, Tabachnick (1980) found that, although the interns deplored the teaching styles and educational outcomes they saw in the schools early in the program, by the end of the internship they had adopted the very teacher roles and styles they originally resisted. Some clearly benefited from the Teacher Corps experience, though not necessarily by staying in the classroom and improving their teaching skills. In one retrospective study of corps members from the University of Maine, Crosby and Massey (1980) found that, without exception, all on-site team leaders who served as supervising teachers for corps members had moved out of the classroom and into administrative positions.

A further complication with Teacher Corps membership was a political one. The heyday of the Teacher Corps program occurred simultaneously with the Vietnam conflict. Membership in the corps provided a deferment from the draft. Hence, many young male Teacher Corps members were probably drawn to the corps as a means to escape military service and participation in a controversial political conflict.

The Teacher Corps differed from both Peace Corps and missionary work in several significant ways. For example, the Teacher Corps focused on domestic rather than international exchange. It was directed primarily at children rather than adults, and its goals were educational rather than social. Like the Peace Corps volunteer and the missionary, the Teacher Corps member felt commissioned to aid the needy. The programs appealed to idealism and altruism in the nation's youth; and like international exchange programs at the community level, the public relations and psychological recruitment of candidates overshadowed a concern for technical expertise and personal motivation (Rhinesmith, 1985).

CROSS-CULTURAL TRAINING FOR TEACHERS

Although little empirical research has been done on the preparation of teachers to work with culturally diverse students, state-mandated, school-created, and university-designed programs intended to train teachers for cross-cultural teaching continue to multiply (Grant & Secada, 1990). These programs operate to achieve a broad range of objectives, and they vary according to length, content, and outcomes. They can be examined across two broad and somewhat overlapping dimensions: programs implemented by state or local school departments, and programs implemented by universities.

One dimension is the work that is being done by state departments and local school districts to train teachers cross-culturally. Some of these programs are designed on-site for specific minority populations in specific environments. For example, Stephan (1987) describes a training program for white secondary teachers in a school that had recently received an influx of black students. The program required of teachers an hour of their time every working day throughout one school year, and it utilized a variety of training methods—all aimed at aiding teachers to work with black students. Stephan (1987) reports the training achieved 69 percent of the goals originally established.

In Montgomery County, Maryland, district officials discovered that a disproportionate number of minority students were being recommended by their teachers for remedial or language-disabled classrooms. Knight (1981) describes the training of white teachers to distinguish between dialectical or linguistic styles of speech and language difficulties that signal neurological learning problems. Inappropriate referrals significantly decreased after this training. One of the best known and perhaps most effective on-site programs is the Kemehameha Early Education Program (KEEP) in Hawaii. The Hawaiian state education department found that native Hawaiian children were at-risk, losing ground academically and dropping out of school at alarmingly high rates. Teachers now undergo "two years of inservice training and consultation" designed specifically to aid native Hawaiian children (Jordan, 1984, p. 69). Although the program periodically undergoes revision to shore up its less effective components, achievement rates have significantly increased among Hawaiian students whose teachers have been trained in KEEP (Jordan, 1984).

These programs focus on specific populations or specific problems and target the training to meet specific needs. What if a school or a district has a mixture of cultures? Can teachers be trained to be effective in culturally diverse schools?

When the student population of King Elementary School in Urbana, Illinois, became 15 percent minority, the range of different cultures was large. Children at King came from twenty-three different countries and sixteen different language backgrounds (Bouton, 1975). An English as a Second Language (ESL) program was started to solve the educational problems, but administrators were not satisfied with the results. The ESL children were more than one academic year behind their peers; they stopped using their native language entirely, and many seemed embarrassed by their home culture. Bouton (1975) describes the solution that the school officials proposed: everyone at King would become multilingual. Six languages are now taught at King, and both teachers and students seem to have benefited. Mainstream and minority students' learning rates have increased since teachers at King have become multilingual.

The Archdiocese of Boston began in 1982 to institute a program to integrate multiculturalism into the city's Catholic schools. The program was based on "the healing power of listening" (Pytowska, 1990, p. 40). Teachers were asked to attend voluntarily six twelve-hour presentations on cultural diversity, for which they received a small stipend. Teachers reported both lower levels of racism in themselves and a greater knowledge of the needs of culturally diverse students. Like the King Elementary solution, the Boston program is ongoing: twenty on-site facilitators are in schools to aid in cross-cultural adjustment for teachers and students. Unlike the King Elementary program, however, the emphasis here is not on language, but on using cultural differences as a means to expand one's spiritual and social views. The program "empowered teachers to experience themselves as cultural researchers, as bearers of cultural knowledge, and, ultimately, as culturally responsive educators" (Pytowska, 1990, p. 42).

A similar program in San Diego, California, was instituted for teachers in twenty-seven school districts composed of Hispanic, white, black, Asian, and Pacific Islander students (Jones, 1985). Teachers were required to attend three two-hour cross-cultural seminars on personal cultural awareness, the impact of cultural diversity on the classroom, and changes in the institutional climate. Additionally, facilitators were available all year to work with the staff, and optional problem-solving seminars were offered. Although this study does not address changes in student achievement or attitudes, teacher attitudes improved substantially (Jones, 1985).

Other state- or district-generated programs produce less well defined results. For example, a half-day observation of thirty-two Denver elementary teachers found that some displayed "promising practices," which included creating culturally diverse bulletin boards and encouraging the study of ethnic heritage. However, no academic or attitudinal results are reported (King, 1983).

As to the other dimensions of cross-cultural teacher training programs, a number of them are being tried in several universities across the country. Some universities target specific cultures and train teachers to interact within them; other universities opt for more generalized training and attempt to train teachers for a broad range of cross-cultural teaching. Many times the decision seems more linked to the particular mix of cultures within the range of the university, rather than an allegiance to a particular theory of cross-cultural training effectiveness.

California universities, for example, largely train for a cultural mix; not surprisingly, California contains one of the most culturally diverse populations in the United States. At San Francisco State University, for example, ways to encourage better communication between students and staff have been explored (Jenkins, 1990). San Diego State has begun a cross-cultural specialist degree program targeting black, Asian, Hispanic, and Native American cultures (Mazon, 1977). At one California university, teacher candidates are required to tutor a minority student before certification (Delgado-Gaitan, 1985).

Other universities in culturally diverse areas have implemented similar programs for their students. At the University of Michigan, the Multiethnic Program Committee holds an annual two-week workshop on teaching multiethnic students (Baker, 1977). The University of Wisconsin offers human relations training to improve general cultural awareness among student teachers (Haberman & Post, 1990; Johnson, 1977; Sleeter, 1989; Williams, 1981). Not all the results from these programs are positive: Sleeter (1988) reports that few long-term gains have been made with Wisconsin teachers; Bennett (1988) reports that high gains made immediately after training are lost within one year of real teaching.

Several universities and research professors "specialize" in training teachers for work with Mexican and Hispanic cultures (Cordova, Jaramillo & Trujillo, 1974; Dawson, 1977; Garcia, 1974; Laosa, 1974). For example, the University of New Mexico established the Cultural Awareness Center to assist public schools with Hispanic cultural contact (Gurule, 1977). The University of Houston offers courses in bilingual education, ethnic studies, humanistic education, and curriculum development to aid teachers in teaching all culturally diverse students, but particularly Hispanic students (Baptiste, 1977). A nongeneralist cultural training program in a California university is the Bay Area Bilingual Education League (BABEL), which sponsors a six-week training program in Guadalajara, Mexico, for teachers of Hispanic students (Reusswig, 1981).

Teachers of rural students receive special training at Southeast Louisiana State University (Anderson, Reiff & McCray, 1988), and teachers of rural Alaskan village students are primarily trained at the University of Alaska at Fairbanks (Barnhardt, 1983; Kleinfeld, McDiarmid, Grubis & Parrett, 1983; Mayne, 1980; Noordhoff & Kleinfeld, 1990; Spears, Oliver & Maes, 1990; Tafoya, 1981). Other researchers and institutions focus on ways to prepare teachers for work with Native American children (Dumont & Wax, 1976; Frazier & DeBlassie, 1984; Mortenson & Wilson, 1980; Osborne, 1989a; Wax, 1976). Universities that offer specialized cross-cultural teacher training programs for work with Native American children include Indiana University (Mahan, 1982; Mahan & Lacefield, 1980), the University of Montana at Missoula (Covington, 1974), and Northeastern Oklahoma State University (Holland, 1974).

While many researchers in recent years have specialized in the educational needs of black children, few universities offer a specialized program designed to train teachers for work with black students. An exception is the Texas A&M University Minority Membership Project or MMP (Larke, 1990; Larke, Wiseman & Bradley, 1990). One of the unique features of the MMP is that candidates make a three-year commitment to mentor a black elementary student; the commitment requires that the candidate be in touch with the child at least once per week throughout the three years (Larke, Wiseman & Bradley, 1990).

Other university programs specialize in learning disabilities and disorders that are linked to or prominent within culturally diverse student populations. For example, language courses are designed to aid teachers of children from diverse language backgrounds (Cere, 1985; Chu & Levy, 1988; Dodge, 1985; Donmall, 1985; English, 1981; Lane, 1980; McCroarty, 1984; Pedersen, 1984). Other courses emphasize the needs of teachers of special needs children (Fox, Kuhlman & Sales, 1988) and of immigrant students (Hinkle, Tipton & Tutchings, 1979), teachers of music (Anderson, 1980), and teachers of adult learners (Orem, 1991). A growing body of research compares cross-cultural teacher training programs in the United States with those in other countries, and isolates the effects of foreign student teaching on U.S. teachers (Hick, 1984; Mahan & Stachowski, 1985, 1990; Neely & Campbell, 1985; Shafer, 1983).

Despite the plethora of cross-cultural teacher training programs, little agreement exists among practitioners regarding the process of candidate selection, the training method, short- and long-term goals, or intended outcomes. Teachers differ from Peace Corps volunteers because teaching is a paid professional career and because teachers teach children at various stages of cultural identity development (Barry, Josephson, Lauer & Marshall, 1987). Teachers and Teacher Corps members—unlike missionaries and Peace Corps volunteers—can retreat into their own cultural enclaves when the workday is over. Like missionaries, teachers have sometimes been drawn to "help" culturally different children; however, culturally different students have been placed in classrooms when teachers did not volunteer to teach them and may even have resented or resisted their presence.

Thus, there exists a very significant difference between teachers and the other cross-cultural workers that have been examined in this chapter. Teachers frequently cannot quit or change districts if they dislike their cultural surroundings; and teachers—unlike Peace Corps volunteers and Teacher Corps members—have no foreseeable time limitations for their cross-cultural contact, except retirement. Hence, unlike any of the cross-cultural workers examined thus far, teachers may be considered—at least to some degree—nonvolunteers. In spite of new teacher training programs and state guidelines that emphasize cross-cultural teacher training (Laughlin, 1980; Wilson, 1983), teachers who began teaching before the training was offered or who selected schools congruent with their own culture may have greater difficulty adjusting to the cultural changes than those who willingly selected a culturally diverse teaching environment (Hood, 1989).

CROSS-CULTURAL TRAINING FOR EXPATS

Personnel in multinational business corporations face the same difficulty. Many of them who were born and educated in the United States—particularly those whose life experiences have been largely confined within their own ethnic group—may feel resistance toward culturally different co-workers. "American executives will not 'pick up' [cross-cultural] skills in the United States educational system, in their normal life experiences, or in their typical working career" (Black & Mendenhall, 1989, p. 512). Transitions into a culturally diverse working environment can be difficult and painful (Armstrong, Sission & Page, 1988).

By 1984, approximately 75 percent of the world's purchasing power was found outside the United States, and more than 33 percent of U.S. corporate profits were earned abroad (Salas, 1984). The Department of Commerce recently estimated that 80 percent of U.S. goods and services are vulnerable to foreign competition (Patterson, 1990). Business is rapidly becoming globalized; furthermore, the cultural changes within the United States during the past four decades have impacted American business profoundly (Blocklyn, 1989). American business is becoming more culturally diverse, and there are indications that American businesses are not faring well in a diverse marketplace (Bradbury, 1988). Fewer than one-third of all failures among expats (American executives working abroad) are attributed to job-related problems (McEnery & DesHarnais, 1990); and not surprisingly, there are estimates that as many as half of all expats who do remain on the job are regarded as marginally efficient or as inefficient (Bird & Dunbar, 1991; Patterson, 1990). In one three-year period, one multinational corporation lost 55 percent of its expats (Patterson, 1990).

Despite the high "blackout" rates (ineffective expats who leave) and "brownout" rates (ineffective expats who stay), relatively few corporations offer cross-cultural training. Among those who do, the training is frequently brief—and, in some cases, misguided. For example, of the corporations that offer training, 66 percent offer it for one week or less (McEnery & DesHarnais, 1990). Less than half of the corporations doing business in foreign countries offer foreign language training (Inman, 1985), and those that do will often hire inexperienced and untrained language coaches (Salas, 1984). According to one estimate, 70–80 percent of all expats and 90 percent of their families are given no cross-cultural training at all (Black & Mendenhall, 1989; Brooks, 1987). A recent study of 320 expats currently working in Pacific Rim and European countries revealed that

> 82 percent received no corporate briefings on management practices in their host countries, and 78 percent weren't even provided factual information on their destination. Only 15 percent were given any language training... Of the largest U.S. corporations... 45 percent don't consider training U.S. managers for overseas markets particularly important although [they may] draw at least a quarter of their annual revenue from international operations. (Patterson, 1990, p. 13)

These expats are often not merely ineffective; they can unwittingly destroy cultural bonds that may have taken years to develop. Black and Mendenhall (1989) estimate that the direct costs of failed expats in the United States stands at $2 billion, and that figure does not include damaged corporate reputations, the loss of international goodwill, and lost business opportunities. Global business is conducted in an atmosphere of political instability, rapid social and economic change, the threat of monopolies, nationalized industries, and indigenous workers (Ronen, 1986). Adding well-intentioned but untrained American business personnel to an already demanding competitive climate may strain cultural ties to the breaking point.

Not only cultural ties may be strained but also personal and company ties (Dillon, 1990; DiMarco, 1974). For many executives, an expat assignment is a professional death knell: while the expat is away, peers are promoted, company culture changes, and the job the expat left behind may disappear. According to McClenahen (1987), four difficulties face the expat. First, expats must leave behind the competitive excitement of company headquarters, from where they are usually sent. The foreign office may be small and slow. Second, expats frequently gain power, experience, and perspectives overseas that their stateside colleagues do not possess. Coming back home to office politics and corporate climbing may seem shallow and unappealing. Third, while away, the expat frequently acquires a sense of loyalty to the foreign office—perhaps even the foreign country. The expat becomes apathetic and ineffective when it is time to return to the home office. Fourth and finally, expats are out of sight and out of mind. The home office does not seek the insights of the returning expat; and U.S. corporate culture, on the whole, resists the new global perspective the expat may bring.

As many have suggested, the difficulty with expat assignments rests in the corporate culture that creates the assignments. For example, according to a survey by Harris (1989), only about 4 percent of companies who have expats say the assignment has a positive impact on the expat's career. American corporations seem to believe not only that the business of America is business, but that the business of the world is American business.

Dunbar and Katcher (1990) suggest that companies tend to minimize the differences between cultures, suggesting to expats that every major city is more or less like Los Angeles. Additionally, companies who have a successful (or at least a mediocre) expat often resist bringing the expat home. Promises about jobs and rewards when the expat gets back can be vague and often misleading which prompts Dunbar and Katcher to conclude that most expats are underused, misused, and ignored. Perhaps most distressing is that the expat chosen for the assignment may possess exactly the qualities valued in American business but prove to be dysfunctional in the foreign office. The corporate star in Boston may be a failure in Bangkok (Black & Porter, 1991; Mendenhall, Dunbar & Oddou, 1987).

Some companies, however, are changing their views of culture and are making cross-cultural training a priority. More and more companies are finding—by listening to their expats—that family relationships are more important than money or other job perquisites (Copeland, 1985). Some companies are beginning to focus on the family before sending an expat abroad—particularly the expat's spouse (McEnery & DesHarnais, 1990; Rodgers, 1984). Spouse dissatisfaction and unhappiness are frequently the key factors in expat productivity. For example, in a recent study of eighty failed expat executives, Tung (1987) found the most frequently given reason for failure to be that the spouse was unhappy living in the new cultural environment. Listed as the least important reason for failure was the expat's personal motivation to work overseas (Tung, 1987). In fact, in one study, a statistically significant prediction of whether an expat family would stay was made, in large part, by asking the spouse if he or she intended to stay (Gregersen & Black, 1990). Concludes Overman (1989), "companies are taking a close look at the entire family issue in relocation . . . The spouse, particularly a non-working spouse, is under the greatest stress." (p. 44).

By studying both American expats living abroad and foreign expats living in the United States (Tung, 1987), researchers have been able to suggest several general guidelines to enhance the chances for expat success. For example, Tung (1981) suggests the following:

- Expats should not be placed in active managerial roles for the first several months.

- Advancement in the company should be available and possible even though the expat is away from headquarters.

- Time should be given to the expat and the family to establish friendships with other expats and with those in the new country.

- Longer, more direct, and more individualized cross-cultural training should be given to the expat.

Grove (1990) further suggests that two people be assigned to guide and protect the expat during the overseas stay. First, the expat should be given a "godfather," a higher ranking executive at the home office who will keep the expat informed on major developments at home and who will watch for opportunities in the company where the returning expat's skills and insights can be best used.

Second, the expat should be given a "guardian angel," an expat peer currently working in the same office whose family can socially and professionally befriend the new expat and family.

As with American colleges and schools of education, schools of business have been rather slow to respond to the need for academically trained practitioners who can succeed in a culturally diverse work environment. True, there are degree offerings in international business, but little is done to prepare every business student for the demands of a multicultural workplace (Seabrook & Valdes, 1988). In Florida where the population is becoming increasingly diverse, a new consortium of forty-five higher educational institutions was formed to address the concerns of multicultural businesses. The constorium contacted 288 major companies in Florida and found that, although more than two-thirds of the companies employed translators and conducted business abroad, fewer than one-quarter offered even foreign language training to their own employees (Campbell, Hallman & Geroy, 1988). More surprising is the recent finding that, according to some business analysts (McEnery & DesHarnais, 1990), few companies value foreign language proficiency in their employees. There are a few exceptions. For example, Frey-Hartel and Kasum (1988) report that a new course at Cardinal Stretch College in Milwaukee has been successful for Milwaukee businesses conducting business in France.

Some firms are taking steps to train their employees. Some firms, in fact, are forcing their employees into cross-cultural training. For example, several public utility companies—Public Service Company of New Mexico, Public Service Company of Colorado, and Southern California Edison Company—have all initiated aggressive, and sometimes mandatory cross-cultural training for their employees. At the Colorado firm, executives were motivated to change not only the attitudes but the cultural composition of their employees when the city of Denver refused to renew the company's contract. The cultural demographics of the company's executives did not match the cultural demographics of Denver (Semien,

1990). In another public service company, some 3,200 Montreal city bus drivers were also given forced cross-cultural training when they refused to pick up immigrant and non-French-speaking riders. The training, according to Stolovitch and Lane (1989), was successful as measured by lowered complaint rates.

Some companies utilize other methods to ease cross-cultural tension. The Nestle and Unilever companies, for example, are trying to staff all their offices with a mixture of multinational employees (Rodgers, 1984). Bechtel focuses on communication training, and utilizes training on an as-needed basis. Additionally, Bechtel assigns a "sponsoring spouse" and a "home sponsor" who fulfill the godfather and guardian angel roles mentioned earlier (Rodgers, 1984). McDonald's hires nationals unless an expat is absolutely necessary, and Parker Pen and KLM strive to keep expat stays shorter than two months (Smith, 1984). Other companies, such as CIBA, Colgate, Dow, Xerox, GE, and Citicorp have moved to integrate overseas assignments into career tracks (Patterson, 1990). Moving up in these companies means, at some point, moving abroad. At Citicorp, for example, "about two-thirds of our top-level executives have worked overseas" (Patterson, 1990, p. 17).

Unlike Peace Corps volunteers, American expats are subject to vast discrepancies in cross-cultural training; frequently, they receive no training at all. To that extent, expats are similar to teachers, many of whom have received little and somewhat sporadic training for a culturally diverse work environment. However, expats are—like missionaries—rather singular in purpose: missionaries spread the gospel; expats create profits. Perhaps the greatest point of differentiation between the American expat and all other cross-cultural workers examined thus far is the growing attention paid to the satisfaction of the expat's spouse and family. Only scant attention is given to spouse or family satisfaction in the missionary literature, and none in the educational literature. Perhaps a more thorough examination of family support would aid other cross-cultural sojourners who face difficult periods of adjustment.

CROSS-CULTURAL TRAINING FOR MILITARY PERSONNEL

Like the expat and the teacher, many in the U.S. military are sent with their families to work in other cultures. For many, the assignment is unwanted. As early as 1964, Humphrey (1964) reported there were growing problems that endangered international goodwill because military personnel in foreign countries spent their off-duty hours getting drunk, destroying flags, and molesting natives. The military tried creating a series of cultural and social functions, and they tried forcing foreign language training on overseas personnel. Neither worked

(Humphrey, 1964). In many military zones worldwide, single military men were forbidden to date local women; married military couples formed a social life on the base.

On military bases in Korea in the late 1950s, relations between locals and the American military reached an impasse. In response, the military began to survey the locals to find out their expectations regarding the U.S. military personnel. To their surprise, military investigators discovered that the locals wanted increased contact with the Americans; they also found that the standard health and sanitation lectures given to military personnel before arrival in Korea lessened the willingness of American personnel to seek local contact (Humphrey, 1964).

The military began to train its personnel by emphasizing the common elements of all cultures (parenting, working, religion, etc.) and the universal current of all human feeling. In Panama, during Operation Friendship—when the United States military was sent to stabilize relations after the 1959 uprising there—soldiers were instructed to "look into [the Panamanian's] face and realize that beneath his darkened, insecure, perhaps black countenance, he is a man who feels as deeply as we do" (Humphrey, 1964, p. 120). In Korea, this kind of training was so successful that although before the cross-cultural training 61 percent of the American military personnel believed the locals were to blame for anti-Americanism, after the training, 60 percent believed Americans were to blame (Humphrey, 1964).

This race relations training had a political component as well (Hayles, 1978). Military personnel were reminded that "the task of helping several hundred thousand overseas Americans to establish better working relations . . . is synonymous with the advancement of . . . [our] interests in the Cold War" (Humphrey, 1964, p. 6). Although large groups of military personnel had to be trained, cross-cultural training was viewed as an "individually-oriented complement to the AA [Affirmative Action]/EO [Equal Opportunity] institutionally-focused activity" (Hayles, 1978, p. 66). International and domestic training were, in a sense, combined. The military strove for a cessation of racial incidents and increased communication both at home and abroad (Hayles, 1978).

The military experimented with different training models; one of them was called the "Army's Alien Presence Model." The goals of this training were as follows:

- developing a positive regard for locals;

- understanding basic human similarities;

- interacting with hosts as individuals rather than as stereotypes;

- providing methods to observe and integrate cultural differences;

- preparing to withstand culture shock;

- developing personal responsibility for better international cultural relations;

- reinforcing training through group involvement; and

- giving specific information about local customs and attitudes.

This training was provided during briefings to senior officers and unit commanders so as to gain support at high levels. In all, sixteen one-hour sessions were given to junior officers and enlisted personnel. At the end of the training, personnel were encouraged (though not forced) to learn the local language, to eat the local food, to refrain from making derogatory jokes, and to keep their peers from doing so. Personnel who responded to these suggestions were then asked to participate in civic projects that the hosts had requested military help in accomplishing (Brislin & Pedersen, 1976).

Measured outcomes of the military training released for publication in recent years have produced some interesting findings. For example, Stewart (1972) found that, even within the hierarchically designed military, Americans were willing to work with all ranks, while locals from other cultures often preferred to retain a hierarchical chain of command and communication. In an evaluation of U.S. Army cross-cultural training, Brislin and Pedersen (1976) found that the trained group expressed significantly more positive attitudes than the control group; however, no behavioral measures (such as fewer fights with nationals) were reported. In a study of eighty U.S. Navy personnel stationed at Yokosuka Naval Base in Japan who were divided randomly into intensive, unstructured, and control training groups, Gudykunst, Hammer, and Wiseman (1977; Hammer, Gudykunst, & Wiseman, 1978) found that those who received intensive training significantly increased their personal satisfaction during the overseas stay. Those who received six hours of unstructured training or no training at all were equally low on outcome measures (Gudykunst, Hammer, & Wiseman, 1977). Harrison (1987)—in a more recent study of sixty-five civilian employees aiding military personnel to settle in Japan—found that those who received a combination of training methods were also significantly better prepared to work overseas. However, Harrison also reports that, the more intense the training, the lower the measures of self-efficacy. Harrison concludes that personnel felt less personally prepared to deal with cultural differences after training because they realized how little they knew.

Like Teacher Corps members and many expats, military personnel are stationed in foreign countries for a relatively short period of time. Like missionaries who live on mission compounds, military personnel can retreat into an American community at the end of the workday. All military personnel stationed abroad receive some cross-cultural training, although the training is not designed to turn the raw recruit into a self-actualized, mediating, multicultural sojourner. The training is limited to specific kinds of interactions the soldier is expected to have with the local. Furthermore, like the missionary and the expat, the soldier is commissioned to create international goodwill. The global perception of the military, corporate, or religious organization takes precedence over the individual's response to the culture; and the individual is encouraged to perceive his or her actions as important in shaping the global perception of the organization.

CROSS-CULTURAL TRAINING FOR MEDICAL/MENTAL HEALTH WORKERS

Among members of the medical and mental health communities, an organizational allegiance is also present, but it is modified by the intensity of contact between majority and minority culture members. For example, Benavides, Lynch, and Velasquez (1980) report that, at the School of Social Work at the University of Minnesota in Minneapolis, graduate students are trained to counsel Native American, Hispanic, and black patients. An integral part of the training requires them to be competent in internal interactional communication (messages they send to themselves, and messages they believe their patients are sending to themselves), external interactional communication (decoding the intended messages of language), and culturally specific communication. This kind of training requires a radical departure from more "traditional" kinds of therapeutic training (Harley & Robinson, 1991). For example, mental health professionals dealing with refugees—as particularly after the Viet Nam War—must be trained to offer help to people who often have under gone torture, isolation, and grueling travel. Because of language barriers, the therapists must hire translators. However, it has frequently occurred that the translators became so upset by the Southeast Asian patient's story, for example, that the translators also needed therapy, thus creating, in effect, two patients (Athey, 1987).

In the early 1980s, the University of California at San Diego discovered that more than 25 percent of the patients served by its medical student interns were Southeast Asian or Hispanic. After securing funding from the California Health Manpower Commission, the Cross-cultural Family Medicine Training Program was started. Professional health workers began receiving cross-cultural training that includes learning Spanish, Mexican history, legends, religious ceremonies, and myths. The residential care of all cross-cultural patients is conducted under the direction of a foreign culture specialist who observes the interaction of the patient with the medical care worker. The program is designed to be intensive and prolonged. Medical students in residency train for three years in cross-cultural activities that include intensive language training and repeated, observed interaction with culturally different patients. Almost half of all graduates of the program choose to practice in underserved Hispanic or Southeast Asian areas of San Diego County (Kristal, Pennock, Foote, & Trygstad, 1983).

Similar programs have been started at Miami's Cross-cultural Training Institute for Mental Health Professionals (Lefley, 1985); at the Vivian Garrison Inner-City Support Systems Project in Newark, New Jersey; at the Therapist Spiritist Training Project in Puerto Rico; at the New Horizons Community Mental Health Center in Miami; and at the Multnomah City Health Division in Multnomah, Oregon (Bliatout, 1988; Lefley, 1981).

At the New Horizons Community Mental Health Center in Miami where Cuban immigrants are facing the new challenges of American life, mental health workers are finding that they must shrink the institution to the size of the neighborhood and that the sessions they offer must "fit" the social and recreational needs of the area. For example, Lefley (1981) reports that, at one center, patients sign up ostensibly for a watercolor class. Although they do watercolor, the class is really group therapy. Lefley also finds that mental health professionals must be trained to be assertive—even authoritative—since this is the leadership style to which Cuban immigrants respond. The more reflective and open style of American counselor–patient relationships is not helpful in Cuban culture.

There are other changes as well. For example, Bliatout (1988) reports that at the Multnomah City Health Division, the Hmong people resist all invasive treatment (drugs, surgery, etc.) because they believe such treatment alters their reincarnation. Furthermore, American males are not allowed to examine or treat Hmong females. In a study of AIDS health care providers in San Francisco, Day (1990) discovered that minority AIDS patients were reluctant to seek treatment from predominantly white physicians and nurses. The patients felt isolated and believed the providers were "insensitive and judgmental about the values and behaviors of culturally different people" (Day, 1990, p. 49). In response to the growing numbers of minority AIDS patients who were not seeking any treatment at all, the San Francisco Department of Health offered free cross-cultural training to ninety AIDS organizations. The training was divided into different kinds of contact the provider had with the patient, and then subdivided into the cultural background from which the patient came. For example, beliefs about homosexuality and dementia are very different in different cultures. Because these are so closely associated with AIDS, much of the training focused on the etiology and outcomes of these among different cultural groups.

One particularly interesting result of cross-cultural training was found by Lefley (1985). In a study of 122 mental health professionals in the Miami Cross-Cultural Training Institute for Mental Health Professionals—sixty-eight of whom were white, and fifty-four of whom were black—Lefley found that the same cross-cultural training produces significantly different effects within the two populations. Using longitudinal measures of changes in agency caseload data, minority agency utilization rates, minority dropout rates, and individual pretest and posttest measures, Lefley found that gaps between blacks and whites widened. For example, after training, whites showed significantly greater tolerance for blacks and Hispanics across all socioeconomic levels on Bogardus's Social Distance Scale. However, on the same scale, blacks showed less tolerance for higher socioeconomic levels across all cultures and a significant increase in intolerance for high socioeconomic peers within their own culture. Furthermore, on a measure of world view change that is sensitive to cultural difference, both blacks and whites originally saw world view as undifferentiated across cultures. After training, white world views shifted closer to black world views. However, blacks who took the same test saw themselves as individuals who had broken with a distinctive black world view. Their views shifted toward their perceptions of white culture. Finally, after training, whites believed blacks should be given preferential treatment; blacks disagreed. This study must be interpreted with caution, however. No behavioral measures are reported. Also, it is possible that the different populations operated under different understandings of the instruments. Nonetheless, it does raise questions about the universality of cross-cultural training among different ethnic groups.

Additional cross-cultural training is being used to aid psychologists and psychiatrists whose patients are increasingly drawn from culturally diverse populations (Christensen, 1984; Johnson, 1983; Johnson, 1987; Merta, Stringham & Ponterotto, 1988; Mio & Morris, 1990; O'Brien, Alexander & Plooij, 1973; Pang, 1981; Petrie, 1987; Ponterotto, 1988; Ponterotto & Casas, 1987; Sabnani, Ponterotto & Borodovsky, 1991; Tanney, 1982; Westwood & Borgen, 1988). As in other occupations, the measurement of success is difficult among counselors. Is an increase in the patient's mental health an indicator that training was successful? If the therapist has a positive attitude but no treatment effects are detected, was the training successful? Neimeyer, Kukuyama, Bingham, Hall, and Mussenden (1986) report that—like the military personnel who reported less self-efficacy in meeting culturally diverse persons—graduate students who completed a class on counseling cultural minorities felt less competent and less likely to continue the therapeutic relationship than students who counseled patients of their own race.

To curb racial violence on its campus, the University of California at Davis created a Cross-Cultural Training Committee in which fifty-six peer counselors (students who received training) were taught to help their peers interact with students from different races. The training included selecting a partner from a different race, keeping a journal, and writing weekly papers. Vohra, Rodolfa, De La Cruz, Vincent, and Bee-Gates (1991) found "it is noteworthy that... the minority students felt a need to explain their own cultural heritage rather than learn about their partner's cultural experience" (p. 83). Again, the issue of whether the same cross-cultural training has similar effects on different ethnic groups seems relevant.

Several psychologists have proposed stage models for increasing the occurrence of counseling interaction among members of different cultures (Ponterotto, 1988; Ponterotto & Benesch, 1988). One of the most elegant is proposed by Gibbs (1985), who views cross-cultural training as a five-stage model across three performance dimensions: task, behavior, and attitude. Hence, the Gibbs model contains fourteen performance attributes along the three dimensions. The task attributes are these five: (1) appraisal; (2) investigation; (3) involvement; (4) commitment; and (5) engagement. These represent the tasks that counselors must undertake with all patients. The behavioral attributes are also five: (1) authenticity; (2) egalitarianism; (3) identification; (4) acceptance; and (5) performance. These represent the style of interaction that therapists must display with patients. Finally, the attitudinal attributes are these four: (1) genuineness; (2) status equalization; (3) positive identification; and (4) empathy. These represent the attitudes that Gibbs (1985) believes are most conducive to therapist–client interaction in a culturally diverse encounter.

Of the vocations examined thus far, medical and mental health providers can be considered unique. While all other workers—with the exception of teachers—may encounter large numbers of culturally diverse people in varying levels of intimacy and intensity, medical and mental health providers may encounter few culturally different patients, but the encounters may be intense, intimate, and prolonged. Furthermore, in the health provider field, contact may be somewhat voluntary and may be at the discretion of the patient. Minority children cannot simply choose other teachers, and locals cannot easily ignore the presence of American military. In contrast, dissatisfied patients can seek other medical help; therapists and doctors who are uncomfortable with patients from other cultures can refer those patients elsewhere.

CONCLUSION

One area of sojourner research unmentioned in this chapter is that conducted on foreign students. This group was intentionally omitted. Foreign students are not employees, as are the other sojourners examined. Rarely do foreign students work in the country of study; they arrive for a specified period of time to study at a university. Many return home to begin a career. While some of the research from this area is included in Chapter 7, foreign students were not included here.

It seems clear that students suffer from culture shock, re-entry shock, and a host of other negative effects from cross-cultural contact; but their methods of solving the problems and adapting to the environment are often more fluid than that of workers (Batchelder, 1978; Batchelder & Warner, 1977). For instance, students can switch classes or return home if the pressures mount. Few other workers have that privilege. Furthermore, while students may enter a foreign country for specialized study, some enter for the experience of living in another country. The stresses of income, family, and career are more likely to be absent. Finally, as Wong-Rieger (1984) points out in a study of eighty students from foreign countries, cultural mismatches are more likely to occur in work contexts than in social contexts. "Work environments [are] more constraining than social ones . . . [and] social situations seemingly allow for greater flexibility" (Wong-Rieger, 1984, p. 181). Students can spend a greater portion of their time in social interaction than can other sojourners; foreign students' interactions with professors may be brief and cursory.

In summary, it seems clear that different vocations have approached the need for cross-cultural training from widely varying viewpoints. Some of the differences can be accounted for, no doubt, by differences in task. However, movement within a different culture is never easy; neither is the specification of skills, attitudes, and behaviors necessary for the success of any given sojourner a simple task. Encouraging, perhaps, is the mixture of seemingly important elements within different organizations. For example, self-selection and nonrigorous training—aspects discovered to be successful in Peace Corps training—seem relevant in many other fields, and certainly within education where the present system of teacher preparation does not incorporate cross-cultural training in every program. The emphasis on spouse and family satisfaction—a new area of importance in the business community—also may be generalizable to other fields.

In Chapter 7, the elements of training that all cross-cultural programs must incorporate will be examined in greater detail. For example, all cross-cultural training programs must have some means of selecting candidates, training them, testing them, and evaluating their performance. The question of whether differences in these elements seem to contribute to changes in training results will shape the inquiry.

7

CHARTING THE ROUTES

> Do not let them sell their stateside house.
>
> —James E. Harris
> "Moving Managers Internationally:
> The Care and Feeding of Expatriates"

In Chapter 6, a general survey of different organizations and groups that have implemented cross-cultural training showed how widely the training programs differ. Why an organization trains its people, and toward what ends will vary by time, task, and goal. Some trainees are volunteers; others are not. Many trainees must live totally within the new culture; some can retreat into a familiar cultural enclave at the end of the workday. Furthermore, the evidence suggests that all trainees undergo some form of culture shock, though the length and intensity of the shock is not uniform. Important as many of these variables are, their importance derives from how well they address the single fundamental question of cross-cultural training: can cross-cultural training create productive, effective, and satisfied people in culturally different or culturally diverse work environments? If so, what elements of training contribute to this outcome?

It is the purpose of this chapter to explore these two questions in depth. These questions seem deceptively simple, but embedded in them are hundreds of other questions. For example, what does "productive" mean? How is it measured? Can it be predicted? What other variables are intervening or interacting or inhibiting?

One seemingly straightforward way to answer these questions might be to consider those organizations that have the lowest failure rates (such as the Peace Corps) and to ignore others (such as expats and teachers) whose failure rates are significantly higher. However, such a comparison would not provide an accurate picture. For example, while Peace Corps failure rates are relatively low, Peace Corps members are stationed for a maximum of two years. A candidate who fulfills the two-year commitment is considered a success. However, teachers in rural Alaskan villages and in minority inner-city areas also stay an average of two years, yet they are considered "failures" because their stay is far shorter than the average length of teachers in other environments (LeCompte, 1985). Some expats are considered cross-cultural training successes if they stay abroad three months (Earley, 1987). Hence, it seems that a broader consideration of training variables may provide insight into what constitutes successful cross-cultural training.

Although questions about the creation of successful training cannot yet be answered definitively, they can be explored across the several dimensions that are part of all cross-cultural training programs. These dimensions include how candidates for training will be selected, what methods of training will be used, whether the training will occur in the home culture or the host culture, who will train, and how long the training will last. In this chapter, several dimensions of training are explored.

METHODS OF TRAINING

In 1983, Landis and Brislin (1983) suggested that all cross-cultural training programs could be categorized into six types. While many within the training field call for the use of combinations of types (Grove, 1982, 1990; Gudykunst, Hammer, & Wiseman, 1977; Triandis, 1977), understanding the distinctions between types can be helpful in analyzing programs. The six types of training are as follows:

1. Information-oriented training—characterized by cognitive acquisition through lectures, video tapes, and reading materials;

2. Attribution training—based on developing internalized perspectives of events from another culture's point of view (for which, a cultural assimilator is used);

3. Cultural awareness training—distinguished by a focus on one's own culture and the nature of cultural differences;

4. Cognitive-behavioral training—designed to teach trainees culturally conditioned systems of rewards and punishments that operate in the target culture;

5. Interactive training—intended to familiarize trainees with the target culture by using experienced sojourners or target culture representatives to teach from their personal perspectives; and

6. Experiential training—characterized by cultural immersion or other forms of participant-oriented activities, such as cultural simulations and role plays.

Information-oriented training is based on what has been called the "intellectual model" (Bennett, 1986b). It incorporates cognitive goals, culture-specific content, and an emphasis on traditional intellectual processes. Because it is relatively easy to staff and because the kinds of learning it involves—rational, abstract, sequential, logical thinking—are foundational within American education, information-oriented training is the favored (and sometimes the exclusive) choice of many organizations. Virtually every cross-cultural training program contains some information training. Its chief advantage lies in the fact that increases in cultural knowledge can be measured rapidly, easily, and quantitatively.

However, there are numerous drawbacks. The most serious weakness of information training is that it fails to produce skills necessary in the field, and it provides no means by which a transfer from knowledge to skills can be made. Another serious drawback is that, frequently, the choice of content is capricious. What should trainees learn? Chu and Levy (1988) make it clear that, rather than relying on research results of cross-cultural effectiveness and then gearing the content to match, many programs capriciously patch together "home-grown curricula" (p. 157).

A close cousin of information-oriented training is *attribution training*. Attribution training has been used by a wide variety of cross-cultural trainers—chiefly by Fieldler, Mitchell, and Triandis (1971), who developed the "cultural assimilator." The cultural assimilator is a series of programmed vignettes. These vignettes are based on single incidents that can prove confusing when different cultures interact. Each vignette, then, presents in story form one incident and asks the reader to select one of four possible explanations for the misunderstanding. Only one explanation is correct: the explanation that is understood within the target culture. It is hoped the trainees who work through these vignettes (and sometimes there are more than 100 vignettes for a culture) will learn to make attributions that are operational in the target culture, rather than in their own (Albert, 1983).

The assimilator has some advantages. It is culture-specific, portable, and not dependent on the skills or style of a trainer. Furthermore, an assimilator includes a broad variety of potentially troubling situations the trainee may encounter, and it allows trainees to understand—at an individualized pace—why some explanations of the vignette are wrong, without risking the loss of relationships and of time in the field. However, like information training, attribution training has its drawbacks. There is little empirical evidence that trainees can transfer the attributions into meaningful field behavior (Harrison, 1987; O'Brien, Alexander & Plooij, 1973), although some studies suggest that trainees become better at recognizing culturally ambiguous situations (Cushner, 1989) and better at communicating within such situations (Brislin, 1986). Furthermore, the assimilator requires that the trainee learn solely by absorbing written information.

One of the most popular forms of training is *awareness training*, sometimes called "cultural awareness training" or "self-awareness training." Although awareness training can incorporate both cultural awareness and self-awareness, there are distinctions between them. Self-awareness training is "designed to encourage change in the individual's self-perception, attitudes, and behaviors" (Bennett, 1986b, p. 125).

While self-awareness encounters can produce strong emotional results, there are numerous disadvantages. For example, trainees may unearth deeply held convictions that are psychologically explosive, and trainers and other trainees may be unprepared to handle the results (Starosta, 1990; Wight & Hammons, 1970). Furthermore, this training relies on trainee adherence to values of openness, equality, directness, and group norms. Not every trainee feels comfortable in this kind of intensive personal exchange. Finally, the training fails to provide a framework for future situations or to prepare trainees to transfer the group experience into future cultural learning. Human relations training relies frequently on self-awareness models and methods (Brislin & Pedersen, 1976; Cere, 1988; Fox, Kuhlman, & Sales, 1988; Oja, 1979; Sleeter, 1989; Williams, 1981).

Similarly, the cultural awareness model relies on an encounter with one's cultural values, usually within a group. Heavily used forms of cultural awareness training were the Contrast American and Alien Presence programs used in the U.S. military. Trainees would be asked to role-play a situation with a trainer who represented someone from a contrasting culture. As the two worked to solve a problem, it became clear that the role-played values of the trainer were operating in contrast to traditional American values (Brislin & Pedersen, 1976; Byram, 1988). Other awareness training emphasizes techniques designed to eliminate or lessen prejudice and ethnocentrism (Lee, 1983; Olsen & Dowell, 1989; Rozema, 1982). Advantages to this training are that many materials are available for implementation, and it sparks lively thought and discussion among participants. However, it requires a skilled trainer to utilize. Furthermore, the effect of the training wanes, since the excitement of the training is lost in the field.

Cognitive-behavioral training is based somewhat on Bandura's theory of social learning (Bandura, 1977). Cultures reward certain kinds of behaviors and punish others. If the trainee can learn to incorporate the skills required in the new culture, it is assumed that adjustment will be easier and effectiveness will be enhanced. Black and Mendenhall (1989) favor this method for use in business training for expats, as do others from various fields (Bogorya, 1985; Cordova, Jaramillo & Trujillo, 1974; Hale-Benson, 1990; Heusinkveld, 1957; Leonard, 1991; Neely & Campbell, 1985; Pedersen, 1984; Ruben, 1976; Westwood & Borgen, 1988).

There are advantages to cognitive-behavioral training. It can be conducted using intercultural communication materials, teaching trainees to analyze intended meanings and to shape their responses toward desired outcomes. Furthermore, it allows trainees to practice and learn about the culture without risking negative responses in the field. However, a drawback is that cultures are complex entities. Discovering and transmitting a packaged set of skills that sum up an entire culture are not easy. Furthermore, this training does not guarantee competence in the field—certainly not competence in any behaviors neglected during training.

Interactive training uses veteran sojourners or target culture representatives as trainers. One advantage of this training is that the trainee participates more directly in the choice of training content to be covered. Veteran sojourners are convincing, and they can speak with personal authority of the adjustments and changes they underwent. Likewise, target culture representatives may be able to translate cultural differences into understandable concepts for trainees. This kind of training is popular and is often used to address particular problems when two cultures are in conflict (Garcia, 1974; Jenkins, 1990; Laosa, 1974; Pang, 1981). However, there are disadvantages. For example, target culture representatives are frequently expected to be cultural exemplars, and their knowledge of their own culture may be limited, inapplicable, or inappropriate for trainees. Veteran sojourners may inadvertently transmit their own biases and negative attitudes surrounding the target culture, rather than teaching trainees to develop their own perspectives.

Experiential training covers a wide spectrum of activities, ranging from short role plays and games to long periods of immersion in the field. This training emphasizes affective and behavioral goals; cognitive acquisition is a by-product of experience. In other words, trainees learn by doing. Learning by doing, however, can be short-lived. For example, although several cross-cultural simulation games have been developed in recent years (Dubin, 1985), Noesjirwan and Freestone (1979) suggest although that the players learn there are differences between two cultures, they may develop a conviction that they could not long survive in either. Without careful intervention from sensitive trainers, role plays that are easily resolved or are unresolvable may produce a negative effect in the long run (Buchanan, 1981; Petrie, 1987; Ponterotto & Benesch, 1988).

Almost everyone agrees that field training is of great benefit to trainees. As early as 1976, the American Association of Colleges for Teacher Education called for all teacher education students to "experience in some depth at least one of the local, regional, or national subcultures" (Wilson, 1983, p. 184). Conn (1984) and Greenway (1983), both missionary trainers, argue that candidates should be trained to be "street smart" by experiencing life as it is lived on the street. Greenway (1983), for example, believes that mission candidates should experience during training one year of street evangelism and one year of ministry within prisons before heading for the foreign or domestic mission field. While experience in the field under training conditions is undoubtedly powerful and effective, one drawback is that trainees need sufficient preparation for the experience. Merely dropping people into an unfamiliar culture will not, even over time, ensure adequate or effective adjustment. Furthermore, not every trainee is available for long-term immersion in the field, particularly if the trainee is not receiving a salary during the training (Bennett, 1986a).

Many programs experiment with combinations of these methods. A thorough examination of these programs would fill several volumes, but a look at some particularly successful programs may show a constellation of elements that seems to produce desirable results. In the field of education, Banks (1991) from the University of Washington, Noordhoff and Kleinfeld (1990) from the University of Alaska at Fairbanks, and Mahan (1984) from Indiana University all employ a variety of techniques to train teachers for culturally different classrooms. All three programs are lengthy; Mahan's (1984), for example, requires a two-year commitment from student teachers. All the programs combine information-oriented training, cultural awareness, attribution training, and some cognitive-behavioral and interactive activities in their programs. Noordhoff and Kleinfeld (1990) and Mahan (1984) both require a lengthy supervised immersion in the field. During the immersion— the final phase of training—trainees are expected to find friends and develop behavioral competencies without retreating into their own native culture.

In a study of Miami's Cross-Cultural Training Institute for Mental Health Professionals, Lefley (1985) discovered that, although the training was only eight days long, it covered a broad range of activities. Professors from the Miami University Department of Psychiatry along with professors from other disciplines, folk healers, and community representatives delivered lectures on ethnic history, cognitive styles, world views, and age and sex roles. Participants learned intercultural communication strategies; they played cross-cultural games; and they simulated cross-cultural encounters. Finally, they made visits to ethnic neighborhoods, bars, restaurants, churches, and homes.

Businesses have tried some creative approaches to field training. Digital Equipment and Fujitsu, for example, have both changed the corporation within the culture. Digital has created a commonality of jobs globally (i.e., people in Cleveland and in Cairo have the same title and perform the same work), while Fujitsu has attempted to create and export a core culture to every office location (Rubin, 1991).

Training in the field, alone, does not guarantee trainee success. Field training usually follows other kinds of preparatory training, and the two seem mutually dependent. When field training is too rapid or too removed from preparation in the native culture, results can be less than satisfactory. In a study of training given to missionaries in the American Baptist Mission, Peters (1990) found that the training occurs in two stages. First there is an initial predeparture stage (of unspecified length), during which a general overview of the area and a history of missiology are provided. This is immediately followed by field training, which consists of local missionaries (as opposed to the mission board or cross-cultural trainers) teaching local customs to the newcomers. As part of the study, Peters (1990) asked the trainees what changes, if any, they believed should be made in their cross-cultural training and orientation. Astonishingly, they complained that they had not received any cross-cultural training and that their spouses (who had been included) received no orientation. Furthermore, they reported feeling rushed into doing work they felt untrained to do.

In summary, training programs employ many different kinds of strategies and learning tools to aid trainees in making the adjustment to a new culture. Some types of training seem to produce results not easily transmitted to the field. For example, information training may increase knowledge, but knowledge alone may not translate into appropriate behavioral skills in the field. Experiential training—unless it is used in concert with other methods—may produce confusing and short-lived results. It seems that the strongest programs are those that utilize a combination of training methods and include a supervised immersion experience as a required part of the training.

SELECTION OF CANDIDATES

Who are the best candidates? One answer might be that, when possible, cultural familiars should work together. Local missionaries should train local ministers; minority children should be taught by minority teachers. Given the difficulty of crossing cultures and the potential damage of culture shock, perhaps same-culture candidates should be preferred. Are the best candidates same-culture candidates, then? Evidence suggests they are not.

Pusch, Seelye, and Wasilewski (1981), who train teachers for cross-cultural classrooms, found that membership in a cultural group does not ensure automatic cultural congruence. Similarly, Hood (1989)—studying cultural bias on teacher competency tests—concludes that it is not the culture of the teacher that best determines candidates, but whether teachers can understand and teach minority children. In an early study of reading comprehension in twenty-six elementary schools, Modiano (1973, 1975) found that children did report feeling more confident and accepted by same-race teachers. "Insiders" (children of the same race as their teacher) were more successful than "outsiders," although the relationship was mediated by language and prior achievement. However, in a study of white teachers on a Zuni reservation, Osborne (1989b) found that minority group membership does not indicate automatic agreement with multicultural teaching goals or styles. Furthermore, many classrooms contain a mixture of cultures; if cultural group membership were a fixed criterion, then any one teacher would not be qualified to teach. In a very real sense, all teachers are "foreigners" in a mixed culture class (English, 1981).

Other seemingly same-based criteria prove insufficient as well. For example, Salas (1984) observes that businesses frequently choose candidates for foreign assignment not because these candidates show the greatest potential at home or abroad, but because they speak a needed language. Nye (1988), a business trainer, and Hesselgrave (1987), a missionary trainer, both caution against choosing women for cross-cultural work simply because their gender seems advantageous in the field. Although Banach (1990) suggests that placing culturally diverse employees in visible positions (such as hiring Asians as bank tellers) may draw a diverse clientele, it is not clear that such placement is beneficial for the employee, the customer, or the organization.

Perhaps it is necessary to add that different-culture candidates have no inherent claims to effectiveness, either. Although some cross-cultural training is aimed at whites (Stephen, 1987), and although whites sometimes exhibit greater changes in knowledge or attitudes during training than do their minority peers (Houston, 1979), no evidence suggests that any racial or cultural membership—alone—contributes to training success or subsequent effectiveness in the field. To discover the best candidates requires a search in directions other than language, gender, and race.

There is some indication that promising candidates come from strong, stable, and supportive families. Families who fail to support, or who oppose the cross-cultural experience, may weaken the chances for successful training and transition (Kane, 1982; Sieveking, Anchor & Marston, 1981). Grove (1982)—in a study of the American Field Service (AFS) International Programs—found that students abroad telephone home an average of three times a week and that often "the advice and counsel offered by parents and other natural family members . . . has been detrimental to the adjustment and intercultural learning of the student" (p. 5). In a study of corporate criteria for selecting expats, Mendenhall, Dunbar, and Oddou (1987) found that one of the top three indicators of success was spouse and family support. A study of corporate expats by Black and Stephens (1989) revealed that of 220 American expats in the Pacific Rim and Europe, the spouse's positive perception of the novelty of the assignment related most strongly to the employee's intent to stay overseas. Furthermore, the spouse's intent to stay was significantly related to employee adjustment. Surprisingly, the intent to stay was unrelated to the presence or absence of prior cross-cultural experience. An even more recent study by Gregersen and Black (1990) confirmed these findings. A study of 228 spouses and expats stationed in the Pacific Rim and Europe showed that "cultural and non-job factors" were most critical in expat adjustment. Of these non-job factors, the strongest predictive variable was the spouse's satisfaction and intent to stay. Perhaps IBM, Ford, Hewlett-Packard, and Westinghouse—all of whom train spouses along with expats—are ensuring a greater likelihood for successful cross-cultural transition (Black & Stephens, 1989).

Many researchers offer lists of personal qualities they believe contribute to cross-cultural success. The qualities most often sought in cross-cultural candidates are high self-esteem and good communication skills (Aronson & Linder, 1965). In a study of 200 Latin American high school students studying in the United States, Crano (1986) found that students with an initially high self-concept expressed fewer and less severe adjustment problems. In a more recent study of foreign students in the United States, Chen (1990) found that "communication flexibility is one of the key elements . . . for individuals to reach a successful adjustment in a new culture" (p. 13). In a study of Japanese students in the United States, Nishida (1985) found that speaking and listening skills were positively correlated to cross-cultural effectiveness.

In an area seemingly related to both self-esteem and communication, O'Brien, Alexander, and Plooij (1973) found that successful individuals were those "likely to have better interpersonal relationships with co-workers from the host culture" (p. 12). Similarly, Kleinfeld, McDiarmid, Grubis, and Parrett (1983), who were studying teachers in rural Alaskan villages, found that "rapport" with students—rather than achievement measures or teaching styles—contributed positively to cross-cultural success.

Other researchers, however, stress a constellation of attributes and personality traits in cross-cultural candidates. Some of these include strong interpersonal relationships, positive family dynamics, communication skills, and high self-esteem. However, the recipes for success often contain a wide variety of other ingredients. A representative list of these attributes follows:

- confidence and initiative, natural family communication, interpersonal interest, interpersonal harmony, and non-ethnocentrism (Hopkins, 1982);

- awareness of personal strengths and weaknesses, sensitivity, strength, interest, and a provocative personality (Pusch, Patico, Renwick & Saltzman 1981);

- problem-solving orientation, attainable and non-ambiguous goals, open, warm, willing to disclose, willing to be directive, authoritative (Lefley, 1985);

- free of bias, open to honoring cultural alternatives, belief in cross-cultural experience for self and others (Hilliard, 1974);

- "inventive and exploratory, and have . . . pioneer mentality aroused . . . some idea of how to pick up foreign languages . . . an analytical and critical attitude" (Aagaard, 1985, p. 11);

- humble, teachable, patient, cooperative (Fernando, 1988);

- willingness to self-disclose, eagerness to communicate (Trautmann, 1978);

- be in good health, have a balanced perspective, bicultural or multicultural personality, willing to be open and human (Heisey, 1990);

- must see cross-cultural work as a "calling"; must accept changing world and role; must prepare for more than one vocation (Ward, 1987);

- "mature, flexible, and stable personality," can create warm personal relationships (Mayne, 1980, p. 3);

- stable, mature, empathetic, demonstrate a commitment to improvement, serve as catalyst and change agent, expand knowledge within new culture (Brooks, 1975);

- express a desire to communicate and show cultural awareness (Rivers, 1988);

- must be aware, positive, culturally congruent, flexible, and experimental (Trueba, 1988); and

- must show potential and commitment to organizational goals (Jones, 1975).

Taken together, these seem to point to three central requirements that recruiters and evaluators seek in potential cross-cultural candidates. First, the successful candidate must be able to communicate. The ability to articulate one's thoughts and feelings to oneself and others, to listen, and to respond with honesty and sensitivity seem crucial to successful transition. Second, the successful candidate must possess a commitment to the goals of the organization providing the contact. The absence of superordinate goals that are internalized by the candidate seems to contribute to ineffectiveness. Third, a candidate who is cooperative seems to have a high potential for selection. The concept of cooperation involves the ability to mix with people easily, to gain a cultural perspective without losing one's personality.

Though certainly few in number, two studies of cross-cultural workers stress a different aspect of personality that may contribute to success. In a study of expats, Sieveking, Anchor, and Marston (1981) found that "the ideal candidate is someone who is stimulated and intrigued by uncertainty. Curiosity is mandatory" (p. 198). Similarly, Natani (1974)—in a study of Peace Corps volunteers—concluded that the best predictor for field success was to choose candidates who had acquired a taste and a preference for "stress-seeking behavior."

In an unusual study of forty-seven Peace Corps volunteers, Masling, Johnson, and Saturansky (1974) found that high oral-dependent males (who, according to Freud, should be sensitive to external cues) proved to be good candidates for cross-cultural experience. Similarly, Dinges and Duffy (1979) advocated measuring a candidate's biological "basic urge" and then administering a psychoanalytic test of "ego identity" as a measure of overall candidate fitness. However, the strongest predictor—and eventually, the only predictor used by Peace Corps—was self-selection. In an early study of Peace Corps volunteers headed for Nigeria, Mischel (1965) found that self-perceptions of authoritarianism and mental strength proved to be the strongest predictors of success. Harris (1975), who conducted several studies of Peace Corps volunteers, confirmed self-selection as the sole reliable predictor for cross-cultural success. As early as 1970, Harris (1970) concluded,

> The assessment-prediction task [of choosing candidates] reduces . . . the human judgmental process from beginning to end, unaided and uncontaminated by objective tests, unassisted beyond the stage of initial invitation by quantitative biographical data (p. 4).

The monumental question was whether the Peace Corps volunteers—largely composed of inexperienced and overly eager collegians—could indeed select themselves. The data seemed to suggest they could. "Virtually every case in which a volunteer resigns while in service," reported Harris (1970), "is an error in self-selection at some earlier phase" (p. 5). Peace Corps volunteers were at one time expected to exhibit more than twenty-four different personal traits and attributes, none of which proved longitudinally to be linked to field success. Although a battery of more than thirty psychological instruments and various assessments were used on volunteers, after 1969 all were dropped because of the lack of predictive validity (Harris, 1973, 1975). Peace Corps dropouts were studied almost as extensively as the successes, so that new recruits could be measured against what was hoped would prove to be polarized character traits (Harris, 1975). Eventually, however, training conditions closely simulated real field conditions, and candidates who continued to choose further training were given further training.

Researchers such as Klineberg and Hull (1979) suggest that a combination of self and system selection is best. In other words, it is possible that some as yet unmeasured attribute was present in the successful, self-selected Peace Corps volunteers—an attribute that the training environment, or some aspect of the training environment, activated. Klineberg and Hull (1979)—in a study of international exchange students from eleven countries—found that attitudes about the country of origin contributed significantly to adjustment in the country of study: "The student who views his home country as being lower in status compared with his host country ... [will undergo] a completely different adjustment pattern and coping process" than the student who views the countries equally or sees his country as superior (p. 69). Although these students chose to study abroad (or in other words, they were self-selected), their attitudes toward both the home and host countries contributed to overall adjustment.

Sabnani, Ponterotto, and Borodovsky (1991) reach similar conclusions in a study of counselors training for work with cross-cultural patients. Furthermore, they suggest that there may be subtle but important differences between those who select themselves for cross-cultural experience and those who are best suited for it. Cross-cultural training research assumes—perhaps incorrectly—that cross-cultural knowledge, beliefs, attitudes, and skills "can be adopted by any counselor at any time, without taking into consideration that [all cultural groups] differ ... in terms of their readiness for the assimilation of these learnings" (Sabnani, Ponterotto & Borodovsky, 1991, p. 77).

However ambiguous the criteria for success may seem to be, there is some consensus about factors that contribute to selection failure. For example, although Hinkle, Tupton, and Tutchings (1979) assert that qualifications for the successful candidate may be "difficult to define, but easy to sense in personal contact," there is skepticism about the ability of anyone to intuit a candidate's success (p. 167). Mischel (1965), in fact, found that the lowest predictor for success was the personal interview, as did Harris (1970, 1975). Another poor predictor seems to be high performance in the candidate's current job, when that variable is isolated from other variables (Hall, 1989; Mayers, 1985, 1987).

LENGTH OF TRAINING

Is there an optimum length of training that contributes to cross-cultural success? Is more training always better? While many researchers agree that training requires a substantial time commitment (Kudirka, 1989; Spears, Oliver & Maes, 1990), there is little consensus on how much time should be spent. In a survey of corporate training, McEnery and DesHarnais (1990) report that 57 percent of corporate training lasts one week or less; only 14 percent of expats are trained for one month. However, lengths of time can be somewhat deceiving. Inman (1985)—in a study of 185 international corporations—found that the average training time spanned one month, but total time in training activities lasted only a total of sixteen hours. The Mars Corporation and Amadeus Global Travel each offer two-day to three-day workshops for employees several times per year (Rubin, 1991).

The Peace Corps requires two to three months of intensive training followed by six months of informal training in the field (Harris, 1975), but that is unusual. Although the Ford Foundation and others advocate long cross-cultural teacher internships (Rinehart & Leight, 1980), most inservice teacher training averages two to three weeks or less (Baker, 1973, 1977; Covington, 1974) and is usually conducted during summer workshops or during staff development days during the academic year. A notable exception is KEEP, designed to train teachers of native Hawaiian children. The KEEP training program, conducted on a part-time basis, lasts two years (Jordan, 1984). The Teacher Corps required one month of formal full-time training (Popkewitz, 1975). Medical and missionary cross-cultural training varies from a few months to several years (Kane, 1982; Luzbetak, 1988).

For student teachers in some universities the training is longer. Mahan (1982) from Indiana University, who trains teachers for work on Native American reservations and who reports an amazingly low failure rate of 3 percent, requires two full years of training. Part of the training consists of a seventeen-week internship when student teachers live and teach on the reservation. Holland (1974) from Northeastern Oklahoma State University, who trains teachers for the Cherokee Indian reservation, also requires a sixteen-week full-time internship, and limits the number of students to forty per year.

Some training is obviously inappropriate regardless of its length. For example, Korn (1972) describes a study of inservice white suburban teachers who were notified three weeks before the beginning of school that they had been transferred to an inner-city minority school. The district did offer training. Teachers who attended the optional one day of training received $15.

LEVELS OF RISK

The question of how much trainees risk may provide an important clue to levels of overall motivation. If failing the cross-cultural training program results in the loss of a job or licensure, are trainees more motivated to succeed? Do trainees who risk more try harder? In the corporate sector, employees may attempt to escape an overseas assignment since it seldom signals advancement potential. A domestic relocation means a move up on the career ladder; an overseas relocation frequently means a prolonged—perhaps permanent—lateral transfer (Mendenhall & Oddou, 1985). While researchers have found that a cross-cultural corporate relocation does involve managing new job roles and responsibilities, they have also found that the higher the level of employee sent, the lower the willingness to stay (Gregersen & Black, 1990). There is an inverse relationship between corporate rank and cross-cultural commitment.

Some teachers and psychologists, in training for cross-cultural positions, risk loss of certification and licensure if they fail training (Mahan, 1982; Ponterotto & Casas, 1987). Increasingly, more practitioners in the teacher training and counselor training fields are calling for higher risks associated with cross-cultural training failure (Banks, 1992; Ponterotto & Casas, 1987)—though, at present, most cross-cultural coursework and certificate designations are still optional (Sleeter, 1989). Teacher Corps training was entirely voluntary, and the training sessions were ungraded (Freiberg, Townsend & Ashley, 1978). However, Teacher Corps membership, like Peace Corps membership—carried its own prestige and publicity as general motivators.

There are other kinds of risks. Students of color at San Francisco State University who are attending classes taught by white professors believe they risk lowered grades if they do not choose "racially expected" majors—or if they do not answer questions about life in the ghetto, even though many come from middle-class families (Jenkins, 1983). Military trainers in the Middle East and Korea were expected to understand the seriousness of their training and the risk of failure in global terms: "The orientation officer must be made intensely aware that his job places him in a crucial position of leadership in the worldwide ideological struggle" (Humphrey, 1964, p. 4).

Some have suggested that, when trainees enter areas where there may be a risk of violence, specialized training may be needed (York, 1993). For example, Quarles (1987) suggests that missionaries who are assigned to potentially violent countries should receive training to prepare them for terrorist attacks and survival as hostages. Adeney (1979) and Gardner (1987) argue that crisis support teams should be available to missionaries to prepare them for kidnapping, murder, crime, and other disasters.

GOALS OF TRAINING

Although trainees in different occupations prepare for different job tasks, the goals of cross-cultural training are somewhat disassociated from performance skills. For example, learning an accounting function or repairing a small engine are job skills employees carry across cultures. However, certain skills, attitudes, and behaviors are desirable in candidates who are embarking on a cross-cultural experience. Understanding what goals are specified by cross-cultural training programs can provide insight into standards for success. If the central goal of cross-cultural training—as stated earlier—is to create effective, productive, and satisfied people, an examination of differences in program goals may explain why standards for success vary between and among programs.

It seems clear that programs can strive for changes in any or all of three areas: attitudinal, cognitive, or behavioral. It is also clear that many programs favor some areas and not others. Few programs incorporate in-the-field behavioral observations and standards, although almost all implicitly or explicitly make behavioral skills a priority. Thus, an examination of goals is not the search for a single objective that excludes all other kinds of change. Programs frequently combine goals; at times they construct training curricula seemingly designed to fulfill different goals than the ones stated. An examination of training goals, then, is a search for different emphases in programs.

Many researchers emphasize cognitive changes. Brislin (1981, 1990), for example, stresses knowledge of the processes of cultural transmission, of the elements of cultural anthropology, and of the ways in which cultural norms are internalized. Orem (1991), who specializes in adult education, stresses knowledge of the specific culture the trainee will enter as well as a general increase in knowledge of current events. Others—particularly in teacher education—stress changes not only in the trainee, but comparable changes in teaching tasks. They expect cross-culturally trained teachers to acquire more culturally sensitive ways of understanding curriculum (Banks, 1991; Baptiste, 1977; International Catholic Migration Commission, 1985; Jones, 1985; Sims, 1983). Rose (1976), in a series of interviews with Fulbright scholars, reports that the most important goals of training are to understand the relationships between cultures and the ways in which these relationships shape social roles and expectations.

Other researchers emphasize attitudinal changes, placing increased self-awareness, cultural awareness, tolerance, or positive feelings as the chief areas of change. Cere (1988) emphasizes self-awareness and cultural awareness as well as professional awareness as the critical goals of training. Professional awareness involves one's attitudes toward institutions, authority, and social power. Humphrey (1964) suggests that, during cross-cultural military training in the early 1960s, the goals of training were somewhat paradoxical. For example, one goal was to achieve an 80 percent rate of positive attitudes among trainees, while another was to use the training "to analyze the nature of the ideological war and to devise techniques to fight it more effectively" (Humphrey, 1964, p. 91).

Several researchers in education specify a variety of attitudinal changes as desirable. These include developing a concern for all human life that transcends culture (Carse, 1969), acquiring a clarified philosophical position of social pluralism (Banks, 1977), and developing a tolerance for others (Haberman & Post, 1990). Some take the position that, while new attitudes may need to be acquired, the lessening of ethnocentrism, prejudice, and racist attitudes must be incorporated into training as well (Rozema, 1982).

Training in several organizations—particularly those for missionaries and expats—seems uniformly to emphasize behavioral goals. Storti (1989) suggests that "we speak of *cultural* adjustment, but in fact it is not to culture that we adjust but to behavior" (p. 14). For example, Elliston (1988) suggests that missionary training goals should include participating in community events within the new culture, tutoring children, and learning how to access social information. Similarly, Smith (1991) emphasizes behavioral effectiveness for expats, as does Wexley (1984) who posits that all expat training is "a planned effort by an organization to facilitate the learning of job-related behavior" (p. 519). In a study of race relations training in the military, Hayles (1978) suggests that one important goal should be training that curbs violent racial incidents.

Grubis (1985) and Grant and Secada (1990), all of whom are involved in teacher training, suggest that an important behavioral goal of training is to "develop skills for social action" (Grant & Secada, 1990, p. 408). This seems in keeping with the Teacher Corps and Peace Corps tradition. Trainees entering other cultures are intended to act as social reconstructionists—people who not only appreciate the variety and richness of cultures, but who will move social machinery toward equal participation and voice for all members of a culture.

LOCATION OF TRAINING

In 1966, after doing an evaluation of Peace Corps training methods, Harrison and Hopkins (1967) published an article that changed the course of Peace Corps training and influenced changes in other organizations as well. In brief, Harrison and Hopkins found that providing training through lectures, textbooks, role plays, and films—all standard teaching methods for American adults—were unsatisfactory and in some cases detrimental to the preparation of successful volunteers. They argued that training needed to be done in context; volunteers needed either to train in the field or in an environment that would simulate field conditions as closely as possible.

In the missionary training field, others had reached similar conclusions several years earlier. As early as 1956, Parsons (1956) suggested that missionary preparation in the home country was largely inadequate and "could offer only generalities and a methodology of how to learn about a culture" (p. 11). Missionaries, he argued, had to learn in the field.

Of all the components of cross-cultural training under examination, the location of the training is one that seems to command almost unanimous agreement: training done in the field (or in field conditions) is preferred to training done in classrooms or conference centers. Furthermore, the evidence overwhelmingly suggests that field training of sufficient rigor and duration produces lower failure rates. That is, candidates who succeed in field training that simulates field conditions are most likely to succeed when they enter the field. Additionally, ongoing but less formalized training in the field seems to contribute to higher and more sustained levels of trainee adjustment (Harris, 1975; Mahan, 1982; York, 1992).

The issue of where cross-cultural training should occur is particularly important in education and other fields where training institutions are located primarily in white suburban areas (Olson, 1988). Barnhardt (1983) who teaches cross-cultural education and rural development at the University of Alaska at Fairbanks offers a course to teachers in rural Alaskan villages. The course requires the teachers to immerse themselves not in the classroom, but in the culture. They attend dog-mushing races; they go to ice-fishing camps; they observe the traditional "stick dance." The point of these activities is partly to make the teachers ethnographers; the important by-product of the research is that they are provided an intelligent forum for reflection and adjustment. Mayne (1980)—also studying teacher life in the Alaskan bush—concludes that it is "impossible to prepare [teachers for village education] . . . unless student teaching is done out here" (p. 98). Barnhardt (1990), in fact, goes so far as to suggest that teacher education faculty should spend time in the Alaskan bush before attempting to prepare student teachers to enter it.

Others—such as Mahan (1982) and Jones (1975)—who prepare teachers for work on Native American reservations require a minimum four-month stay on the reservation for student teachers. During this period, the student teachers are surrounded by Native Americans who are supervising teachers, principals, neighbors, and strangers. Mahan (1982), in fact, requires that the student teachers make at least one Native American friend. Importantly, little contact is maintained with the university. As mentioned earlier, Mahan (1982) reports a failure rate of only 3 percent among cross-cultural trainees.

Rosenblum and Jastrzab (1980) found that Teacher Corps members spent an average of only 20 percent of their training time engaged in formal classwork; the remainder was invested in the school and community. The Peace Corps utilized training sites within the target country and in countries where the conditions were similar to the target country. They emphasized a process of self-selection in the field; if the trainee could not function in the training field, it was clear that the impairment would follow into the real field (Burnes, 1985; Harris, 1975; Jones & Burnes, 1970; Maretzki, 1969). Self-selection in the field is sometimes surprising. For example, Harris (1975) points out that some individuals who could, by almost any standard measure, be considered maladaptive within American culture were frequently the ones who flourished within the field conditions of another culture.

There seems to be no optimum training time. However, structured and supervised training—of any length—is preferable to allowing trainees to move unaided through cross-cultural contact. Clearly, there are training programs that too briefly address the magnitude of change the trainee will face in the field. However, a relatively short combined-methods program that includes an immersion experience seems to produce a better candidate than a longer single method program.

AGE OF CANDIDATES

The preponderance of cross-cultural trainees are young adults. Most Peace Corps and Teacher Corps volunteers, teacher trainees, missionaries, and military personnel are under the age of thirty-five. Do young adults make the best trainees? Is there any research indicating that older, more seasoned people adapt better? Kane (1982), in a study of missionaries, found that most were young students recruited during college chapel services. Rhinesmith (1985), however—a specialist in international community-exchange programs—recruits people of all ages. He suggests people of all ages can be attracted to cross-cultural experience by appealing to their sense of altruism and idealism, being honest about the personal risks and time commitments, and promising that many non-age-specific needs for affiliation, power, and influence can be met through cross-cultural experience. In a survey of expat recruiting, Rubin (1991) found that Hewlett-Packard recruits college students to work abroad during summers, and British Petroleum sends all new hires (many of them just beginning their careers) circulating throughout Europe. Dyer (1986, 1989), a missionary trainer, urges career missionaries to search for younger replacements to mentor.

Thus, there seems to be a great deal of evidence suggesting that many cross-cultural sojourners are young. This may be attributable, at least in part, to programs designed for people with few family, economic, and career responsibilities. Many cross-cultural training programs, in fact, train for careers. There is little evidence, however, that the young make better or more rapid adjustments than older sojourners. On the contrary, in a study of adolescent immigrants who might be expected to make a fairly rapid transition, Athey (1987) found that, even after four years, many were still experiencing psychological trauma from the move. One of the strongest corporate expat volunteer programs is for retired business managers and executives who wish to act as volunteer consultants in all areas of the world (Schleier, 1980). The average age of these volunteers is sixty-eight. This program, International Executive Service Corps—funded in part by the U.S. State Department—has used senior sojourners to complete almost 13,000 projects in ninety-two countries since 1954. By 1980, the program conducted "800 to 900 projects a year . . . [drawing on] a skill bank of about 11,600 volunteers" (Schleier, 1980, p. 47).

TRAINERS, CONSULTANTS, AND PROFESSORS

There exist few programs for cross-cultural trainers apart from those offered by the Society for Intercultural Education, Training, and Research (SIETAR) (Casse, 1979). Almost anyone who wants to be called a "cross-cultural trainer" can be. For that reason, professors from a wide variety of academic and professional disciplines, human resources personnel, communication and productivity consultants, and others from within all levels and areas of different organizations create and deliver cross-cultural training programs. Are some of these trainers better than others? Do some, in general, seem to possess more qualifications or a better "feel" for the needs of their trainees?

Few specify what the necessary qualifications for trainers might be. Needed credentials and characteristics seem as elusive for trainers as for trainees. Paige (1986; Paige & Martin, 1983), however, suggests that cross-cultural effectiveness in trainees is influenced by the trainer's knowledge of the target culture, qualities of openness and flexibility, tolerance of ambiguity, awareness of his or her own values and beliefs, and sense of humor.

Trainers should help the trainees to maintain their own cultural identity while cultivating a multicultural perspective. Bryant, Houston, and Andrews (1978) suggest that a trainer should have the "ability to relate well to participants and to communicate warmth, caring, and interest" (p. 43). Rosenberg (1991) suggests that, when cultures mix in the American workplace, the higher ranking employee should be seen as a facilitator or a coach, but not as a boss.

A trainer is likely to encounter resistance, defensiveness, and confrontive behavior: "Learners will take their frustrations out on the trainers. . . . They will resist certain learning activities. They may reject the program in its entirety" (Paige,

1986, p. 139). Trainers, it seems, need neither a thick skin (since they must be sensitive to the needs and feelings of trainees) nor a thin one (since they may be the targets of misdirected anxiety) (Greening, 1983).

Starosta (1990) suggests that programs designed to reveal deeply lodged convictions about racism or prejudice can challenge trainers beyond the limits of their professional expertise. Starosta describes the experience of having attended a workshop designed to combat racism and prejudice. The leaders asked provocative questions, challenged participants, and encouraged active participation. The trainees responded, but many grew antagonistic and hostile. The trainees were clearly at a loss to aid participants who were recalling painful memories and deeply felt anger. Starosta concluded that many participants left the workshop feeling vulnerable, embarrassed, and more calcified in their negative beliefs than at the beginning of the sessions. The trainers may have succeeded in unearthing fundamental feelings and primary memories, but the trainers were not trained as psychologists and, hence, could not aid the trainees to resolve inner conflicts.

Many "trainers" are, in fact, university professors. They frequently hold the power of trainee grades and credentials in their hands; and hence, their trainees may edit frustrations or refuse to disclose negative reactions and thoughts. However, there are trainer–trainee relationships within the university community that seem less susceptible to withholding. For example, Koester (1984) teaches a class at the University of New Mexico for students returning to the United States from having studied abroad. The class is optional, and its purpose is to teach the students to communicate their experience abroad and to relate to friends and family members who seem changed or who cannot accept changes in the returning student. Grubbs (1985)—in a less academically charged context—looks at foreign students in residence halls and suggests that university staff should be familiar with and accept cultural differences while allowing the foreign student to feel comfortable relinquishing the old cultural identity. Finally, as indicated in an earlier discussion of teacher trainers in the Alaskan bush, several researchers—including missiologist Mulholland (1984)—suggest that professorial trainers need to go to the field themselves to observe and interact with the target culture.

Others advocate the use of veteran sojourners, co-workers, or those who might teach using an apprenticeship model of training. For example, Tanney (1982), a trainer for community mental health and health management centers, suggests that those currently working in the facility should apprentice new trainees. Ideally, minority mentors should train mainstream proteges. However, it is unrealistic to believe that, in the case of counselors and other mental health providers, white trainees would all have the opportunity to learn under a minority mentor, since only 2 percent of all doctorates in psychology are held by minorities (Tanney, 1982). Dammers (1955), a missionary trainer, believes that missionaries should be trained by locals living in the area. Finally, in an interesting study of bus drivers in Montreal, Stolovitch and Lane (1989) conclude that the strongest trainers may be co-workers. In their study, outside consultants were called in to train a few selected bus drivers, who then taught the rest of the bus drivers cross-cultural skills. The training—as measured by lowered complaint rates from riders—was successful.

Many organizations use only outside consultants for cross-cultural training as a matter of policy. In some cases, consultants are called not because the consultant possesses particular qualifications that in-house employees lack, but because organizations believe that outside consultants send the employees a stronger message of the importance of the training. Organizations also believe their employees will respond more freely during training in the presence of a stranger.

The American Psychological Association, for example, suggests that training institutions either acquire or hire outside trainers specializing in African-American, Hispanic, Native American, and Asian-American culture to teach graduate students in psychology (Merta, Stringham & Ponterotto, 1988). In a survey of ninety Fortune 500 companies, Seabrook and Valdes (1988) found that no firms used in-house trainers; all hired outside consultants. The Teacher Corps used outside consultants for much of its training, and the San Diego County school system continues to do so (Jones, 1985).

There are no clear qualifications for trainers, and no clear indications that the presence or lack of any particular set of credentials aids or impedes training. However, many organizations seem to feel that an outside consultant or professor is preferable to an in-house employee. Several factors may account for this preference, including the traditional view that cross-cultural training can be quick and can be "added on" to the current institutional culture. Furthermore, hiring the services of a trainer for two days or two weeks is certainly cheaper than creating a long-term position. Nevertheless, cultural change—particularly in domestic institutions—requires personal as well as institutional change. Such change requires not only the expertise of a qualified trainer, but adequate time as well.

VARIABLES IN THE HOST ENVIRONMENT

There is a growing suspicion among cross-cultural researchers that more success for trainee adjustment may be attributable to variables in the host environment than to specific aspects of training (Bhawuk, 1990; Klein, 1979; Lambert, 1989). Cross-cultural training is not a mechanical process; it is a human enterprise. It attempts to teach people to build cultural bridges, to forge a community of contacts, and to feel at home in an entirely new work context.

Some trainers are beginning to suggest that failure rates can be lowered by searching for cultural climates that "match" personality styles (McIlduff & Coghlan, 1989; Wong-Rieger, 1984). Black and Mendenhall (1989) report that the adjustment to a new culture is far more difficult for expats than the adjustment to a new job. In a study of social support systems and their relationship to expat stress, Fontaine (1986) found that expats who could identify and find ways to meet their social needs for support experienced fewer psychological problems than expats who felt isolated. Similarly, in a study of 122 inservice teachers who spent a summer teaching on a Native American reservation, Mahan (1984) reports that prior to the experience none of the teachers had a Native American friend. By the end of the summer, 100 percent had made at least one friend, and 98 percent of the teachers described the Navajo and Apache as warm, friendly, and socially outgoing people. Contact seems to lessen the distance between people (Albrecht & Adelman, 1987; Byrne & Nelson, 1965; Schneider & Jordan, 1981).

In fact, there are indications that simply giving people the chance to engage in simple conversation may aid adjustment. In a summative assessment of a four-year Teacher Corps project at a California elementary school, Jones (1980) found that the most positive outcome the teachers reported was that they had created more extended contacts with parents. In a separate Teacher Corps study conducted by Rosenblum and Jastrzab (1980), administrators cited the most important program benefit as having the opportunity to talk about problems with other principals and program participants. Interestingly, the success of Teacher Corps members was directly proportionate to the level of interest the principal took in the individual Teacher Corps member (Rosenblum & Jastrzab, 1980). Northfield (1957), a missionary trainer, argues that building "colleagueship" is as important in cross-cultural adjustment as individual thought, feeling, and action. However, a study of 150 foreign students living in London (Furnham & Bochner, 1982) revealed that, of the ten most difficult problems the students faced, the students cited making friends with Londoners as the most difficult. Three additional problems that the students also ranked within the top ten were approaching others to start a friendship, getting to know people, and understanding jokes.

Of the factors listed by Foust, Fieg, Koester, Sarbaugh, and Wendinger (1980) as contributing to cross-cultural adjustment, situational variables—which include finding a support system and maintaining other sojourner contact—are first. Bosco and Harring (1983) stressed the importance of the school climate in the overall success of Teacher Corps members, and Guthrie and Zektick (1967) suggested that successful Peace Corps volunteers were simply those fortunate enough to have been placed in—or to have created for themselves—a supportive climate.

What constitutes a supportive social climate, and whether such a climate is created by sojourners or hosts or both, are questions currently under investigation. In a study of 121 international students, Gao and Gudykunst (1990) suggest that a favorable climate is one that is "intimate rather than casual, is pleasant rather than unpleasant, and in which the individuals have common goals" (p. 314). Albentis (1983) and Schofield (1986) suggest that a favorable climate must be created by supportive institutions that are willing to work at building equality among ethnic groups into the superstructure. Similarly, Berman (1980) attributes experiences that are less than satisfactory to levels of "psychic distance" between training institutions and field sites.

UNSOLVED PROBLEMS

Among the persistent and unsolved problems of cross-cultural training is the mystery of reentry. Returning sojourners are not entering an unfamiliar culture, yet they overwhelming report great difficulties readjusting to life at home. Many contend that the adjustment back to the United States is far more prolonged and difficult than the adjustment to life away (Adler, 1981; Clague & Krupp, 1980).

Some suggest that part of the difficulty may lie in the distance between the work done abroad and the work at home. Harris (1989)—describing his own repatriation experience after living as an expat for several years—draws a picture of job role discrepancy that suggests returning home is not always easy: "[As an expat] I had half-million dollar signing authority . . . but when I came home I wanted a dictionary and I had to get my boss to sign for it out of the supply room" (p. 51).

Foust, Fieg, Koester, Sarb, and Wendt (1981) have suggested that sojourners typically adopt one of three reentry styles. One style is alienation: the returnee rejects the home culture and reacts negatively to it. The second style is reversion: the returnee rejects all changes in thought and attitude that occurred during the cross-cultural experience. The third style is renewal: the returnee may integrate the experiences and forge a new identity. In a reentry research study conducted on international students, Sussman (1986) found that individuals who adapted most successfully to the new culture had more severe reentry problems than those who did not adapt. However, those who did not adapt in the new culture were less effective in it than those who did.

Other problems center on whether training is actually used in the field, and to what extent it is used. In a study of Texas teachers who had received cross-cultural training, Yao (1985) found that, although school libraries stocked multicultural materials, they were seldom used. Teachers were reluctant to develop their own culturally sensitive materials or to draw on cultural sources within the community. At times, training may have the opposite effect to that it was designed to produce. For example, trainees may emerge with more negative feelings toward the target culture (Pettigrew, 1971, 1974). In a study of 700 teachers involved in teacher education programs, Kennedy (1991) concludes that multicultural coursework may produce serious unintended outcomes: "Sometimes through these courses teachers even [become] more persuaded that certain children cannot learn certain content. . . . Information can inadvertently reinforce, rather than alter, latent prejudices" (p. 15).

Another area of explanation for the problem of unapplied or misapplied training is that functioning within a foreign culture does not signal full acceptance of it or full acceptance within it. For example, in a study of Sioux Indian males disciplined by white teachers, Wax (1976) suggests that these boys require long knowledge of a person before they consent to obey. They cannot "make short-term superficial social adjustments with strangers" (Wax, 1976, p. 218). Dumont and Wax (1976)—in a study of Cherokee Indian education—observe that white teachers encounter "not simply a clash of cultural traditions, but a cold war between rival definitions of the classroom" (p. 212). Larke (1990)—studying teachers in the Minority Membership Project (MMP) at Texas A&M—found that, while teachers want parental input in education, they seem not to respect the cultural knowledge of parents. These teachers believe that minority parents are ill equipped to assess a child's abilities. Finally, teachers—even teachers who seek cross-cultural work among minority children—may misinterpret minority behavior, dress, language, and conversational style (Irvine, 1990; Kleifgen, 1988; Lieberman & Miller, 1990; York, 1992).

TRAINING OUTCOMES

The Peace Corps is one of the most frequently reviewed cross-cultural training programs in U.S. history (Meyers, 1975). According to Peace Corps policy, every review of programs and participants has to produce research that is usable and is improvement oriented. Researchers must track down volunteers all over the world, and the data must be gotten quickly and confidentially (Meyers, 1975). In one sense, the Peace Corps researchers cannot ignore two aspects of cross-cultural training that other agencies and organizations can either disregard or downplay: that cross-cultural training creates social change; and that social change operates within the larger context of political power (Meyers, 1975). An examination of training outcomes, then, is inadequate if social and political dimensions are ignored.

Cultures are self-sustaining; and although cultures do change, they preserve their traditions, their rituals, and their myriad small social exchanges from which status and power are constructed. Chapters 1 and 2 surveyed briefly some of the larger social and political machinery operational in the United States. All Americans—regardless of ethnic group membership—are linked to a tradition of slavery and attempted genocide in our racial and ethnic history. We continue to feel the reverberations of older racial conflict as we respond to the contradictory and often confusing cultural codes in which we create our political lives, our social rhetoric, and our private thoughts. Our immediate lives skim the surface of a deep and swift river. Evidence of the press of larger realities can be seen both in outcomes from domestic cross-cultural programs and in the outcomes of training Americans for cross-cultural work around the world.

In 1978, Fox, Grant, Lufler, Melnick, Mitchell, and Thompson (1978) found ten former Teacher Corps interns who had been through the training more than three years earlier. The researchers wanted to assess the long-term impact of training on the interns—five of whom were black, two were Hispanic, and three were white. The ten reported, in retrospect, that they believed the training had given each of them an entirely new way of looking at culture. One of them, a white, had adopted two Vietnamese children. All of them believed the training had changed them as individuals and that they, as individuals, had changed society. The researchers wondered if the interns had been change agents in the schools they were trained to enter—the places they had worked, and the rooms where they had touched the lives of poor and minority children. Unanimously, the interns said they had not. Interestingly perhaps, they recommended that future interns might successfully change schools if they were given more cross-cultural experiences during training.

Larke (1990) recently assessed the training outcomes of student teachers involved in the Minority Membership Project (MMP) at Texas A&M. These teachers are required to mentor a minority student for three years, in addition to taking cross-cultural coursework. Their cross-cultural training experience—though not broad—is considerably longer than that of Teacher Corps trainees. Of the fifty-one student teachers Larke (1990) studied (forty-six of whom were white, and five were Hispanic), 92 percent said they believed it was important in education to identify the cultural backgrounds of students, and almost 70 percent reported they supported testing in a student's native language. However, although 90 percent said that they would teach a culturally different child, 43 percent preferred to work with students whose cultural background was identical to their own. More than 65 percent reported feeling uncomfortable working in a different culture, and almost 90 percent said that it would surprise them if minority students participated in traditionally non-minority school activities.

In a 1984 study of twenty-eight teachers who teach exclusively Native American students on an Apache reservation, Frazier and DeBlassie (1984) discovered that the teachers—all of whom had received some inservice cross-cultural training—reported many of their students were sullen and socially maladaptive. Using hypothetical case studies in which children were described with identical symptoms but from different cultures, Frazier and DeBlassie found that teachers were more likely to target the Native American children as behavior disordered. In a more recent study of how teachers view "ideal student behavior," Carlson and Stephens (1986) found that teachers form different ideas of ideal behavior for children in different cultures. This finding is somewhat ambiguous, however. Merely establishing difference does not indicate that the teachers' ideals were culturally congruent or incongruent.

In a 1978 study of fifty-six Teacher Corps projects held during July 1977, Andrews, Houston, and Bryant (1978) found that the effects of training seemed positive. In a comparison of pretest and posttest measures of the interns' degree of familiarity with multicultural education, the researchers found that an awareness of culturally different communication styles, a respect for multiple cultural perspectives and richness, and an ability to describe cultural conflicts between the school and the community all increased significantly. The long-term effects of the training, the impact on student progress, and the question of whether these attitudes became behavioral competencies in the classroom were left unaddressed (Brooks & Weber, 1975).

Mahan's (1982) successful program at Indiana University has been discussed at some length earlier in the chapter. The outcomes of the program have been measured a variety of ways. For example, Mahan reports that 83 percent of cross-culturally trained teachers receive job offers, compared to only 53 percent of their peers who opted for traditional training. Furthermore, of the total pool who receive offers, the cross-cultural teachers are more likely to get the position they really want—by a margin of two to one (Mahan, 1982; Mahan & Lacefield, 1980). Interestingly, 90 percent of the cross-cultural group were offered the position of their choice, regardless of whether they chose predominantly minority or mainstream schools in which to teach; over 40 percent choose minority schools. Mahan (1982) concludes that, "if education majors can be moved out of mainstream settings and into culturally different settings, they will react positively to student teaching work, social interactions, and their new role as the 'minority person in town'" (p. 107).

In 1981, the Bay Area Bilingual Education League (BABEL), in conjunction with the California Department of Education, provided six weeks of cross-cultural training at the Universidad Autónoma de Guadalajara for ninety public school educators to aid them in working with Hispanic children (Reusswig, 1981). The educators were allowed to speak only Spanish, and they lived in conditions similar to the Limited English Proficiency (LEP) Hispanic students in their own districts. Every morning the educators were given classes in Spanish culture, bilingual instruction, writing lesson plans, psychology, and parent conferences. All classes were in Spanish. In the afternoons, they were sent to barrio schools to teach reading, mathematics, and culture. All teaching had to be in Spanish as well. At the end of the six weeks, the educators averaged a 40 percent gain in Spanish language proficiency, a 150 percent gain in their understanding of bilingual psychology, and a 220 percent gain in bilingual testing and assessment knowledge. Of the thirty-four educators who attempted it, thirty-three received California's Bilingual Certificate of Competence.

A more recent study of teachers in Texas and New Mexico who had undergone a Hispanic immersion experience produced results that suggest the competencies learned during supervised immersion translate into classroom teaching (Cooper, Beare & Thorman, 1990). These teachers, for example, were more likely to visit student's families than their nontrained peers, and they had higher expectations for their nonwhite students.

In a 1985 study of Texas teachers who had received at least one cross-cultural training course as a required part of certification, Yao (1985) found that the teachers "are not well-prepared for the ethnic reality of the classroom and . . . fail to respond to the needs of culturally different learners and to promote cultural understanding" (p. 3). A similar study by Sleeter (1989)—examining 416 Wisconsin teachers (406 of whom were white) who had completed a state-mandated cultural awareness training course as part of their student teaching education—revealed that 78 percent of the teachers taught classes of 95 percent white children; only 7 percent taught 75 percent or more minority classes. Another interesting result was that teachers of minority children taught more multicultural education and more lessons on the importance of tolerance than teachers of white children.

Baker (1973) tested 299 student teachers to find if cross-cultural training might change their attitudes. The teachers were given a two-week workshop during which lectures on multicultural education, observations of minority children, films, discussions, and videos were geared at making teacher attitudes toward minority students more favorable. Using a pretest and posttest measure, Baker found that the teachers displayed significantly more positive attitudes toward all minority groups except black students. The teachers' attitudes toward black students were unchanged. In a similar study of thirty-nine secondary teachers who received two weeks of information-oriented and cultural-awareness training, Bennett (1979) found that teachers' perceptions of ethnic groups, as a whole, were significantly more positive. However, there was no significant difference in the perception of any individual ethnic group.

Two studies by Mahan and Stachowski (1985, 1990) suggest that student teachers who teach overseas display similar competencies to domestic subculture immersion teachers; immersed student teaching groups are markedly different from their traditionally trained peers. The internationally trained teachers reported their most important knowledge about teaching came from areas unrelated to the classroom, such as community activities and cultural events. Furthermore, more than half of them indicated that the most important knowledge they learned about how to teach came from non-school-related people; less than 40 percent of the traditionally trained teachers reported similar nonacademic learning.

In a intercultural relations (ICR) training session for eighty Navy personnel stationed in Japan, trainees were divided into three groups: one group was given a six-hour information-centered orientation; one group was provided three days of intensive training, including a brief immersion into the culture; one group was given no training. In the results of testing designed to measure learning about self, learning how to communicate, and learning about life in Japan, little difference was found between the group that received no training and the group that received six hours of training. The group receiving the intensive training scored higher on all measures and significantly higher on measures of personal satisfaction (Gudykunst & Hammer, 1983; Gudykunst, Hammer & Wiseman, 1977).

In a study of a treatment/no-treatment condition for thirty-one white graduate psychology students, Christensen (1984) found different results. The students in the treatment group received eleven hours of cultural-awareness and information-oriented training. Both groups were then videotaped counseling a culturally dissimilar black "patient." The video was judged and compared to a self-report of anxiety. There was no significant difference between the trained and untrained group, leading Christensen to conclude that cultural empathy is not a by-product of training. A similar study by Neimeyer, Fukuyama, Bingham, Hall, and Mussenden (1986) found that, among graduate psychology students enrolled in a course on cultural minorities, most reported feeling confused and incompetent after counseling a culturally dissimilar patient. They also reported that they believed the patient was not likely to continue therapy. Similar findings were reported by Benavides, Lynch, and Velasquez (1980) in a study of social workers trained at the University of Minnesota. Johnson (1987), who trains psychologists at the Minnesota Multiethnic Counseling Education Curriculum Center, believed that too much of the training given to psychology students focuses on cultural differences, rather than on cultural expertise.

The AIDS health providers mentioned in Chapter 6, tended to divide in terms of their receptivity to cross-cultural training (Day, 1990). For example, professionally trained doctors and nurses rated the training lowest; agencies dealing with abused and jailed clients rated the training highest in terms of overall usefulness. This may only indicate that the training was geared to one audience's needs.

In a large study of more long-term child welfare workers serving more than 300 children in six states, Wilson and Green (1983) conclude that "the effect of cross-cultural training on staff appears to be a function of the intensity and duration of the training experience and its connection with an identified need" (p. 310).

Training outcomes vary. Other elements of training seem only tangentially linked to research results rather than directly linked. The links between training, transition, and effectiveness are uncertain; the knowledge base—despite thousands of programs over a span of four decades—remains weak. Levine and Havighurst (1989) suggest—as do many others—that cross-cultural training must be contextualized. They conclude that very little generalization of findings from program results is possible, since world views, economic status, location, and life experience differ widely in cross-cultural contexts.

The question of generalizability has produced a solipsistic tendency in the field of cross-cultural training. Past training—even within the same field—is viewed as irrelevant; findings from other programs seem immaterial within the context of current needs, current conflicts, and the current cultures under examination. Yet, training produces changes in individual people and in the social milieu. White teachers on a Native American reservation change the reservation as well as themselves. Black managers in a formerly white office change the office and change themselves. This change is interpreted differently by different individuals and by different groups of people.

Nevertheless, a thread of effectiveness can be found. Trainees—of whatever age—who are self-selected either by occupational choice, degree decisions, or program policy seem to be not only the available pool, but the pool of strongest candidates. Trainees need knowledgeable trainers who can manage the ambivalence and anxiety of adjustment. Trainees need exposure to a variety of training methods; they need time; they need to reflect alone and with their peers. They need to immerse themselves in the new culture; but they need to be supervised during the immersion, both by hosts and by program directors. This constellation of the strongest and most promising elements of cross-cultural training is explored in greater detail in Chapter 8.

8

SOME SUGGESTIONS FOR BUILDING A BETTER WORLD

> Conversation was impossible for a long time; and when it was slowly resumed, it was that regrettable sort of conversation that results from talking with your mouth full. The Badger did not mind that sort of thing at all, nor did he take any notice of elbows on the table, or everybody talking at once. As he did not go into Society himself, he had got an idea that these things belonged to the things that really didn't matter. (We know of course that he was wrong, and took too narrow a view; because they do matter very much, though it would take too long to explain why.)
>
> —Kenneth Grahame
> *The Wind in the Willows*

The pundits claim there is no such thing as a free lunch. In this study, I have tried to advance the argument that there is no such thing as a culture-free lunch. Our places of work are permeated with our culture. Our ways of processing and prioritizing tasks and our understanding of achievement and reward are embedded in the work we do and the status we assign to the tasks. We may be able to forge a personal identity apart from our work; we cannot forge a work identity apart from our culture.

This chapter proposes some guidelines for cross-cultural training for use in a wide variety of occupations. This need for effective cross-cultural training is critical as Americans approach the twenty-first century. Given that minority and immigrant populations are escalating in both size and breadth of diversity, it seems only logical to conclude that the world of work will change. Our understanding of task orientation, reward, power, and performance may be dramatically altered by the energy and vision of new world views, new values, and new ideas. The question is whether we, as a nation, are prepared for the magnitude of the changes we face.

We need a new vision of the workplace that is responsive to the needs of all workers—but particularly minority and immigrant workers, whose work styles and preferences may not be congruent with the culture of the existing workplace. We must begin by acknowledging the social perceptions and cultural norms we bring to our places of work and to the tasks we perform. However well-intentioned we may be, we live in a society in which racism was historically sanctioned and in which, in some measure, it continues to be practiced. Companies, colleges, and other training institutions must struggle to provide a context for effective and productive performance with minorities and immigrants who have traditionally been excluded from the mainstream and who are the continuing victims of institutional and structural racism. These needs must command our attention.

EDUCATION AS AN EXAMPLE OF CULTURAL CHANGE

Nowhere has the press of new cultures been felt more strongly than in American schools, and nowhere has the need been greater for immediate and effective change. Because of the intense scholarly and popular attention paid to schools in recent years, a fairly accurate picture of the totality of challenges that educators continue to face can be drawn. Hence, a brief overview of the history of cultural change in the schools since Brown v. Board of Education of Topeka, Kansas ([Brown], 1954) serves as an example for many fields of the kinds of structural, institutional, and personal changes that cultural diversity requires.

While the assimilation of culturally different children has a long history in American education, the decades since World War II have witnessed a resurgence of cultural concerns in education. In the years following the war, national attention focused on the nation's schools and on the challenges teachers faced in classrooms with culturally different and economically disadvantaged children. The Brown (1954) case—which ended *de jure* racially separate schooling—and the enactment of several pieces of social legislation (including the Civil Rights Act of 1965, the Economic Opportunity Act of 1964, the Voting Rights Act of 1965, and the Elementary and Secondary Education Act [ESEA] of 1965) gave American cultural minorities political visibility and voice. These changes suggested that schools had served as a social vehicle for maintaining an elitist status quo. The Teacher Corps was one attempt to dismantle social, political, and educational institutions that had been steeped in the doctrines of racial superiority. American schools would continue to be the target of cultural and educational reform.

In the 1960s, evidence of racial discrimination seemed to surface in every corner of American education. Educators faced growing difficulties in redistributing school populations in compliance with federal orders for desegregation, and questions surfaced about the means by which educational dollars and programs were appropriated among competing racial and ethnic groups. The practice of student assessment and academic placement based on aptitude and achievement tests came under fire; and the processes governing the selection, training, certification, and employment of educational personnel were examined. This focus on educational personnel would affect the nation's teachers and the institutions that trained them (Ravitch, 1983).

Institutions of teacher training were not inattentive to these changes. Although the populations of teacher candidates increased in size during the 1960s and 1970s, the racial and ethnic composition of teachers remained largely unchanged. Thus, despite the growing presence of minority children in traditionally white schools, white teacher candidates selected predominantly white schools in which to teach; minority candidates were employed in predominantly minority schools (Warren, 1990). Nevertheless, federal funding and corporate research dollars helped create teaching certifications and specializations aimed at the education of culturally different students. Courses focusing on education as a sociological and political phenomenon began, and the psychological impact of schooling—which had been at the crux of the Brown (1954) decision—came under closer scrutiny (Goodlad, 1990; Travers & Rebore, 1987). However, despite new research foci, new certification options, new courses, and the early promise of the Teacher Corps, the training and employment of teachers remained largely unchanged. Teacher trainers continued to use models and methods nearly a century old (Goodlad, 1990).

Although the direction and focus of teacher training institutions may have shifted slightly, state departments of education have gained increasing control over university requirements for teacher certification, and many state departments have generated their own certification standards, which supersede those imposed by teacher training institutions. Despite this shift in power, the training of teachers remains—in large measure—a cottage industry. Each institution and state department determines the individual design of local teacher education. Institutions that provide coursework or field experiences that deviate from local norms often risk high funding costs, the loss of state certification, low enrollments, and nonaccreditation. In 1972 Congress passed the Ethnic Heritage Studies Bill—legislation aimed at encouraging Americans living in a multiethnic society to understand their history from a multiethnic perspective (Yao, 1985).

New energy boosted these cross-cultural initiatives when, in 1979 a report released by President Jimmy Carter's commission on the declining status of foreign languages and international study brought immediate and varied response. Business and community leaders cited the need for multilingual and multicultural training, and increased media attention gave birth to speculations that the United

States was edging toward the periphery of the global village (Cere, 1988). Later in 1979, the prestigious National Council for Accreditation of Teacher Education (NCATE)—which included nearly half of all teacher training institutions in its membership—issued a revision in its guidelines (Gollnick, 1991). Teacher education institutions seeking accreditation would have to show evidence that multicultural education was included in the required coursework for all teacher candidates (National Council for Accreditation of Teacher Education [NCATE], 1977). Designed to aid teachers in preparing children for "culturally diverse and complex human encounters," this revision served to acknowledge both the growing cultural complexity of school populations and the growing inability of traditional teacher training programs to satisfy the educational needs of these minority students (NCATE, 1977, p. 4). Effectively, the confinement of minority concerns to a small population of teachers seeking special certifications, or enrolled in Teacher Corps, ended; instead, minority issues and their educational implications permeated all grade levels and content areas.

During the early years of the Reagan administration, the levels and types of federal funding for education changed. Furthermore, a series of national reports during the 1980s called for sweeping educational reform. These reports included Mortimer Adler's (1982) *Paideia Proposal*; the National Commission on Excellence in Education 1983 report, *A Nation at Risk* (U.S.A. Research, Incorporated, Staff, 1984); John Goodlad's (1984) *A Place Called School*; the report of the Twentieth Century Fund Task Force on Federal Elementary and Secondary Education Policy called *Making the Grade* (1983); the National Science Board Commission on Pre-college Education in Mathematics, Science, and Technology's (1983) *Educating Americans for the 21st Century*; the Task Force on Education for Economic Growth's (1983) *Action for Excellence*; the Carnegie Foundation for the Advancement of Teaching's 1983 report, *High School* (Boyer, 1985); and the College Board's (1983) *Academic Preparation for College*. Although these reports addressed a variety of social and political concerns, each report unequivocally emphasized excellence in education, thus redirecting—and, in large measure, replacing—the thirty year focus on equality in education.

These reports and the cuts in federal spending that accompanied them have had a tremendous impact on minority education in this country. Despite the flourish of national attention during the 1960s and 1970s, minority and culturally sensitive education has largely fallen from favor. Nevertheless, the educational needs of minority children continue to grow. The 1980s heralded increasing proportions of immigrant and minority children in public schools, and demographic projections show continuing growth of these populations well into the twenty-first century (Coates & Jarratt, 1987; National Center for Education Statistics, 1989).

How well the nation's teachers are prepared to educate culturally diverse children is an area of increasing concern (Haberman, 1991). The Holmes Group (1986)—a consortium of higher education institutions committed to educational reform—estimates that more than 200,000 new teachers will be needed in the years ahead, but that successful teachers will be those who "relinquish the norms of professional colleges of education without a struggle" (p. 62). According to a Metropolitan Life survey of more than 1,000 new teachers in the late 1980s, 75 percent of them believed culturally diverse students had problems that would interfere with learning; furthermore, one out of every five of these teachers reported that they "felt unprepared" to teach culturally diverse students (Diegmueller, 1990). In a national survey of new teachers, Olson (1988) estimated that fewer than one in ten beginning teachers is motivated to teach in urban or culturally different schools. Furthermore, most teacher training institutions are located in white suburban areas, and many required courses in multicultural education amount to a "disjointed series of 'add-ons' to the curriculum or . . . a 'foods and fiestas' approach to increasing teachers' cultural awareness" (Olson, 1988, p. 21). In a recent survey of twenty-nine teacher training institutions, Cummings and Bridges (1986) found that all of the institutions considered cross-cultural experience and knowledge essential in teacher preparation, but only 66 percent provided even optional cross-cultural fieldwork and only 17 percent offered optional classes in comparative education. In a study of thirty-two Wisconsin teacher training institutions, Sleeter (1988) found that teachers were likely to enter and complete a fieldwork experience with minority students only when required to do so. Nonetheless, teaching is changing, and teacher training must change as well (Cetron, Soriano & Gayle, 1990). By 1983, a survey of almost 400 of the nation's teacher training institutions revealed that, despite their lack of training and sense of unpreparedness, 77 percent of student teachers were teaching culturally different students (Wilson, 1983).

The impact of the lack of cross-cultural teacher training is evident in a growing body of research literature. Law and Lane (1987)—mentioned in Chapter 1— who used a social distance measure on more than 140 new teachers, reported that white preservice teachers not only harbor negative feeling toward all American subcultures, but that their feelings are more negative than student teachers tested a decade earlier and lower still than measures obtained in any of the previous six decades of national studies. Haberman (1991) found that, after 120 hours of state-mandated human awareness training for minority education, many of the student teachers "became more insensitive and hardened in their positions by attributing more negative values to school children, their parents, and their neighborhoods" (p. 29). Results from a global awareness measure given to undergraduate students revealed that "the global awareness of undergraduate majors in education was lower than that of students in any other undergraduate specialization" (Torney-Purta, 1985, p. 384).

Inservice teachers fare little better. In an early study of inservice teachers, Pettigrew (1974) found that they harbor "negative assumptions about minority pupils and their cultures" (p. 80). In a more recent study of Texas teachers, Yao (1985) concluded that "they have vague ideas of human differences ... [but] they are not well-prepared for the ethnic reality in the classroom and ... fail to respond to the needs of the culturally different [child]" (p. 3). LeCompte (1985) has hypothesized that many inservice teachers leave teaching because of these cultural differences: "Many teachers burn out because of stress deriving from contact with children from cultures different from their own" (p. 121). In short, the problem with both student teacher and inservice teacher training is that culturally limited teachers are ill equipped to instruct culturally different children (Boateng, 1990).

This history of American educators' attempts to redefine and restructure education along more culturally tolerant lines proves instructive for those in other occupations who face similar challenges. Taken together, these events suggest four strands that are critical in organizational change: (1) the political and legal climate in which the organization functions; (2) the level of cultural sensitivity embedded in the policies, practices, and processes that operate within institutions themselves; (3) the cross-cultural skills, attitudes, and behaviors practiced by members of the institution; and (4) the malleability of individuals to become more culturally tolerant and to display appropriate cultural styles within certain contexts.

PERSPECTIVES OF CHANGE

In 1980, Mortenson and Wilson (1980) published an article describing the education of Native American children. In it, they examined teacher training given by Northern Arizona University for teachers of Native American students. Mortenson and Wilson proposed five essential components for training teachers cross-culturally. Their typology forms the basis of all effective cross-cultural training. From this base, specific kinds of cross-cultural training programs for a variety of workers can be recommended.

The five characteristics Mortenson and Wilson (1980) recommended are as follows:

1. *Cross-cultural training must be job-embedded.* Culture must become a prism through which we can view one aspect of the work we do. Who we are when we are working, why we work, and what rewards or out-

comes we anticipate will result from our labor must be redefined in cultural terms. Cultural issues can no longer be relegated to brief shots of "one big global family" motivational presentations. Cultural differences at work, as in our larger society, are points of tension. They must be fully addressed.

2. *Cross-cultural training must be job related.* This implies more than the inclusion of a few folk dances, bulletin boards, foods, and holidays. The outside world must come inside; leaders must invite leaders from culturally different groups to participate in shaping a just and highly productive workplace. The task we perform must be seen from a constructionist perspective: workers from different cultural groups constructing tasks within dynamic work environments.

All employees work from within their own cultural perspectives, and their culture influences what they know how to do, how they view their tasks, and the perspectives they acquire to order and prioritize their work. Employers who fail to respect and integrate the culture of the employee into the tasks at hand cannot effectively participate for long in building a strong organization.

3. *Cross-cultural training must be credential oriented.* Organizations that offer opportunities for cultural growth, and that tie those opportunities to reward structures, are most likely to produce employees whose morale is high and whose commitment to the organization is strong.

Establishing minimal cross-cultural criteria constitutes professional negligence. We are failing to prepare employees for the world of work. As long as we persist in providing minimum training, we produce employees who are ill equipped, undertrained, and ineffective. Credentials that certify intercultural competence must be linked to cross-cultural behavioral competence in real work situations.

4. *Cross-cultural training must be oriented to professional organizations.* Employee organizations and other groups that function within the organization must be invited to participate in making the workplace more culturally tolerant. Their ability to affirm cultural sensitivity at work is an important component of program success.

5. *Cross-cultural training must be self-directed.* This is another critical component for program success. Mortenson and Wilson (1980) sug-

gest that those in culturally diverse work situations should be viewed not only as employees, but as colleagues, students, professionals, and artisans. Each of these roles should be called into play in the training of employees for cross-cultural work. Employees must be taught to identify their problems in the workplace, and they must participate in a creative dialogue with their colleagues and others who can aid them in generating possible solutions for their areas of need.

Cross-cultural training does not require amputation of unworking or offensive perspectives; but it requires a supportive, encouraging, challenging climate for positive change. In other words, the trainee does not need something (like racism or ethnocentrism) removed or something else (like tolerance or patience) added. Those changes are necessary; but that approach, by itself, is too narrow. A more holistic perspective is needed. Over time, the trainee needs to adapt to new work strategies, new perspectives, and a new understanding of job competence. To that extent, trainees must participate in the training they receive. Cross-cultural work is not easy, and employees must be trained to craft their skills in a fluid and dynamic cultural environment.

Below are some practical suggestions, designed to aid organizations in creating a context in which the cross-cultural training of employees can occur. These suggestions do not constitute a tallying of research results to find the strongest formula for success. Instead, they represent a synthesis of hundreds of studies from several occupational perspectives; the suggestions I propose are an attempt to mark a moderate path for change, rather than a radical one.

Before constructing this path, three mythological barriers must be removed:

1. *Ethnic groups are monolithic.* This myth presupposes a standardization of world view, values, norms, and interests imposed, created, and sustained by culture. The truth is that not all Hispanic employees think alike; not all blacks share the same political views; not all Native American workers are from the same social class. Thus, an organization employing different minority and immigrant groups (and training all its employees to work in a culturally diverse environment) must adapt cross-cultural training to the particular mix of cultures in singe work environments. Furthermore, not every employee can cross all cultures in all situations. Cross-cultural training is (and must be) highly contextualized.

2. *Effective minority-owned-and-operated organizations possess strategies that can be exported to other organizations employing minorities*

and immigrants. This myth presumes that effective management and operational methods within minority-run organizations can be superimposed on all organizations. Minority-operated firms (like all other organizations) establish their policies and practices within the peculiar constraints of the communities in which they operate. Neither ethnic groups nor institutions are monolithic; the print of each organization's own culture will be distinguishable from every other's.

3. *Exemplary employees will act as individual, institutional, and perhaps even cultural change agents.* This myth suggests that minority employees and culture must change and that productive or technically competent employees should be trained to usher in the changes. In contrast, cross-cultural training assumes that employees need to learn to interact within the new culture. Again, task orientation should be constructed by the employees themselves utilizing cultural norms that increase organizational health and productivity. Cultural diversity should provide new energy and direction to the task.

CROSS-CULTURAL TRAINING WITHIN ORGANIZATIONS

The first action an organization wishing to create a positive cultural climate must take is to make a commitment to cross-cultural training. This involves creating both a program and a philosophy for change. This philosophy must reflect mobility and some leniency: there are few people in any occupation who choose to spend an entire career working in another culture. If left too long with cultural unfamiliars, the employee may become less comfortable in the home culture, may become increasingly less effective or may resign. "Success" rates should be shortened to three years or possibly five years. Some employees will stay longer; others will not.

The second action the organization must take is to survey thoroughly the existing cultural climate and listen to both their mainstream and their minority employees. Finding leadership (even informal leadership) among different cultural groups is critical to the success of the program. Without the help and input of supportive employees, appropriate and adequate preparation of organizational members will be difficult and perhaps impossible. In other words, cultural group leaders must become partners in the training process. These leaders understand the needs and desires of their communities; in a very real sense, they possess a unique expertise on the problems and potential for organizations in their areas.

The third action on the part of an organization is more in the way of an inaction. Insofar as it is possible, candidates should be self-selected for training. Forcing employees to participate may undermine the positive changes in volunteer employees and may hamper effective organizational change.

HELPING EMPLOYEES SUCCEED IN CULTURALLY DIVERSE SETTINGS

Training employees in any organization is difficult, because cross-cultural training often involves unlearning or modifying job styles and interpersonal strategies that have worked in the past. Veteran employees are frequently far more willing to listen to strategies on how to change minority employees rather than on how to change themselves and their work styles. Cross-cultural training is difficult also because many employees want quick pragmatic solutions for problems that are complex, abstract, and long-standing. The levels of conscious and unconscious racism and resistance that employees bring to work cannot be dismantled in a day or two of workshops. What Sleeter (1992) disparagingly refers to as the "flash and dash" method of multicultural training is not merely inadequate, but may be detrimental to any real progress that can be made. Below is compiled not an exhaustive list of remedies, but a list of suggestions culled from the research. This training can be seen in four stages. These stages are all crucial to cross-cultural teaching growth; each should be present in every training session and should be implemented in the order presented:

1. *Identification.* During this stage, employees should meet to discuss and formulate the problems they experience working with culturally different workers.

2. *Information.* During this stage, employees should receive information about the target culture(s), and family life in the culture. Other forms of training (such as attribution or awareness) should be used as well, so that the employees can challenge themselves to think of others in the target culture(s) in new and different ways. This stage should include activities that are designed to gain and retain interest in cultural issues.

3. *Evaluation.* During this stage, the trainer should present the problems the employees identified and help them solve these issues based on the information and new perspectives gained.

4. *Experimentation.* During this stage, employees should attempt to implement the solutions they and their trainer formulated. Employees should note which strategies were successful and which were not. Further problems should be presented in the next training session.

This method of training has several advantages. First, it is highly contextualized. Employees are addressing problems they face in the organization where they work. It is anticipated that the problems will be specific ones—perhaps even personal ones. One advantage of allowing employees to express and define their problems is that they begin to admit that culture is problematic. This is often not an easy confession to make. Some employees may resist admitting problems of any kind. Furthermore, employees may fear that problems with culturally different co-workers or clients may invite suspicions of prejudice and discrimination or may suggest professional weakness or inability. Once employees accept that cross-cultural work is not easy, they can begin to share their difficulties and their solutions with each other.

Second, it allows employees to gain knowledge about the lives and background of the people with whom they work. The values and norms of the culture, and the language, dress, and aspirations of others, become more real as employees learn about other cultures. The information that employees learn about the culture of their co-workers aids them in finding solutions to problems on the job.

Third and finally, this training is ongoing. Because it is problem centered and solution driven, it is highly pragmatic. It allows employees to confront their problems and to share them in a supportive environment. It is cyclical. It does not attempt to change attitudes or to broaden cultural perspectives. Instead, it focuses on the needs employees face as they recognize and articulate them.

DIMENSIONS OF CHANGE

In short, while cross-cultural training requires several changes in the content and type of training given to employees, these changes can be broadly grouped into three dimensions: institutional changes; interpersonal changes; and personal changes. In each of these, new information and perspectives in training should produce changes in behaviors that make the workplace more culturally sensitive and more cooperative. These dimensions of change suggest not only that the employees themselves must be trained, but also that their relationships inside and outside their culture must be informed by their training. Additionally, changes in institutional policies and practices may be necessary to achieve cultural equity.

Hence, each dimension is important as a separate aspect of the workplace; however, an organization can only function synergistically when all three dimensions are examined and changed as needed.

YORK'S SALAMANDER MODEL OF CROSS-CULTURAL TRAINING

Taken as a whole, the research from many disciplines and organizations seems to suggest that there are ten components of successful cross-cultural training programs. I have chosen the acronym SALAMANDER underscoring several similarities between salamanders and cross-cultural workers.

Salamanders are amphibians, and—like all cold-blooded creatures—they possess a variety of adaptational skills. For example, salamanders must be attentive to their external and internal limitations in temperature. Also, they can switch between water or land climates. Like salamanders, cross-cultural workers must function in different cultural environments, and they must learn to move between them to maintain an internal cultural equilibrium. According to legend, salamanders are able to survive being burned in flames. Like salamanders, sojourners must survive a kind of fiery culture shock. Hence, productive sojourners acquire some of the traits of salamanders.

The components of the SALAMANDER model are listed below:

S = Self-selection. High turnover rates, high failure rates, and the lessons of Peace Corps recruitment suggest that the strongest candidates are self-selected candidates. Unhappy, misplaced candidates who complete training will probably—at some not too distant point—select another position.

A = Accreditation. Strong programs are those that not only build in some form of professional risk attached to training failure (such as loss of certification or licensure), but also formally acknowledge completion of the cross-cultural program.

L = Length. Lengthy programs do not necessarily produce the strongest outcomes. Time can be wasted, and activities might be called "training" that, in fact, are not, (such as touring a culturally different area). However, sufficient preparation time is very necessary to prepare strong candidates.

A = Affiliation. This component either exists within individual candidates or it does not. Candidates who do not display an interest or willingness to establish relationships and ties within new cultures are not good candidates for training success.

M = Mixed Methods. Strong programs are those that incorporate a repeated mixture of training methods, including information-oriented, attribution, cultural awareness, cognitive-behavioral, interactive, and experiential.

A = Approval. One surprising aspect of strong candidate selection involves finding volunteers whose family and friends approve of the cross-cultural work. This approval and support seem critical in the persistence of the cross-cultural worker.

N = New Culture Partnership. This refers not to the candidates, but to the institutions that support and send them. More connections must be made between the training institution or suprastructure and the cultural communities touched by it. Cross-cultural workers need mentors, guides, examples, and interpreters—and these relationships occur only by happenstance unless there are channels of institutional support for the relationships to be formed.

D = Direction. All aspects of training must be directed and supervised. People will not learn to be at home in a new culture if they are left alone to flounder in it or to "pick up" cultural nuances through casual contact.

E = Experiential Training. A successful program is one that builds experiential learning into the training sequence. Cultural immersion that is supervised, prolonged, and directed seems to produce the strongest candidates.

R = Reflection. To train employees for culturally different work environments is to ask for tremendous changes in perspective, and perhaps even in personal identity. Cross-cultural training is a process of transition, and some of the transitions may be difficult or painful ones to make. Candidates need a safe and sustained context in which they can reflect by themselves, with their cultural familiars, and with colleagues from the new culture.

In summary, the SALAMANDER model describes ten components of successful cross-cultural training. Earlier sections of this chapter specified the dimensions and chronology of successful training; the SALAMANDER model outlines ten critical aspects of good programs. It does not address or explain some difficulties organizations face. For example, it does not address the shortages of minority candidates for certain fields, nor does it offer ways to stabilize organizations during periods of social (particularly, racial) unrest. However, the model does address institutional, interpersonal, and personal aspects of training that seem to contribute to creating the strongest and most persistent candidates.

CONCLUSION

This study describes factors related to cross-cultural training. The gap between our legal and political ideologies and the social and institutional forms of racism was described in Chapter 1, with particular attention given to demographic changes, ongoing racial violence, the lack of minority representation in positions of leadership, and the high failure rates of workers in cross-cultural environments. In Chapter 2, the complexities of culture study—the myriad theories attending the conceptualization, operationalization, and evaluation of culture and its consequences—were described. These complexities create a tangled and somewhat problematic base for training. Cross-cultural contact on both aggregate and individual terms was explored in Chapters 3 and 4, and the growth models describing movement toward a bicultural or multicultural perspective were outlined as an antidote to culture shock. Chapters 5, 6, and 7 addressed the history of cross-cultural training, the organizations that have created and utilized training since World War II, and the dimensions of training and the research results pertinent to them. This final chapter—Chapter 8—suggested strategies for training employees to be effective in cross-cultural organizations.

The cross-cultural training of any workers is not a simple straightforward task. The necessary components of successful training seem to be rooted in a supportive training environment and a supportive host environment. Candidates must be committed people who are willing and able to undergo the kinds of changes in thought, attitude, and action necessary to ensure the success of the organizations in which they participate.

Successful organizations will be those that are comfortable adapting to the language, dress, and behavioral styles of culturally diverse workers. These organizations must be committed to the participation and well-being of all their members. They must be willing to welcome the cultural expressions of their members, and channel that diversity into effective and productive work. Cross-cultural training for employees is not the only area of needed reform in the workplace, but it is our single best choice.

REFERENCES

Aagaard, J. 1985. Renewing the missionary calling. *Aeropagus: A Living Encounter*, 1:13–15.
Abbasi, S. M., and Hollman, K. W. 1991. Managing cultural diversity: The challenge of the '90s. *American Records Management Quarterly*, 25:24–32.
Abe, H., and Wiseman, R. L. 1983. A cross-cultural confirmation of the dimensions of intercultural effectiveness. *International Journal of Intercultural Relations*, 7:53–67.
Abell, T., and Lyon, L. 1979. Do the differences make a difference? An empirical evaluation of the culture of poverty in the United States. *American Ethnologist*, 6:602–620.
Aberle, D. F. 1960. The influence of linguistics on early culture and personality theory. In *Essays in the science of culture in honor of Leslie A. White,* edited by G. E. Dole and R. L. Carneiro, 1–29. New York: Crowell.
Ackermann, J. M. 1976. Skill training for foreign assignment: The reluctant U.S. case. In *Intercultural communication: A reader*, edited by L. A. Samovar and R. E. Porter, 298–306. Belmont, CA: Wadsworth Publishing.
Adams, G. R., and Schvaneveldt, J. D. 1985. *Understanding research methods*. New York: Longman.
Adelman, M. B. 1988. Cross-cultural adjustment: A theoretical perspective on social support. *International Journal of Intercultural Relations*, 12:183–204.
Adeney, D. H. 1979. The preparation of missionaries to cope with political change. In *Christ and Caesar in Christian missions*, edited by E. L. Fiezen, Jr. and W. T. Coggins, 49–54. Pasadena, CA: William Carrey Library.
Adler, M. 1982. *The Paideia proposal*. New York: Macmillan Co.
Adler, N. 1981. Re-entry: Managing cross-cultural transitions. *Group and Organization Studies*, 6:341–356.
_____. 1983. Cross-cultural management. *International Studies of Management and Organization*, 12:1–173.

———. 1986. Cultural synergy: Managing the impact of cultural diversity. *Developing Human Resources*, 1986 Annual, 229–238.
Adler, P. S. 1972. Culture shock and the cross-cultural learning experience. *Readings in intercultural communication, Vol. 2*, 6–21. Philadelphia: Intercultural Communication Network.
———. 1975. The transitional experience: An alternative view of culture shock. *Humanistic Psychology*, 15:13–23.
———. 1976. Beyond cultural identity: Reflections upon cultural and multi-cultural man. *Topics in Culture Learning*, 2:23–41.
Adorno, T. W., Frendel-Bruswick, E., Levinson, D. J., and Sanford, R. N. 1950. *The authoritarian personality*. New York: Harper and Row.
Albentis, M. H. 1983. The training of Italian teachers in the Federal Republic of Germany: An alternative approach. *European Journal of Teacher Education*, 6:71–77.
Albert, R. D. 1983. The intercultural sensitizer or culture assimilator: A cognitive approach. In *Handbook of intercultural training: Vol. 2. Issues in training methodology*, edited by D. Landis and R. W. Brislin, 186–217. Elmsford, NY: Pergamon Press.
Albert, R. D. 1986. Conceptual framework for the development and evaluation of cross-cultural orientation programs. *International Journal of Intercultural Relations*, 10:197–213.
Albrecht, T. L., and Adelman, M. B. 1987. Communicating social support: A theoretical perspective. In *Communicating social support*, edited by T. L. Albrecht, M. B. Adelman & Associates, 18-40. Newbury Park, CA: Sage Publications.
Allport, G. W. 1954. *The nature of prejudice*. Reading, MA: Addison-Wesley.
Alvirez, D., Bean, F. D., and Williams, D. 1981. The Mexican-American family. In *Ethnic families in America: Patterns and variations*, edited by C. H. Mindel and R. W. Habenstein, 269–292. New York: Elsevier.
Amir, Y. 1969. Contact hypothesis in ethnic relations. *Psychological Bulletin*, 71:319–342.
Anderson, P. J. 1984. The lessons of 27 years' gleaning among Muslims. *Evangelical Missions Quarterly*, 20:362–366.
Anderson, P. L., Reiff, H., and McCray, A. D. 1988. Project AIME: Developing a multicultural training program. *Rural Special Education Quarterly*, 9:7–12.
Anderson, W. M. 1980. Multicultural training: A missing link in graduate music education. *Music Educators Journal*, 67:38–43.
Andrews, T., Houston, R., and Bryant, B. 1978. *Description of CMTI [Corps Member Training Institute]. Vol. 1*. Omaha Nebraska University: Center for Urban Education. (ERIC Document Reproduction Service ED 183 544.)
Argyle, M. 1982. Intercultural communication. In *Cultures in contact: Studies in cross-cultural interaction*, edited by S. Bochner, 61–79. Elmsford, New York: Pergamon Press.
Argyle, M., and Kendon, A. 1967. The experimental analysis of social performance. In *Advances in experimental social psychology. Vol. 3,* edited by L. Berkowitz, pp. 55–98. New York: Academic Press.
Armes, K., and Ward, C. 1988. Cross-cultural transitions and sojourner adjustment in Singapore. *The Journal of Social Psychology*, 129:273–275.

Armstrong, R. N., Sission, R., and Page, J. H. 1988. *Cross-cultural training in business: A sensitizing module. Proceedings of the Seventh Annual Eastern Michigan University Conference on Language for Business and the Professions.* (ERIC Document Reproduction Service ED 304 903).

Arntson, P., and Droge, D. 1987. Social support in self- help groups: The role of communication in enabling perceptions of control. In *Communicating social support,* edited by T. L. Albrecht, M. B. Adelman & Associates, 148–171. Newbury Park, CA: Sage.

Aronson, E., and Linder, D. 1965. Gain and loss of esteem as determinants of interpersonal attractiveness. *Journal of Experimental Social Psychology,* 1:156–171.

Arrendondo-Dowd, P. M. 1981. Personal loss and grief as a result of immigration. *Personnel and Guidance Journal,* 59:376–378.

Arrow, K. J. 1971. *Some models of racial discrimination in the labor market.* Santa Monica, CA: Rand Corporation.

Ascher, C. 1985. The social and psychological adjustment of Southeast Asian refugees. *Urban Review,* 17:147–152.

Athey, J. H. 1987. Comment on Dr. Westermeyer's paper. *Journal of Traumatic Stress,* 2:543–547.

Atkins, A. 1990. Know your own culture: A neglected tool for cross-cultural ministry. *Evangelical Missions Quarterly,* 26:266–271.

Atkinson, P. 1990. *The ethnographic imagination: Textual constructions of reality.* London: Routledge.

Aylesworth, L. S., and Ossorio, P. G. 1983. Refugees: Cultural displacement and its effects. *Advances in Descriptive Psychology,* 3:45–93.

Baba, P. 1981. Frontier mission personnel. In *Seeds of Promise: World consultation on frontier missions, Edinburgh '80,* edited by A. Starling, 114–124. Pasadena, CA: William Carey Library.

Badgero, R. 1986. Teaching tips and tools. *Evangelical Missions Quarterly,* 22:76–69.

Baker, G. C. 1973. Multicultural training of student teachers. *Journal for Teacher Education,* 24:306–307.

———. 1977. Development of the multicultural program: School of education, University of Michigan. In *Pluralism and the American teacher: Issues and case studies,* edited by F. H. Klassen and D. M. Gollnick, 163–170. Washington, DC: Society for Intercultural Education and Research.

Baker, W. L. 1979. Prefield training to enable future missionaries to cope with political change. In *Christ and Caesar in Christian missions,* edited by E. L. Fiezen, Jr. and W. T. Coggins, 55–59. Pasedena, CA: William Carey Library.

Ballantine, J. H. 1983. *The sociology of education: A systematic analysis.* Englewood Cliffs, NJ: Prentice-Hall.

Ball-Rokeach, S. 1973. From pervasive ambiguity to a definition of the situation. *Sociometry,* 36:43–51.

Banach, E., (Ed.) 1990. Today's supply of entry-level workers reflects diversity. *Savings Institutions,* 111:74–75.

Bandura, A. 1977. *Social learning theory.* Englewood Cliffs, NJ: Prentice-Hall.

Banks, J. A. 1977. The implications of multicultural education for teacher education. In *Pluralism and the American teacher: Issues and case studies*, edited by F. H. Klassen and D. M. Gollnick, 1-30. Washington, D.C.: Society for Intercultural Education and Research.
———. 1984. Multiethnic education in the U.S.A.: Practices and promises. In *Education in multicultural societies*, edited by T. Corner, 68-95. London: Croom Helm.
———. 1988. *Multiethnic education: Theory and practice.* Boston: Allyn & Bacon.
———. 1991. Teaching multicultural literacy to teachers. *Teacher Education*, 4:135-144.
———. 1992. Multicultural education: For freedom's sake. *Educational Leadership*, 49:32-36.
Baptiste, H. P., Jr. 1977. Multicultural education evolvement at the University of Houston: A case study. In *Pluralism and the American teacher: Issues and case studies*, edited by F. H. Klassen and D. M. Gollnick, 174-182. Washington, D.C.: Society for Intercultural Education and Research.
Barnabas. 1983. World evangelization and the success syndrome. *Fundamentalist Journal*, 2:43-45.
Barnes, A. 1987. Home thoughts of a broad. *Women in Management Review*, 3:78-84.
Barnes, R. L. 1985. Across cultures: The Peace Corps training model. *Training and Development Journal*, 39:46-49.
Barnhardt, R. 1983. A field-based fieldwork course. *Anthropology and Education Quarterly*, 14:206-208.
———. 1990. *Domestication of the ivory tower: Institutional adaptation to cultural distance.* Unpublished manuscript. University of Alaska, Fairbanks.
Barnlund, D. C. 1982. The cross-cultural arena: An ethical void. In *Handbook of intercultural training. Vol. 2*, edited by D. Landis and R. W. Brislin, 19-49. New York: Pergamon.
Barry, H., Josephson, L., Lauer, E., and Marshall, C. 1987. Agents and techniques for child training: Cross-cultural codes. *Ethnology*, 16:191-230.
Batchelder, D. 1978. Training United States students going abroad. In *Overview of intercultural education, training, and research*, edited by D. S. Hoopes, P. B. Pedersen, and G. Renwick, 45-63. Washington, D.C.: Society for Intercultural Education, Training, and Research.
Batchelder, D., and Warner, E. C. Eds. 1977. *Beyond experience.* Brattleboro, VT: Experiment in International Living.
Becker, G. S. 1971. *The economics of discrimination,* 2nd ed. Chicago: University of Chicago Press.
Befus, C. P. 1988. A multilevel treatment approach for culture shock experienced by sojourners. *International Journal of Intercultural Relations*, 12:381-400.
Belbin, E., and Belbin, R. M. 1972. *Problems in adult retraining.* London: Heinemann.
Bell, H. 1986. White teacher, black learner: The influence of the cross-cultural context on teaching practice. *Australian Journal of Adult Education*, 26:29-32.
Benavides, E. III, Lynch, M. M., and Velasquez, J. S. 1980. Toward a culturally relevant fieldwork model: The community learning center project. *Journal of Education for Social Work*, 16:55-62.
Benedict, R. 1946. *The chrysanthemum and the sword.* Boston: Houghton Mifflin.
Bennett, C. I. 1990. *Comprehensive multicultural education: Theory and practice* 2nd ed. Boston: Allyn & Bacon.

Bennett, C. T. 1979. The preparation of preservice secondary social studies teachers in multicultural education. *The High School Journal*, 62:232–237.

Bennett, M. J. 1986a. A developmental approach to training for intercultural sensitivity. *International Journal of Intercultural Relations*, 10:179–196.

_____. 1986b. Modes of cross-cultural training: Conceptualizing cross-cultural training as education. *International Journal of Intercultural Relations*, 10:117–134.

Benson, P. G. 1978. Measuring cross-cultural adjustment: The problem of criteria. *International Journal of Intercultural Relations*, 2:21–37.

Bergera, G. L. 1988. What you leave behind: Six years at the MTC [Missionary Training Center]. *Dialogue: A Journal of Mormon Thought*, 21:146–155.

Berman, J. 1982. *Preparing to teach in low-income area schools: A case study user's manual*. Cambridge, MA: American Institutes for Research in the Behavioral Sciences. (ERIC Document Reproduction Service ED 212 578).

Berry, J. W. 1990. Psychology of acculturation: Understanding individuals moving between cultures. In *Applied cross-cultural psychology*, edited by R.W. Brislin, 232–253. Newbury Park, CA: Sage Publications.

Bhawuk, D. P. S. 1990. Cross-cultural orientation programs. In *Applied cross-cultural psychology*, edited by R.W. Brislin, 325–346. Newbury Park, CA: Sage Publications.

Billingsley, A. 1968. *Black families in white America*. Englewood Cliffs, NJ: Prentice-Hall.

Bird, A., and Dunbar, R. 1991. Getting the job done over there: Improving expatriate productivity. *National Productivity Review*, 10:145–156.

Black, J. S. 1991. Returning expatriates feel foreign in their native land. *Personnel*, 68:17.

Black, J. S., and Mendenhall, M. 1989. A practical but theory-based framework for selecting cross-cultural training methods. *Human Resource Management*, 28:511–534.

_____. 1991. The U-curve adjustment hypothesis revisited: A review and theoretical framework. *Journal of International Business Studies*, 22:225–247.

Black, J. S., and Porter, L. W. 1991. Managerial behaviors and job performance: A successful manager in Los Angeles may not succeed in Hong Kong. *Journal of International Business Studies,* 22:99–113.

Black, J. S., and Stephens, G. K. 1989. The influence of the spouse on American expatriate adjustment and intent to stay in Pacific Rim overseas assignments. *Journal of Management*, 15:529–544.

Bliatout, B. T. 1988. *Hmong refugees: Some barriers to Western health care services*. Paper presented at Southeast Asians in the United States Conference, March 5, 1988, Tempe, AZ. (ERIC Document Reproduction Service ED 306 317).

Blocklyn, P. L. 1989. Developing the international executive. *Personnel*, 66: 44–47.

Boas, F. 1940. *Race, language and culture*. New York: Macmillan.

Boateng, F. 1990. Combatting deculturalization of the African-American child in the public school system: A multicultural approach. In *Going to school: The African-American experience*, edited by K. Lomotey, 73–84. Albany, NY: State University of New York Press.

Bochner, S. 1973. *The mediating man*. Honolulu: East-West Center.

———. 1982. The social psychology of cross-cultural relations. In *Cultures in contact: Studies in cross-cultural interaction*, edited by S. Bochner, 5–44. Elmsford, New York: Pergamon Press.

———. 1986. Coping with unfamiliar cultures: Adjustment or culture learning? *Australian Journal of Psychology,* 38:347–358.

Bochner, S., and Cairns, L. G. 1976. An unobtrusive measure of helping behaviour toward Aborigines. In *Aboriginal cognition: Retrospect and prospect*, edited by G. E Kearney and D. W. McElwain, 204–234. Canberra: Australian Institute of Aboriginal Studies.

Bogardus, E. S. 1959. *Social distance.* Yellow Springs, OH: Antioch Press.

Bogdan, R. C., and Biklen, S. K. 1982. *Qualitative research for education: An introduction to theory and methods.* Boston: Allyn & Bacon.

Bogorya, U. 1985. Intercultural training for managers involved in international business. *Journal of Management Development*, 4:17–25.

Bonk, J. 1984. Rich, poor, and missions. *Evangelical Missions Quarterly*, 20:389–391.

———. 1991. *Missions and money: Affluence as a Western missionary problem.* Maryknoll, NY: Orbis Books.

Bosco, J. J., and Harring, L. R. 1983. Afloat of the sea of ambiguity: The Teacher Corps experience. *Education and Urban Society*, 15:331–349.

Bouton, L. F. 1975. Meeting the needs of children with diverse linguistic and ethnic backgrounds. *Foreign Language Annals,* 8:306–316.

Bowlby, J. 1969. *Attachment and loss.* London: Hogarth Press.

Boyer, E. L., and the Carnegie Foundation for the Advancement of Teaching Staff. 1985. *High School: A Report on Secondary Education in America.* New York: Harper Collins.

Bradbury, N. 1989. The faces of change. *Canadian Business*, 62:133–136.

Brein, N., and David, K. H. 1972. Intercultural communication and the adjustment of the sojourner. *Psychological Bulletin*, 76:215–230.

Brereton, V. L. 1981. Preparing women for the Lord's work: The story of three Methodist training schools, 1880–1940. In *Women in new worlds*, edited by H. F. Thomas and R. S. Keller, 178–199, Nashville, TN: Abingdon.

Brewer, M. B., and Campbell, D. T. 1976. *Ethnocentrism and intergroup attitudes: East African evidence.* New York: Wiley.

Briggs, N. E., and Harwood, G. R. 1983. *Furthering adjustment: An application of inoculation theory in an intercultural context.* Paper presented at the Annual Meeting of the Western Speech Communication Association, Albuquerque, NM. (ERIC Documentation Reproduction Service ED 225 221.)

Brislin, R. W. 1981. *Cross-cultural encounters.* Elmsford, NY: Pergamon Press.

———. 1986. A culture general assimilator: Preparation for various types of sojourns. *International Journal of Intercultural Relations*, 10: 215–234.

———. 1990. Applied cross-cultural psychology: An introduction. In *Applied cross-cultural psychology*, edited by R. W. Brislin, 9–33. Newbury Park, CA: Sage Publications.

Brislin, R., and Pedersen, P. 1976. *Cross-cultural orientation programs.* New York: Gardner Press.

Brooks, B. 1987. Exporting: Abroad is different. *Industrial Marketing Digest,* 12:75–80.

Brooks, S. L. 1975. Role descriptions of Teacher Corps personnel. In *Programmatic issues in teacher education: Texas Teacher Corps experience*, edited by R. D. Olivarez, 31–44. Washington, D.C.: Office of Education. (ERIC Document Reproduction Service ED 186 392.)

Brooks, S. L., and Weber, W. A. 1975. The instructional system and assessment. In *Programmatic issues in teacher education: The Texas Teacher Corps experience*, edited by R. D. Olivarez, 67–98. Washington, D.C.: Office of Education. (ERIC Document Reproduction ED 186 392.)

Brown v. Board of Education of Topeka, Kansas. [Brown]. 347 U.S. 483. 1954.

Bryan, J. H., and Test, M. A. 1976. Models and helping: Naturalistic studies in aiding behaviour. *Journal of Personality and Social Psychology*, 6: 400–407.

Bryant, B., and Houston, R. 1979. Evaluating training programs. In *Designing short-term instructional programs*, edited by F. T. Waterman, T. E. Andrews, W. R. Houston, B. L. Bryant, and R. S. Pankratz, 49–74. Washington, DC: Association of Teacher Educators. (ERIC Document Reproduction Service ED 183 552.)

Bryant, B., Houston, R., and Andrews, T. 1978. *Engaging in the study of organizations: A temporary systems approach to the description and analysis of Teacher Corps' pilot trainer workshops*. Washington, DC: Office of Education. (ERIC Document Reproduction Service ED 185 028.)

Buchanan, D. R. 1981. Forty-one years of psychodrama at St. Elizabeth's Hospital. *Journal of Group Psychotherapy, Psychodrama, and Sociometry*, 34:134–147.

Buchanan, K. 1990. *Vocational English-as-a-second-language. ERIC Digest.* Washington, DC: Office of Educational Research and Improvement. (ERIC Document Reproduction Service ED 321 551.)

Bullard, S. 1992. Sorting through the multicultural rhetoric. *Educational Leadership*, 49:4–7.

Burry, J. 1978. *Evaluation report of the Teacher Corps Cycle XII and Program 78 developmental training conference*. Nebraska University at Omaha: Center for Urban Education. (ERIC Document Reproduction Service ED 173 301.)

Byram, M. 1988. Foreign language education and cultural studies. *Language, Culture, and Curriculum*, 1:15–30.

Byrne, D. 1971. *The attraction paradigm*. New York: Academic Press.

Byrne, D., and Nelson, D. 1965. Attraction as a linear function of proportion of positive reinforcement. *Journal of Personality and Social Psychology*, 1:659–663.

Byrnes, F. 1966. Role shock: An occupational hazard of American technical assistants abroad. *Annals of the American Academy of Political and Social Science*, 368:95–108.

Campbell, A. E., Hallman, C. L., and Geroy, G. D. 1988. Needs assessment of Florida's international business community's foreign language and cross-cultural training. *Performance and Instruction*, 27:22–25.

Carlson, P. E., and Stephens, T. M. 1986. Cultural bias and identification of behaviorally disordered children. *Behavioral Disorders*, 11:191–198.

Carnegie Foundation for the Advancement of Teaching. 1988. *An imperiled generation: Saving urban schools*. New York: Carnegie Foundation for the Advancement of Teaching.

Carse, W. 1969. Teacher education in culture change. In *Culture change, mental health, and poverty*, edited by J.C. Finney, 117–124. Lexington: University of Kentucky Press.

Casse, P. 1979. *Training for the cross-cultural mind*. Washington, DC: Society of Intercultual Education, Training, and Research.

Cere, D. 1985. *Program development for special purpose foreign language culture courses*. Paper presented at Eastern Michigan University Conference on Language for Business and the Professions, Dearborn, MI, May 2–4. (ERIC Document Reproduction Service ED 271 990).

———. 1988. A new dimension for international and professional studies: Foreign language intercultural courses (FLICS). *Canadian Foreign Language Review*, 44:316–333.

Cetron, M. J., Soriano, B., and Gayle, M. 1990. Schools of the future. *Education*, 102:226–231.

Chaffee, C. 1978. Cross-cultural training for Peace Corps volunteers. In *Overview of intercultural education, training, and research,. Volume 3: Education and training*, edited by D. Hoopes, P. Pedersen, and G. Renwick, 104–126. Washington, DC: Society for Intercultural Education, Training and Research.

Chen, G. M. 1990. *Communication adaptability and interaction involvement as predictors of cross-cultural adjustment*. Paper presented at the Annual Meeting of the Speech Communication Association, Chicago, November 1–4, 1990. (ERIC Document Reproduction ED 327 907).

Christensen, C. P. 1984. Effects of cross-cultural training on helper response. *Counselor Education and Supervision*, 23:311–320.

Christie, A. 1987. *Mr. Parker Pyne, Detective*. New York: Bantam Books.

Chu, H., and Levy, J. 1988. Multicultural skills for bilingual teachers: Training for competency development. *NABE [National Association of Bi-lingual Education] Journal*, 12:153–69.

Church, A. 1982. Sojourner adjustment. *Psychological Bulletin*, 91:540–572.

Clague, L, and Krupp, N. 1980. International personnel: The repatriation problem. *Bridge*, 5:11–13, 37.

Clark, K. B. 1965. *Dark ghetto: Dilemmas of social power*. New York: Harper and Row.

Clinton, J. R. 1984. *Training models*. Pasadena, CA: Fuller Theological Seminary.

Coates, J. F., and Jarratt, J. 1987. *Future search: Forces and factors shaping education*. Washington, DC: National Education Association.

Cochrane, R. 1983. *The social creation of mental illness*. London: Longman.

Coffman, T. L., and Harris, M. C., Jr. 1980. Transition shock and adjustments of mentally retarded persons. *Mental Retardation*, 18:3–7.

Coleman, J. S. 1966. *Equality of Educational Opportunity*. Washington, D.C.: Office of Education.

College Board. 1983. *Academic preparation for college*. New York: College Board.

———. 1988. *Equality and excellence: The educational status of Black Americans*. New York: The College Board.

Collier, M. J., and Thomas, M. 1988. Cultural identity: An interpretive perspective. In *Theories in intercultural communication*, edited by Y. Y. Kim and W. B. Gudykunst, 99–120. Newbury Park, CA: Sage Publications.

Collins, M. 1990. Enrollment, recruitment, and retention of minority faculty and staff in institutions of higher education. *Action in Teacher Education*, 12:57–62.

Collins, T. 1979. From courtrooms to classrooms: Managing school desegregation in a Deep South high school. In *Desegregated schools: Appraisals of an American experiment*, edited by R. Rist, 89–114. New York: Academic Press.

Conn, H. 1984. World missions. *Evangelical Missions Quarterly,* 20:395–398.

———. 1985. I changed the message and God changed me. *Evangelical Missions Quarterly*, 21:182–184.

Cook, S. W. 1962. The systematic study of socially significant events: A strategy for social research. *Journal of Social Issues*, 18:66–84.

Cook, S. W. 1978. Interpersonal and attitudinal outcomes in cooperating interracial groups. *Journal of Research and Development in Education*, 12:97–113.

Cooper, A., Beare, P., and Thorman, J. 1990. Preparing teachers for diversity: A comparison of student teaching experiences in Minnesota and South Texas. *Journal of the Association of Teacher Educators*, 12:1–4.

Copeland, L. 1985. Cross-cultural training: The competitive edge. *Training*, 22:49–53.

Cordova, I., Jaramillo, M., and Trujillo, R. 1974. Competency-based teacher education for Mexican American students. In *Multicultural education through competency-based teacher education*, edited by W. A. Hunter, 174–193. Washington, DC: American Association of Colleges for Teacher Education.

Corn, D., and Morley, J. 1988. Less of the same. *The Nation*, December 5, p. 592.

Coustas, M. A. 1992. Qualitative analysis as a public event: The documentation of category development procedures. *American Educational Research Journal*, 29:253–266.

Covington, R. J. 1974. Inservice model for training public school teachers of Indian students. In *Multicultural education through competency-based teacher education*, edited by W. A. Hunter, 206–208. Washington, DC: American Association of Colleges for Teacher Education.

Coyle, K. 1989. Formation for mission: An Asian perspective: A program for women. *SEDOS Bulletin*, 4:113–122.

Crano, S. L. 1986. *Self-concept and adjustment in international exchange students, Research report 32*. New York: American Field Service International/Intercultural Programs, Inc. (ERIC Document Reproduction Service ED 283 745) .

Cremin, L. A. 1988. *American education: The metropolitan experience, 1876–1980*. New York: Harper and Row.

Crosby, J., and Massey, S. 1980. *Did Teacher Corps make a difference? Ninth cycle Teacher Corps project, University of Maine*. Washington, DC: Office of Education. (ERIC Document Reproduction Service ED 194 523).

Crump, L. 1989. Japanese managers—Western workers: Cross-cultural training and development issues. *Journal of Management Development*, 8:48–55.

Cummings, D. 1987. Programmed for failure—mission candidates at risk. *Evangelical Missions Quarterly*, 23:240–246.

Cummings, R. L. and Bridges, E. F. 1986. *Multiculturalism and teacher education: The rhetoric and a reality*. Madison: University of Wisconsin. (ERIC Document Reproduction Service ED 269 513).

Cushner, K. 1989. Assessing the impact of a culture-general assimilator. *International Journal of Intercultural Relations*, 13:125–146.

Daley, J. M., and Labit, C. 1979. Factors influencing the success of intercultural community development. *Journal of the Community Development Society*, 10:67–82.

Daly, M. E. 1975. The teacher as innovator: A report on urban Teacher Corps, D.C. public schools. *The Journal of Negro Education*, 44:385–390.

Dammers, A. H. 1955. Where should missionary recruits be trained? *International Review of Missions*, 44:185–186.

Darity, E. R. 1985. *Multiethnic perspectives on education.* Paper presented at the National Conference of the National Association of Women Deans, Chicago, May 2–4. (ERIC Document Reproduction Service ED 259 858).

David, K. 1972. Intercultural adjustment and applications of reinforcement theory to problems of "culture shock." *Trends*, 4:1–64

Davidson, G., Hansford, B., and Moriarty, B. 1983. Interpersonal apprehension and cultural majority-minority communication. *Australian Psychologist*, 18:97–105.

Davis, F. J. 1963. Perspectives of Turkish students in the United States. *Sociology and Social Research*, 48:47–57.

Dawson, M. E. 1977. From compensatory to multicultural education: The challenge of designing multicultural educational programs. *Journal of Research and Development in Education,* 11:84–101.

Day, N. A. 1990. Training providers to serve culturally different AIDS patients. *Family and Community Health*, 13:46–53.

Dayton, E. R. 1984. Recruiting and training of cross-cultural missionaries. In *Missions and theological education in world perspective*, edited by H. M. Conn and S. F. Rowen, 389–404. Farmington, MI: Association of Urbanus.

Deer, D. S. 1978. The missionary language-learning problem. *Missiology*, 3:87–102.

Dege, D. B. 1981. *Format and evaluation of the cross-cultural component of a foreign teaching assistant training program.* Paper presented at the Annual Meeting of the International Communication Association, Minneapolis, MN, May 21–25. (ERIC Document Reproduction Service ED 207 100).

Delgado-Gaitan, C. 1988. Preparing teachers for inter-ethnic communication. *Equity and Choice*, 2:53–59.

Dennis, R. 1987. Racism on the rise. *Black Enterprise*, April 17, p. 17.

Diegmueller, K. 1990. New teachers say they are prepared to teach ethnically diverse students. *Education Week*, September 26, p. 6.

Dillon, L. S. 1990. The Occidental tourist. *Training and Development Journal*, 44:72–80.

DiMarco, N. 1974. Stress and adaptation in cross-cultural transition. *Psychological Reports*, 35:279–285.

Dinges, N. 1983. Intercultural competence. In *Handbook of intercultural training. Vol. 1: Issues in theory and design*, edited by D. Landis, 176–202. Elmsford: NY: Pergamon.

Dinges, N., and Duffy, L. 1979. Culture and competence. In *Perspectives on cross-cultural psychology*, edited by A. J. Marsella, R. G. Tharp, and T. J. Ciborowski, 209–232. New York: Academic Press.

D'Innocenzo, M., and Sirefman, 1992. *Immigration and ethnicity: American society—"melting pot" or "salad bowl"?* Westport, CT: Greenwood Press.

Dodge, D. T. 1985. *A classroom teacher's handbook for building English proficiency.* Washington, DC: Office of Bilingual Education and Minority Languages Affairs. (ERIC Document Reproduction Service ED 275 134).

Donmall, B. G. 1985. *Some implications of language awareness work for teacher training, pre-service and in-service.* London: Center for Information on Language Teaching and Research. (ERIC Document Reproduction Service ED 277 243).

Dorotich, D., and Stephan, W. 1984. Multicultural education and society in Canada and Yugoslavia. In *Education in multicultural societies*, edited by T. Corner, 96–116. London: Croom Helm.

Dougherty, M. A. 1981. The social gospel according to Phoebe: Methodist deaconesses in the metropolis, 1885–1918. In *Women in new worlds*, edited by H. F. Thomas and R. S. Keller, 200–218. Nashville, TN: Abingdon.

Dovidio, J. F., and Gaertner, S. L. 1981. Changes in the expression and assessment of racial prejudice. In *Opening doors: Perspectives on race relations in contemporary America*, edited by H. J. Knopke, R. J. Norrell, and R. W. Rogers, 119–148. Tuscaloosa: University of Alabama Press.

Downs, J. F. 1969. Fables, fancies, and failures in cross-cultural training. *Trends*, 2:3. (ERIC Document Reproduction Service No. ED 034 935).

Dumont, R. V., Jr., and Wax, M. L. 1976. Cherokee school society and the intercultural classroom. In *Schooling in the cultural context: Anthropological studies in education*, edited by J. I. Roberts and S. K. Akinsanya, 205–216. New York: David McKay.

Dunbar, E., and Katcher, A. 1990. Preparing managers for foreign assignments. *Training and Development Journal*, 44:45–47.

Dyer, K. 1986. Crucial factors in building good teams. *Evangelical Missions Quarterly*, 22:254–258.

———. 1989. Leadership transition: Painful, but necessary. *Evangelical Missions Quarterly*, 25:172–173.

Earley, P. C. 1987. Intercultural training for managers: A comparison of documentary and interpersonal methods. *Academy of Management Journal*, 30:685–698.

Edwards, A. 1991. The enlightened manager: How to treat all your employees fairly. *Working Woman*, 16:45–55.

Elkins, S. M. 1959. *Slavery: A problem in American institutional and intellectual life.* Chicago: University of Chicago Press.

Ellis, D. 1992. L. A. Lawless. *Time*, May 11, p. 26–27.

Ellison, C. W. 1978. Psychology, Christianity, and urban need. *Journal of Psychology and Christianity*, 6:283–290.

Elliston, E. J. 1988. Designing leadership education. *Missiology: An International Review*, 16:203–215.

English, S. L. 1981. Critical incidents workshop for ESL teacher intercultural awareness training. In *On TESOL '80. Building bridges: Research and practice in teaching English as a second language*, edited by J. Fisher, 159–167. Washington, DC: Georgetown University. (ERIC Document Reproduction Service ED 208 643.)

Faison, J. J. 1993. *Unmeasured, but essential: A study of distinguishing factors between graduate school African-American persistors and non-persistors.* Unpublished manuscript. Emory University.

Feather, N. T. 1980. Value systems and social interaction: A field of study in a newly independent nation. *Journal of Applied Social Psychology*, 10:1–19.

Feldman, R. E. 1968. Response to compatriots and foreigners who seek assistance. *Journal of Personality and Social Psychology*, 10:202–14.

Feleppa, R. 1988. *Convention, translation, and understanding: Philosophical problems in the comparative study of culture.* Albany: State University of New York Press.

Fendrich, J. M. 1967. A study of the association among verbal attitudes, commitment, and overt behavior in different experimental situations. *Social Forces*, 45:347–355.

Fernando, A. 1988. Missionaries still needed—but of a special kind. *Evangelical Missions Quarterly*, 24:18–25.

Ferrell, R. J. 1984. Anthropology—a two-edged sword. *Evangelical Missions Quarterly*, 20:279–282.

Festinger, L. 1957. *A theory of cognitive dissonance.* Evanston, IL: Row, Peterson.

Fiedler, F. E., Mitchell, T., and Triandis, H. C. 1971. The culture assimilator: An approach to cross-cultural training. *Journal of Applied Psychology*, 55:95–102.

Fiske, E. B. 1988. The undergraduate Hispanic experience: A case of juggling two cultures. *Change*, 20:29–33.

Fontaine, G. 1986. Roles of social support systems in overseas relocation: Implications for intercultural training. *International Journal of Intercultural Relations*, 10:361–378.

Foust, S., Fieg, J., Koester, J., Sarbaugh, L., and Wendinger, L. eds.. 1981. Dynamics of cross- cultural adjustment: From pre-arrival to re-entry. In *Learning across cultures: Intercultural communication and international educational exchange*, edited by G. Althen, 7–29. Washington, DC: National Association for Foreign Student Affairs.

Fox, C. L., Kuhlman, N. A., and Sales, T. B. 1988. Cross-cultural concerns: What's missing from special education training programs. *Teacher Education and Special Education*, 11:156–161.

Fox, C. T., Grant, C. A., Lufler, H. S., Melnick, S. L., Mitchell, N. J., and Thompson, F. 1978. *Residual impact of the 1975 Corps Member Training Institute [CMTI].* Washington, DC: Office of Education, Teacher Corps. (ERIC Document Reproduction Service ED 185 019).

Frazier, D., and DeBlassie, R. R. 1984. Diagnosing behavior-disordered early adolescents as a function of cultural differences. *Adolescence*, 19:385–390.

Freeman, L. C., and Winch, R. F. 1957. Societal complexity: An empirical test of a typology of societies. *American Journal of Sociology*, 62:461–466.

Freiberg, H. J., Townsend, K., and Ashley, I. 1978. *Field-based clinical inservice education: Eleventh cycle Teacher Corps.* Paper presented at the National Council of States on Inservice Education Conference, San Francisco, November 16–18. (ERIC Document Reproduction Service ED 161 849).

Frey-Hartel, C., and Kasum, D. 1988. *The highlights and pitfalls of developing an intercultural workshop in France.* In Proceedings of the Seventh Annual Eastern Michigan University Conference on Language Business and the Professions. April. (ERIC Document Reproduction Service ED 304 931).

Fry, P. S. 1984. Stress ideations of Vietnamese youth in North America. *Journal of Social Psychology*, 125:35–43.

Furnham, A. 1988. The adjustment of sojourners. In *Cross-cultural adaptation: Current approaches*, edited by Y. Y. Kim and W. B. Gudykunst, 42–61. Newbury Park, CA: Sage Publications.

Furnham, A., and Bochner, S. 1982. Social difficulty in foreign culture: An empirical analysis of culture shock. In *Cultures in contact: Studies in cross-cultural interaction*, edited by S. Bochner, 161–198. Elmsford, NY: Pergamon.

———. 1986. *Culture shock: Psychological reactions to unfamiliar environments*. London: Methuen.

Gangel, K. O. 1989. Developing new leaders for global tasks. *Evangelical Missions Quarterly*, 25:166–171.

Gao, G., and Gudykunst, W. B. 1990. Uncertainty, anxiety, and adaptation. *International Journal of Intercultural Relations*, 14:310–317.

Garcia, E. 1974. Chicano cultural diversity: Implications for competency-based teacher education. In *Multicultural education through competency-based teacher education*, edited by W. A. Hunter, 146–157. Washington, DC: American Association of Colleges for Teacher Education.

Gardner, L. M. 1987. A practical approach to transitions in missionary living. *Journal of Psychology and Theology*, 15:342–349.

Gay, G. 1977. Curriculum for multicultural teacher education. In *Pluralism and the American teacher: Issues and case studies*, edited by F. H. Klassen and D. M. Gollnick, 31–62. Washington, DC: American Association of Colleges of Teacher Education.

Geertz, C. 1973. *The interpretation of cultures*. New York: Basic Books.

Gemson, C. 1991. How to cultivate today's multi-cultural work force. *Employment Relations Today*, 18:157–160.

Genovese, E. D. 1974. *Roll, Jordan, roll: The world the slaves made*. New York: Pantheon.

Gest, T. 1987. Is an ugly past returning to haunt America? *U.S. News and World Report*, February 12, p. 12.

Gibbs, J. T. 1985. Can we continue to be color-blind and class-bound? *Counseling Psychologist*, 13:426–435.

Giffin, K. 1970. Social alienation by communication denial. *Quarterly Journal of Speech*, 56:247–357.

Glass, G., McGraw, B., and Smith, M. 1981. *Meta-analysis in social research*. Newbury Park, CA: Sage Publications.

Glazer, N. 1983. *Ethnic dilemmas, 1964–1982*. Cambridge, MA: Harvard University Press.

Glazer, N. and Moynihan, D. P. eds.. 1975. *Ethnicity: Theory and experience*. Cambridge, MA: Harvard University Press.

Goldsmith, J. 1989. The environment: Three options. *Vital Speeches*, 56:221–224.

Gollnick, D. 1991. [Author's interview with Donna Gollnick, Vice-President of the National Council for the Accreditation of Teacher Education]. January.

Goodlad, J. I. 1984. *A Place Called School*. New York: McGraw-Hill.

———. 1990. *Teachers for our nation's schools*. San Francisco: Jossey-Bass Publishers.

Gouldner, A. W. 1977. Stalinism: A study of internal colonialism. *Telos*, 4:5–48.

Grahame, K. 1982. *The wind in the willows*. New York: Gallery Books.

Grant, C. A., and Secada, W. G. 1990. Preparing teachers for diversity. In *Handbook of research on teacher education*, edited by W. R. Houston, 403–422. New York: Macmillan.

Greenway, R. S. 1983. Don't be an urban missionary unless. *Evangelical Missions Quarterly*, 19:86–94.

Gregersen, H. B., and Black, J. S. 1990. A multifaceted approach to expatriate retention in international assignments. *Group and Organization Studies*, 15:461–485.

Grove, C. L. 1982. *Improving intercultural learning through the orientation of sojourners*. New York: American Field Service International/Intercultural Programs. (ERIC Document Reproduction Service ED 221 613).

———. 1990. An ounce of prevention: Supporting international job transitions. *Employment Relations Today*, 17:111–119.

Grove, C. L., and Torbiorn, I. 1985. A new conceptualization of intercultural adjustment and the goals of training. *International Journal of Intercultural Relations*, 9:205–233.

Grubbs, L. L. 1985. Multicultural training in university residence. *Journal of College and University Student Housing*, 15:21–25.

Grubis, S. F. 1985. Teaching in the Alaskan village: The challenge. *Rural Educator*, 7:17–20.

Grundmann, C. 1985. The role of medical missions in the missionary enterprise: A historical and missiological survey. *Mission Studies*, 2:39–48.

Gudykunst, W. B. 1983. Toward a typology of stranger-host relationships. *International Journal of Intercultural Relations*, 7:401–413.

Gudykunst, W. B., and Hammer, M. R. 1983. Basic training design: Approaches to intercultural training. In *Handbook of intercultural training, Vol. 2: Issues in theory and design*, edited by D. Landis, 118–154. Elmsford, NY: Pergamon.

Gudykunst, W. B., Hammer, M. R., and Wiseman, R. L. 1977. An analysis of an integrated approach to cross-cultural training. *International Journal of Intercultural Relations*, 1:99–110.

Gullahorn, J. T., and Gullahorn, J. E. 1963. An extension of the U-curve hypothesis. *Journal of Social Issues*, 14:33–37.

Gurule, E. 1977. Case study: The cultural awareness center at the University of New Mexico. In *Pluralism and the American teacher: Issues and case studies*, edited by F. H. Klassen and D. M. Gollnick, 217–238. Washington, D.C.: American Association of Colleges for Teacher Education.

Guthrie, G. A. 1976. A behavioral analysis of culture learning. In *Cross-culture perspectives on learning*, edited by R. Brislin, S. Bochner, and W. Lonner, 95–113. New York: Wiley.

Guthrie, G. M., and Zektick, I. N. 1967. Predicting performance in the Peace Corps. *Journal of Social Psychology*, 71:11–21.

Gutman, H. G. 1977. *The black family in slavery and freedom, 1750–1925*. New York: Pantheon.

Haberman, M. 1991. Can cultural awareness be taught in teacher education programs? *Teacher Education*, 4:25–31.

Haberman, M., and Post, L. 1990. Cooperating teacher's perceptions of the goals of multicultural education. *Action in Teacher Education*, 12:31–35.

Haines, D. W. 1985a. Initial adjustment. In *Refugees in the United States*, edited by D. W. Haines, 17-35. Westport, CT: Greenwood Press.

———. 1985b. Refugees and the refugee program. In *Refugees in the United States*, edited by D.W. Haines, 3–15. Westport, CT: Greenwood Press.

———. 1985c. Toward integration into American society. In *Refugees in the United States*, edited by D. W. Haines, 37–55. Westport, CT: Greenwood Press.

Hainsworth, J. 1978. A Teacher Corps project on multiple talents. In *Teaching for talents and gifts, 1978 status: Developing and implementing multiple talent teaching*, edited by C. W. Tayler, 85-90. Washington, DC: National Institute of Education. (ERIC Document Reproduction Service ED 172 475).

Hale-Benson, J. 1990. Visions for children: Educating black children in the context of their culture. In *Going to school: The African-American experience*, edited by K. Lomotey, 209–222. Albany: State University of New York Press.

Hall, E. T. 1976. *Beyond culture*. New York: Doubleday.

Hall, M. N. 1989. Being there: The value of teacher exchange programs. *Social Studies and the Young Learner*, 1:7–8.

Hall, P. H. 1989. The relationship of perceived ethnocentrism in corporate cultures to the selection, training, and success of international employees. *International Journal of Intercultural Relations*, 13:183–201.

Hammer, M. R., Gudykunst, W. B., and Wiseman, R. 1978. Dimensions of intercultural effectiveness. *International Journal of Intercultural Relations*, 2:99–110.

Hammersley, M. 1992. *What's wrong with ethnography? Methodological explorations*. London: Routledge.

Haney, C., Banks, W. C., and Zimbardo, P. G. 1973. Interpersonal dynamics in a simulated prison. *International Journal of Criminology and Penology*, 1:69–97.

Hankin, J. N. 1990. Moving your institution into the 21st century. *Vital Speeches*, 57:253–256.

Hannigan, T. P. 1990. Traits, attitudes, and skills that are related to intercultural effectiveness and their implications for cross-cultural training: A review of the literature. *International Journal of Intercultural Relations*, 14:89–111.

Hansen, J. T., and Hansen-Krening, N. 1988. Difficult appointments abroad. *ADE Bulletin*, 88:71–79.

Harley, B. L., and Robinson, C. D. 1991. Multinational managers on the move. *Medical Marketing and Media*, 26:44–51.

Harnden, P. 1986. Mission to the missionary: OMSC [Overseas Missions Study Center] innovates with the old, old story. *Other Side*, 22:7–8.

Harris, J. E. 1989. Moving managers internationally: The care and feeding of expatriates. *Human Resources Planning*, 12:49–53.

Harris, J. G, Jr.. 1970. Prediction of success on a lonely Pacific island: Peace Corps style. *Trends*, 3:1–69.

———. 1973. A science of the South Pacific: Analysis of the character structure of the Peace Corps volunteer. *American Psychologist*, 28: 232–247.

———. 1975. Identification of cross-cultural talent: The empirical approach of the Peace Corps. *Topics in Culture Learning*, 3:66–78.

References

Harrison, J. K. 1987. An examination of the individual and combined effects of behavior modeling and the cultural assimilator as cross-cultural training techniques. (Doctoral dissertation, University of Maryland). *Dissertation Abstracts International*, 48:08A.

Harrison, R., and Hopkins, R. 1967. The design of cross- cultural training: An alternative to the university model. *Journal of Applied Behavioral Science*, 3:431–460.

Harshman, H. W. 1974. Influencing teacher-training programs: A possible model. *Journal of Special Education*, 8:33–37.

Hart, J. 1991. *Damage*. New York: Ivy Books.

Hatch, E. 1973. *Theories of man and culture*. New York: Columbia University Press.

———. 1983. *Culture and morality: The relativity of values in anthropology*. New York: Columbia University Press.

Haughton, R. 1982. Divine love breaking through into human experience. *International Review of Missions*, 71:20–28.

Hautaluoma, J. E., and Kaman, V. 1975. Description of Peace Corps volunteers' experience in Afghanistan. *Topics in Culture Learning*, 3:69–73.

Hawes, R., and Kealey, D. J. 1981. An empirical study of Canadian technical assistance: Adaptation and effectiveness on overseas assignment. *International Journal of Intercultural Relations*, 5:239–258.

Hayles, R. 1978. Inter-ethnic and race relations education and training. In *Overview of intercultural education, training, and research*, edited by D. S. Hoopes, P. B. Pedersen, and G. Renwick, 64–87. Washington, D.C.: Society for Intercultural Education, Training, and Research.

Heger, K. 1989. A tale of two Lucys. *International Association of Business Communication Communication World*, 6:32–35.

Heider, F. 1958. *The psychology of interpersonal relations*. New York: Wiley.

Heisey, N. 1990. 19th century commitment and 21st century perspective: Attributes of a Christian internationalist. *Evangelical Missions Quarterly*, 26:292–303.

Heiss, J., & Nash, D. (1967). The stranger in laboratory culture revisted. *Human Organization*, 26, 47–51.

Helmes, J. E. 1985. Toward a theoretical explanation of the effects of race on counseling: A black and white model. *Counseling Psychologist*, 12:153–165.

Henry, J. 1960. A cross-cultural outline of education. *Current Anthropology: A World of the Sciences of Man*, 1:267–305.

Hertz, D. G. 1984. Psychological and psychiatric aspects of remigration. *The Israel Journal of Psychiatry and Related Sciences*, 21:57–68.

Hesselgrave, D. J. 1983. Missionary psychology and counseling—A timely birth? *Trinity Journal*, 4:72–81.

———. 1987. Missionary education: Women educators speak out on issues from their perspectives. *Evangelical Missions Quarterly*, 23:82–89.

Heusinkveld, M. 1957. The new missionary committee and field orientation. *International Review of Missions*, 46:283–289.

Hewstone, M., and Brown, R. 1986. Contact is not enough: An intergroup perspective on the "contact hypothesis." In *Contact and conflict in intergroup encounters*, edited by M. Hewstone and R. Brown, 1–44. New York: Basil Blackwell.

Hick, D. 1984. The emergence of cultural diversity in Australia. In *Education in multicultural societies*, edited by T. Corner, 117–136. London: Croom Helm.

Hiebert, P. E. 1989. Anthropological insights for whole ministries. In *Christian relief and development: Developing workers for effective ministry*, edited by E. J. Elliston, 75–92. Dallas, TX: Word Publishing.

Higbee, H. 1969. Role shock—a new concept. *International Educational and Cultural Exchange*, 4:71–81.

Hilliard, A. G. III. 1974. Restructuring teacher education for multicultural imperatives. In *Multicultural education through competency-based teacher education*, edited by W. A. Hunter, 40–56. Washington, DC: American Association Colleges for Teacher Education.

———. 1992. Why we must pluralize the curriculum. *Educational Leadership*, 49:12–16.

Hinkle, G. E., Tupton, R. L., Tutchings, T. R. 1979. *Who cares? Who counts? A national study of migrant students' educational needs*. Washington, D.C.: Office of Education. (ERIC Document Reproduction Service ED 180 705).

Hodgkinson, H. L. 1986. *Future search: A look at the present*. Washington, D.C.: National Education Association.

———. 1989. *The same client: The demographics of education and service delivery systems*. Washington, DC: Institute for Educational Leadership, Center for Demographic Policy.

Hofstede, G. 1980. *Culture's consequences: International differences in work related values*. Beverly Hills, CA: Sage Publications.

Hoke, S. T. 1985. The introduction to missions course—how to prepare "world" Christians. *Evangelical Missions Quarterly*, 21:68–80.

Holland, F. 1974. Preservice and inservice model for training Indian teachers. In *Multicultural education through competency-based teacher education*, edited by W. A. Hunter, 202–205. Washington, DC: American Association of Colleges for Teacher Education.

Holmes Group. 1986. *Tomorrow's leaders*. East Lansing, MI: Holmes Group.

Honeycutt, R. L. 1989. Training missionaries through the cooperative program. *Baptist History and Heritage*, 24:45–46.

Hood, S. 1989. Minority bias review panels and teacher testing for initial certification: A comparison of two states' efforts. *Journal of Negro Education*, 58:511–519.

Hoopes, D. S. ed.. 1977. *Readings in intercultural communication: Vol. 2: Teaching intercultural communication, concepts and courses*. Pittsburgh, PA: Society for Intercultural Education, Training, and Research.

Hoopes, D. S., and Pusch, M. D. 1981. Teaching strategies: The methods and techniques of cross-cultural training. In *Multicultural education: A cross-cultural approach*, edited by M. D. Pusch, 106–203. Chicago: Intercultural Press.

Hoopes, D. S., and Ventura, P. eds.. 1979. *Intercultural sourcebook*. Washington, DC: Society for Intercultural Education, Training, and Research.

Hopkins, R. 1982. *Defining and predicting overseas effectiveness for adolescent exchange students*. Washington, DC: Youth for Understanding.

Horner, G. R. 1953. The need for anthropologically trained missionaries. *Practical Anthropology*, 1:93–97.

Horowitz, I. L. 1976. *Genocide: State power and mass murder*. New Brunswick, NJ: Transaction Books.

References

Houston, W. R. 1979. Empirical study of institute strategies. In *Designing short-term instructional programs*, edited by F. T. Waterman, T. E. Andrews, W. R. Houston, B. L. Bryant, and R. S. Pankratz, 87–146. Washington, DC: Association of Teacher Educators. (ERIC Document Reproduction Service ED 183 552).

Houston, W. R., Andrews, T., and Bryant, B. 1977. *Synthesis and analysis of data, Volume 2: Corps Member Training Institute*. Washington, DC: Office of Education. (ERIC Document Reproduction Service ED 185 010).

Howard, C. 1980. The expatriate manager and the role of the MNC [multinational corporation].. *Personnel Journal*, 59:838–844.

Howard, E. D. 1987. Extremism on campus: Symbols of hate, symbols of hope. *The Christian Century*, July 15, p. 625–626.

Howell, W. S. 1981. *Ethics of intercultural communication*. Paper presented at the Annual Meeting of the Speech Communication Association, Anaheim, CA. (ERIC Document Reproduction Service ED 209 689).

Hughes-Weiner, G. 1986. The "learning-how-to-learn" approach to cross-cultural orientation. *International Journal of Intercultural Relations*, 10: 485–505.

_____. 1988. *An overview of international education in the schools*. Washington, D.C.: Office of Education. (ERIC Document Reproduction Service ED 185 010).

Hui, H. C. 1990. Work attitudes, leadership styles, and managerial behaviors in different cultures. In *Applied cross-cultural psychology*, edited by R. W. Brislin, 186–208. Newbury Park, CA: Sage Publications.

Hull, F. W. IV. 1978. *Foreign students in the United States: Coping behavior within the educational environment*. New York: Praeger.

Humphrey, R. L. 1964. *Fight the Cold War, a handbook for overseas orientation officers: How Americans serving abroad can help the Free World win the battle of ideas in the Cold War*. Office of the Chief of Research and Development, Department of the Army. (Contract No. DA-49-092-ARO-15). Washington, DC: American Institutes for Research.

Inman, M. 1985. Language and cross-cultural training in the American multinational corporations. *Modern Language Journal*, 69:247–256.

International Catholic Migration Commission. 1985. *Intensive English as a second language/cultural orientation training program. Guide for instruction*. Washington, DC: Department of State, Bureau of Refugee Programs. (ERIC Document Reproduction Service ED 263 342).

Irvine, J. J. 1990. *Black students and school failure: Policies, practices, and prescriptions*. New York: Praeger.

Irving, K. J. 1984. Cross-cultural awareness and the English-as-a-second-language classroom. *Theory into Practice*, 23:138–143.

Jackson, R. 1987. We have a serious problem that isn't going away. *Sports Illustrated*, May 11, p. 40–42.

Jenkins, M. M. 1983. *Guidelines for cross-cultural communication between students and faculty*. San Francisco: San Francisco State University. (ERIC Document Reproduction Service ED 265 595).

_____. 1990. Teaching the new majority: Guidelines for cross-cultural communication between students and faculty. *Feminist Teacher*, 5:8–14.

References

Johnson, J. W. 1977. Human relations preparation in teacher education: The Wisconsin experience. In *Pluralism and the American teacher: Issues and case studies*, edited F. H. Klassen and D. M. Gollnick, 185–204. Washington, DC: American Association of Colleges for Teacher Education.

Johnson, S. D., Jr. 1983. *The cross-cultural counseling specialization at Teachers College, Columbia University*. Paper presented at the Annual Convention of the American Psychological Association, Anaheim, CA, August 26–30. (ERIC Document Reproduction Service ED 241 860).

——. 1987. Knowing that versus knowing how: Toward achieving expertise through multicultural counseling.*Counseling Psychologist*, 15:320–331.

Jones, C.M. 1985. *Practical applications of multicultural communication theory in the classroom setting*. Paper presented at the Annual Meeting of the Western Speech Communication Association, Fresno, CA, February 16–19. (ERIC Document Reproduction Service ED 257 147).

Jones, J. 1975. Recruitment. In *Programmatic issues in teacher education: The Texas Teacher Corps experience*, edited by R. D. Olivarez, 12–19. Washington, DC: Office of Education. (ERIC Document Reproduction Service ED 186 392).

Jones, R. R., and Burnes, W. J. 1970. Volunteer satisfaction with in-country training for the Peace Corps. *Journal of Applied Psychology*, 54:533–537.

Jordan, C. 1984. Cultural compatibility and the education of Hawaiian children: Implications for mainland educators. *Education Research Quarterly*, 8:59–69.

Joyce, B. R. 1980. *The social ecology of the school: The dynamics of the internal/external systems*. Paper presented at the Annual Meeting of The American Educational Research Association, Boston, April 7–11. (ERIC Document Reproduction Service ED 194 776).

Juntune, J. and Worthley, L. 1978. A theoretical model for training of multiple talent teachers. In *Teaching for talents and gifts, 1978 status: Developing and implementing multiple talent teaching*, edited by C. W. Taylor, 119–120. Washington, DC: National Institute of Education. (ERIC Document Reproduction Service ED 172 475).

Kagitcibasi, C., and Berry, J. W. 1989. Cross-cultural psychology: Current research and trends. *Annual Review of Psychology*, 40:493–531.

Kahl, J. A. 1968. *The measurement of modernism: A study of values in Brazil and Mexico*. Austin: University of Texas Press.

Kane, J. H. 1982. *Understanding Christian missions*, 3rd Ed. Grand Rapids, MI: Baker Book House.

Kanter, E. M. 1977. Some effects of proportions on group life: Skewed sex ratios and responses to token women. *American Journal of Sociology*, 82:965–990.

Kealey, K. J., and Ruben, B. D. 1983. Cross-cultural personnel selection criteria, issues, and methods. In *Handbook of intercultural training,Vol. 1: Issues in theory and design,* edited by D. Landis and R. W. Brislin, 155–175. Elmsford, NY: Pergamon.

Kennedy, M. M. 1991. Some surprising findings on how teachers learn to teach. *Educational Leadership*, 49:14–17.

Keys, B., and Wolfe, J. 1988. Management education and development: Current issues and emerging trends. *Journal of Management*, 14:205–229.

Kim, Y. Y. 1985. On theorizing intercultural communication. In *Theories in intercultural communication*, edited by Y. Y. Kim and W. B. Gudykunst, 11–21. Newbury Park, CA: Sage Publications.

Kincheloe, J., and Staley, G. 1983. Teaching on a rural reservation: An authentic learning experience. *Momentum*, 14:18–19.

King, E. W. 1983. Promising practices in teaching ethnically diverse children. *Momentum*, 14:38–40.

Kinsler, R. 1989. *Kairos* in theological education: Changing perspectives from the underside. [The appointed time]. *Ministerial Formation*, 45:4–27.

Klein, J. 1990. Race: The mess. *New York*, May 28, p. 32–37.

Klein, M. H. 1979. Adaptation to new cultural environments. In *Overview of intercultural education, training and research, Vol. 1: Theory*, edited by D. S. Hoopes, P. B. Pedersen and G. Renwick, 49–55. Washington, DC: Society for Intercultural Education, Training, and Research.

Kleinfeld, J., McDiarmid, G. W., Grubis, S., and Parrett, W. 1983. Doing research on effective cross-cultural teaching: The teacher tale. *Peabody Journal of Education*, 61:86–108.

Kleifgen, J. A. 1988. Learning from student teachers' cross-cultural communicative failures. *Anthropology and Education Quarterly*, 19:218–234.

Klineberg, O. 1971. Black and white in international perspective. *American Psychologist*, 26:119–128.

———. 1980. Historical perspectives: Cross-cultural psychology before 1960. In *Handbook of cross-cultural psychology*, edited by H. C. Triandis and W. W. Lambert, 31–68. Boston: Allyn & Bacon.

———. 1982. Contact between ethnic groups: A historical perspective of some aspects of theory and research. In *Cultures in contact: Studies in cross-cultural interaction*, edited by S. Bochner, 45–55. Elmsford, NY: Pergamon.

Klineberg, O., and Hull, W. F. IV. 1979. *At a foreign university: An international study of adaptation and coping*. New York: Praeger.

Kluckhohn, F., and Strodbeck, F. 1961. *Variations in value orientations*. Chicago: Row, Peterson.

Knight, E. M. 1981. *The case for teacher training in non-biased, cross-cultural assessment*. Paper presented at the Council for Exceptional Children Conference on the Exceptional Bilingual Child, New Orleans, LA, February 18–20. (ERIC Document Reproduction Service ED 209 829.)

Koehler, G. 1980. Personality needs of German wives and satisfaction with life in the Philippines. *Psychologia*, 23:78–86.

Koester, J. 1984. Communication and the intercultural reentry: A course proposal. *Communication Education*, 33:251–256.

Kohls, L. R. 1979. *Survival kit for overseas living*. Yarmouth, ME: Intercultural Press.

———. 1987. Four traditional approaches to developing cross-cultural preparedness in adults: Education, training, orientation, and briefing. *International Journal of Intercultural Relations*, 11:89–106.

Konner, M. 1982. *The tangled wing: Biological constraints on the human spirit*. New York: Harper and Row.

Korn, K. 1972. Culture shock and the transfer of teaching. *Bureau of School Service Bulletin*, 45:5–16.

Kovel, J. 1984. *White racism: A psychohistory*. New York: Columbia University Press.
Kozol, J. 1991. *Savage inequalities: Children in America's schools*. New York: Harper Perennial.
Kracke, W. 1987. Encounter with other cultures: Psychological and epistemological aspects. *Ethos*, 15:58–81.
Kristal, L., Pennock, P. W., Foote, S. M., and Trygstad, C. W. 1983. Cross-cultural family medicine residency training. *Journal of Family Medicine*, 17:683–687.
Kudirka, J. C. 1989. *Cross-cultural communication in the workplace: Can we stay home without it?* Paper presented at the Annual Conference of the National Alliance of Business. Washington, DC, October 3. (ERIC Document Reproduction Service ED 319 897.)
Kuntzer, K. S. 1986. The day of salvation in the Third World: Amsterdam '86 trains national evangelists for national evangelism. *Christianity Today*, 30:14–15.
Laboratory of Comparative Human Cognition [LCHC]. 1986. Contributions of cross-cultural research to educational practice. *American Psychologist*, 41: 1049–1057.
Lambert, J. W. 1989. Accepting other's values in the classroom: An important difference. *Clearing House*, 62:273–274.
Lane, S. 1980. *"But it's English, isn't it?" Teaching English as a second language and/or developmental English—Same method?* Paper presented at the Annual Conference of the New York State English to Speakers of Other Languages and Bilingual Educators Association, New York, October 24–26. (ERIC Document Reproduction Service ED 213 261).
Landis, D., and Brislin, R. W. eds.. 1983. *Handbook of intercultural training, Vol. 2: Issues in training methodology.* Elmsford, NY: Pergamon.
Langer, T. 1962. A 22-item screening score of psychiatric symptoms indicating impairment. *Journal of Health and Social Behaviour*, 111:269–276.
Laosa, L. M. 1974. Toward a research model of multicultural competency-based teacher education. In *Multicultural education through competency-based teacher education*, edited by W. A. Hunter, 135–145. Washington, DC: American Association of Colleges for Teacher Education.
Larke, P. J. 1990. Cultural diversity awareness inventory: Assessing the sensitivity of preservice teachers. *Action in Teacher Education*, 12:23–30.
Larke, P. J., Wiseman, D., and Bradley, C. 1990. The minority mentorship project: Changing attitudes of preservice teachers for diverse classrooms. *Action in Teacher Education*, 12:5–11.
Larson, D. N. 1984. Missionary preparation: Confronting the presuppositional barrier. In *Missions and theological education in world perspective*, edited by H. M. Conn and S. F. Rowen, 298–309. Farmington, MI: Association of Urbanus.
Latourette, K. S. 1957. Re-thinking missions after twenty-five years. *International Review of Missions*, 46:164–170.
Laughlin, M. A. 1980. *An examination of state requirements for multicultural/human relations in elementary and secondary teacher education*. Paper presented at the Annual Midwest Regional Conference of the National Association of Interdisciplinary Ethnic Studies, Ames, IA, December 4. (ERIC Document Reproduction Service ED 202 975.)

Law, S. G., and Lane, D. S. 1987. Multicultural acceptance by teacher education students: A survey of attitudes toward 32 ethnic and national groups and a comparison with 60 years of data. *Journal of Instructional Psychology*, 14:3–9.

LeCompte, M. D. 1985. Defining the differences: Cultural subgroups within the educational mainstream. *Urban Review*, 17:111–127.

Lee, C. 1983. Cross-cultural training: Don't leave home without it. *Training*, 20:20–21, 23–25.

Lee, Y., and Larwood, L. 1983. The socialization of expatriate managers in multinational firms. *Academy of Management Journal*, 26:657–665.

Leeds-Hurwitz, W. 1990. Notes in the history of intercultural communication: The Foreign Service Institute and the mandate for intercultural training. *Quarterly Journal of Speech*, 76:262–281.

Lefley, H. P. 1981. Psychotherapy and cultural adaptation in the Caribbean. *International Journal of Group Tensions*, 11:3–16.

———. 1984. Cross-cultural training for mental health professionals: Effects on the delivery of services. *Hospital and Community Psychiatry*, 35:1227–1229.

———. 1985. Impact of cross-cultural training on black and white mental health professionals. *International Journal of Intercultural Relations*, 9:305–318.

Leonard, B. 1991. Ways to make diversity work. *HR [Human Resource] Management*, 36:37–39, 98.

Levine, D. N. 1979. Simmel at a distance. In *Strangers in African societies*, edited by W. Shack and E. Skinner. Berkeley: University of California Press.

Levine, D. U., and Havighurst, R. J. 1989. *Society and education*. 7th Ed. Boston: Allyn & Bacon.

Lewis, D. K. 1976. The multicultural education model and minorities: Some reservations. *Anthropology and Education Quarterly*, 7:32–37.

Lewis, O. 1966. The culture of poverty. *Scientific American*, 215:19–25.

Lieberman, A., and Miller, S. 1990. The social realities of teaching. In *Education and society: A reader*, edited by K. J. Dougherty and F. M. Hammack, 193–204. San Diego, CA: Harcourt Brace Jovanovich.

Lindquist, S. E. 1982. Prediction of success in overseas adjustment. *Journal of Psychology and Christianity*, 1:22–25.

Littlewood, R., and Lipsedge, M. 1982. *Aliens and alienists: Ethnic minorities and psychiatry*. Harmondsworth, England: Penguin.

Livingston, A. 1991. 12 companies that do the right thing. *Working Woman*, 16:57–61.

Locke, S. A., and Feinsod, F. M. 1982. Psychological preparation for young adults traveling abroad. *Adolescence*, 17:815–819.

Lomotey, K. 1990. Qualities shared by African-American principals in effective schools: A preliminary analysis. In *Going to school: The African-American experience*, edited by K. Lomotey, 181–196. Albany: State University of New York Press.

Long, P. B. 1984. Equipping nationals for cross-cultural ministry. *Evangelical Missions Quarterly*, 20:283–288.

Longstreet, W. 1978. *Aspects of ethnicity: Understanding differences in pluralistic classrooms*. New York: Teachers College Press.

Lonner, W. J. 1980. The search for psychological universals. In *Handbook of crosscultural psychology*, edited by H. C. Triandis and W. W. Lambert, 143–204. Boston: Allyn & Bacon.

Luzbetak, L. J. 1988. What can anthropology offer to the missions? In *Anthropology and mission*, edited by J.G. Piepke, 49–58. Nettetal: Steyler Verlag-Wort und Werk.

———. 1989. *The church and cultures: New perspectives in missiological anthropology*. Maryknoll, NY: Orbis Books.

Lysgaard, S. 1955. Adjustment in a foreign society: Norwegian Fulbright grantees visiting the United States. *International Social Sciences Bulletin*, 7:45–51.

Machida, S. 1986. Teacher accuracy in decoding nonverbal indicants of comprehension and noncomprehension in Anglo and Mexican-American children. *Journal of Educational Psychology*, 78:454–464.

Mahan, J. M. 1982. Native Americans as teacher trainers: Anatomy and outcomes of a cultural immersion project. *Journal of Educational Equity and Leadership*, 2:100–110.

———. 1984. *Cultural immersion for inservice teachers: A model and some outcomes*. Paper presented at the Annual Meeting of the Association for Supervision and Curriculum. (ERIC Document Reproduction Service ED 254 923).

Mahan, J. M., and Lacefield, W. E. 1980. *Employability and multi-cultural teacher preparation*. Paper presented at the Annual Meeting of the American Educational Research Association, Boston, MA, April 7–11. (ERIC Document Reproduction Service ED 186 405.)

Mahan, J. M., and Stachowski, L. L. 1985. Overseas student teaching: A model, important outcomes, recommendations. *International Education*, 15: 9–28.

———. 1990. New horizons: Student teaching abroad to enrich understanding of diversity. *Action in Teacher Education*, 12:13–22.

Making the Grade: Report of the Twentieth Century Fund Task Force on Federal Elementary and Secondary Education Policy. 1973. New York: Twentieth Century Fund Press/Priority Press Publications.

Malinowski, B. 1962. *Sex, culture, and myth*. New York: Harcourt, Brace and World.

Maretzki, T. W. 1969. Transcultural adjustment of Peace Corps volunteers. In *Culture change, mental health, and poverty*, edited by J. C. Finney, 203–221. Lexington: University of Kentucky Press.

Martin, J. 1984. The intercultural reentry: Conceptualization and directions for future research. *International Journal of Intercultural Relations*, 8115–134.

Martin, J. N., and Hammer, M. R. 1989. Behavioral categories of intercultural communication competence: Everyday communicators' perceptions. *International Journal of Intercultural Relations*, 13:303–322.

Masling, J., Johnson, C., and Saturansky, C. 1974. Oral imagery, accuracy of perceiving others, and performance in Peace Corps training. *Journal of Personality and Social Psychology*, 30:414–419.

Mayers, M. K. 1985. The missionary as cross-cultural educator. In *Missionaries, anthropologists, and cultural change [Part I]: Studies in Third World societies*, edited D.L. Whiteman, 387-395. Williamsburg, VA: College of William and Mary, Department of Anthropology. (ERIC Document Reproduction Service ED 271 355).

———. 1987. Training missionaries for the twenty-first century. *Evangelical Missions Quarterly*, 22:306–319.
Mayes, N. H. 1978. Teacher training for cultural awareness. In *Overview of intercultural education, training, and research*, edited D. S. Hoopes, P. B. Pedersen, and G. Renwick, 35–44. Washington, DC: Society for Intercultural Education, Training, and Research.
Mayne, D. H. 1980. *Recommendations from teachers in small rural high schools for modification of the teacher training program of the University of Alaska: A survey.* Fairbanks: University of Alaska. (ERIC Document Reproduction Service ED 211 458.)
Mazon, M. R. 1977. Community, home, cultural awareness and language training: A design for teacher training in multicultural education. In *Pluralism and the American teacher: Issues and case studies*, edited by F. H. Klassen and D. M. Gollnick, 205–216. Washington, D.C.: American Association of Colleges for Teacher Education.
McCaffery, J. A. 1986. Independent effectiveness: A reconsideration of cross-cultural orientation and training. *International Journal of Intercultural Relations*, 10:159–178.
McCaffrey, J. A., and Hafner, C. R. 1985. When two cultures collide: Doing business overseas. *Training and Development Journal*, 39:26–31.
McClenahen, J. S. 1987. Why U.S. managers fail overseas. *Industry Week*, 235:71–74.
McCroarty, M. 1988. Issues in design and evaluation of cross-cultural workshops for ESL teachers and administrators. *Canadian Modern Language Review*, 44:295–315.
McDermott, R. 1987. Achieving school failure: An anthropological approach to illiteracy and social stratification. In *Education and cultural process: Anthropological approaches*, 2nd Ed., edited by G D. Spindler, 173-209. Prospect Heights, IL: Waveland Press.
McDermott, R. P., and Godpodinoff, K. 1979. Social contexts for ethnic borders and school failure. In *Non-verbal behavior: Applications and cross-cultural implications*, edited by A. Wolfgang, 175–195. New York: Academic Press.
McEnery, J., and DesHarnais, G. 1990. Culture shock. *Training and Development Journal*, 44:43–47.
McGroarty, M. 1984. *Design and evaluation of cross-cultural workshops for ESL teachers and administrators.* Paper presented at the Annual Meeting of the Teachers of Speakers of Other Languages, Houston, TX, March 6–11. (ERIC Document Reproduction Service ED 245 566).
McGuire, M., and McDermott, S. 1988. Communication in assimilation, deviance, and alienation states. In *Cross-cultural adaptation: Current approaches*, edited by Y. Y. Kim and W. B. Gudykunst, 90–105. Newbury Park, CA: Sage Publications.
McIlduff, E., and Coghlan, D. 1984. Process and facilitation in a cross-cultural communication workshop. *Person-centered Review*, 4:77–98.
Mead, M., and Wolfenstein, M. 1955. *Childhood in contemporary cultures.* Washington, DC: U.S. Government Printing Office.
Meintel, D. A. 1973. Strangers, homecomers, and ordinary men. *Anthropological Quarterly*, 46:47–58.

Mendenhall, M., Dunbar, E., and Oddou, G. R. 1987. Expatriate selection, training, and career-pathing: A review and critique. *Human Resource Management*, 23:331–345.

Mendenhall, M., and Oddou, G. 1985. Dimensions of expatriate acculturation: A review. *Academy of Management Review*, 10:39–47.

Menninger, W. W. 1988. Adaptation and morale: Predictable responses to life change. *Bulletin of Menninger Clinic*, 52:198–210.

Merta, R. J., Stringham, E. M., and Ponterotto, J. G. 1988. Simulating culture shock in counselor trainees: An experiential exercise for cross-cultural training. *Journal of Counseling and Development*, 66:242–245.

Meyers, W. R. 1975. The politics of evaluation research: The Peace Corps. *Journal of Applied Behavioral Science*, 11:261–280.

Milburn, T. W. 1979. Conflict in cross-cultural interaction. In *Overview of intercultural education, training and research, Vol. 1: Theory*, edited by D. S. Hoopes, P. B. Pedersen and G. Renwick, 72–79. Washington, D.C.: Society for Intercultural Education, Training, and Research.

Milgram, S. 1974. *Obedience to authority: An experimental view*. London: Tavistock.

Miller, D. C. 1983. The measurement of international patterns and norms: A tool for comparative research. *Southwestern Social Science Quarterly*, 48:531–547.

Miller, M. D. 1988. *Reflections on reentry after teaching in China*. New York: Center for the Study of Intercultural Learning. (ERIC Document Reproduction Service ED 306 174.)

Miller, S. 1987. Hi-tech racism. *Black Enterprise*, October 17, p. 22.

Mio, J. S., and Morris, D. R. 1990. Cross-cultural issues in psychology training programs: An invitation for discussion. *Professional Psychology: Research and Practice*, 21:434–441.

Mischel, W. 1965. Predicting the success of Peace Corps volunteers in Nigeria. *Journal of Personality and Social Psychology*, 1:510–517.

Mitchell, B. M. 1987. Multicultural education: A second glance at the present American effort. *Educational Research Quarterly*, 11:8–12.

Modiano, N. 1973. *Indian education in the Chiapas highlands*. New York: Holt, Rinehart, and Winston.

———. 1975. Using native instructional patterns for teacher training: A Chiapas experiment. In *Proceedings of the first inter-American conference on bi-lingual education*, edited by R. C. Troike and N. Modiano, 349–355. Arlington, VA: Center for Applied Linguistics.

Moore, M. 1988. Scapegoats again. *The Progressive*, February, p. 25–27.

Moreno, J. L. 1934. *Who shall survive?* New York: Beacon House.

Morris, R. T. 1960. *The two-way mirror: National status in foreign students' adjustment*. Minneapolis: University of Minnesota Press.

Mortenson, R., and Wilson, R. 1980. Inservice teacher education on the Navajo reservation. In *Reservation schools and 95-561: The administrator and the curriculum*, edited by C. G. Foster, 34-44. Washington, DC: Office of Education. (ERIC Document Reproduction Service ED 192 945).

Mulholland, K. B. 1984. Mission agencies and missions professors need to work together. *Evangelical Missions Quarterly*, 25:200–203.

Mungo, S. J. 1983. Stress, burnout, and culture shock: An experiential, pre-service approach. *Journal of Experiential Education*, 6:27–31.

Murdock, G. P. 1949. *Social structure*. New York: Macmillan.

Murnane, R. J., Singer, J. D., Willett, J. B., Kemple, J. J., and Olsen, R. J. 1991. *Who will teach? Policies that matter*. Cambridge, MA: Harvard University Press.

Myrdal, G. 1944. *An American dilemma: The Negro problem and modern democracy*. 2 Vols. New York: Harper and Row.

Naroll, R. 1968. Some thoughts on comparative method in cultural anthropology. In *Methodology in social research*, edited by H. M. Blalock, and A. B. Blalock, 236–277. New York: McGraw-Hill.

Naroll, R., Michik, G. L., and Naroll, F. 1976. *Worldwide theory testing*. New Haven, CT: Human Relations Area Files.

Natani, K. 1974. A voice from the field. *American Psychologist*, 29:59–63.

National Center for Education Statistics. 1989. *Digest of education statistics*. Washington, D.C.: U. S. Government Printing Office.

National Council for Accreditation of Teacher Education [NCATE]. 1977. *Standards for the accreditation of teacher education*. Washington, DC: American Association of Colleges for Teacher Education.

National Education Association. 1987. *Status of the American public school teacher, 1985–86*. Washington, DC: National Education Association.

National Museum of National History. 1991. Refugee children in school: Understanding cultural diversity in the classroom. *Anthropological Notes: National Museum of Natural History Bulletin for Teachers*, Spring, 1–15.

Neal, A. G., and Seeman, M. 1969. Organizations and powerlessness: A test of the mediation hypothesis. *American Sociological Review*, 29:216–226.

Neely, R., and Campbell, W. 1985. A comparative look at teacher education in the United States, Latin America, and the United Kingdom. *Reflection on teacher education: Monograph 3.*, edited by M. M. Dupuis, 102–109. University Park: Pennsylvania State University. (ERIC Document Reproduction Service ED 266 105).

Neimeyer, G. J., and Fukuyama, M. A. 1984. Exploring the content and structure of cross-cultural attitudes. *Counselor Education and Supervision*, 23:214–224.

Neimeyer, G. J., Fukuyama, M. A., Bingham, R. P., Hall, L. E., and Mussenden, M. E. 1986. Training cross-cultural counselors: A comparison of the pro-counselor and anti-counselor triad models. *Journal of Counseling and Development*, 64:437–439.

Newbigin, L. 1950. The evangelization of eastern Asia. *International Review of Missions*, 39:137–145.

———. 1978. Christ and the cultures. *Scottish Journal of Theology*, 31:1–22.

Nichols, C. 1982. God's blueprint for the church. *Journal of Christian Education*, 2:29–31.

Nishida, H. 1985. Japanese intercultural communication competence and cross-cultural adjustment. *International Journal of Intercultural Relations*, 9:247–269.

Noblit, G. W., and Hare, R. D. 1988. *Meta-ethnography: Synthesizing qualitative studies*. Newbury Park, CA: Sage Publications.

Noesjirwan, J., and Freestone, C. 1979. The culture game: A simulation of culture shock. *Simulation and Games*, 10:189–206.

Noordhoff, K., and Kleinfeld, J. 1990. Shaping the rhetoric of reflection for multicultural settings. In *Encouraging reflective practice in education: An analysis of issues and programs*, edited by R. T. Clift, W. R. Houston and M. C. Puback, 163–185. New York: Teachers College Press.

Northfield, H. D. 1957. The training of men missionaries. *International Review of Missions*, 46:59–67.

Novak, M. 1973. Probing the new ethnicity. In *White ethnics: Their life in working-class America*, edited by J. Ryan. Englewood Cliffs, NJ: Prentice-Hall.

Nunes, S. A. 1987. Toward a theoretical framework for cross-cultural training programs. (Doctoral dissertation, Florida State University). *Dissertation Abstracts International*, 48:03A.

Nye, D. 1988. The female expat's promise. *Across the Board*, 25:38–43.

Oakes, J. 1988. *Keeping track: How schools structure inequality*. New Haven, CT: Yale University Press.

Oberg, K. 1960. Culture shock: Adjustment to new culture environments. *Practical Anthropology*, 7:179–182.

Obot, I. S. 1988. Value systems and cross-cultural contact: The effect of perceived similarity and stability on social evaluations. *International Journal of Intercultural Relations*, 12:363–379.

O'Brien, G. E., Alexander, R., and Plooij, D. 1973. The critical incident approach to cross-cultural training. *New Guinea Psychologist*, 5:5–14.

Ogbu, J. U. 1988. Cultural diversity and human development. In *Black children and poverty: A developmental perspective*, edited by D.T. Slaughter, 11–28. San Francisco: Jossey-Bass.

Oja, S. N. 1979. Deliberate psychological education and its impact on teachers and students in a junior high school. *Humanist Educator*, 18: 64–73.

Ojile, C. S. 1984. Intercultural training: An overview of the benefits for business and anthrolopogists' emerging role. *Studies in Third World Societies*, 28:35–51.

Olivarez, R. D. 1981. Teacher Corps and inservice education: A national experiment. *Journal of Research and Development in Education*, 14:92–98.

Olsen, L., and Dowell, C. 1989. *Bridges: Promising programs for the education of immigrant children*. Menlo Park, CA: Walters Johnson Foundation. (ERIC Document Reproduction Service ED 314 544).

Olson, J., and Tucker, M. F. 1974. *Results of overseas diplomacy measurement surveys*. Denver, CO: Center for Research and Education.

Olson, L. 1988. The unbalanced equation: Trained to instruct the "ideal" student, new teachers encounter the "at risk." *Education Week*, June 22, p. 19–24.

O'Reilly, B. 1988. Japan's uneasy U.S. managers. *Fortune*, 117:245–264.

Orem, R. A. 1991. Preparing adult educators for cultural change. *Adult Learning*, 2:8–10.

Organization for Economic Cooperation and Development [OECD]. 1981. *Educational policy and planning: Compensatory education programmes in the United States*. Washington, DC: OECD Publications. (ERIC Document Reproduction Service ED 202 132).

Osborne, B. 1989a. Cultural congruence, ethnicity and fused biculturalism: Zuni and Torres Strait. *Journal of American Indian Education*, 28:7–20.

———. 1989b. Insiders and outsiders: Cultural membership and the micropolitics of education among the Zuni. *Anthropology and Education Quarterly*, 20:196– 215.
Ostow, M. 1991. A psychoanalytic approach to the problems of prejudice, discrimination, and persecution. In *Opening doors: Perspectives on race relations in contemporary America*, edited by H. J. Knopke, R. J. Norrell, and R. W. Rogers, 79–99. Tuscaloosa: University of Alabama Press.
Overman, S. 1989. Shaping the global workplace. *Personnel Administrator*, 34:40–44, 101.
Paige, R. M. 1986. Trainer competencies: The missing conceptual link in orientation. *International Journal of Intercultural Relations*, 10:135–158.
Paige, R. M., and Martin, J. N. 1983. Ethical issues and ethics in cross-cultural training. In *Handbook of intercultural training, Vol. 1: Issues in theory and design*, edited by D. Landis and R.W. Brislin, 36–60. Elmsford:NY: Pergamon.
Palinkas, L. A. 1982. Ethnicity, identity, and mental health: The use of rhetoric in an immigrant Chinese church. *Journal of Psychoanalytic Anthropology*, 5:235–258.
Palmer, C. 1984. The homeland church—partner or pawn? *Evangelical Missions Quarterly*, 20:244–250.
Pang, D. B. 1981. *Developing interculturally skilled counselors: Process and productivity of the project*. Paper presented at the Annual Meeting of the Western Psychological Association, Los Angeles, April 9–12. (ERIC Document Reproduction Service ED 214 044).
Parsons, R. T. 1956. The missionary and the cultures of man. *International Review of Missions*, 45:161–168.
Partridge, W. L., and Eddy, E. M. 1987. The development of applied anthropology in America. In *Applied anthropology in America*, edited by E. M. Eddy and W. L. Partridge, 3–58. New York: Columbia University Press.
Patico, A., Renwich, G. W., and Saltzman, C. 1981. Cross-cultural training. In *Learning across cultures: Intercultural communication and educational exchange*, edited by M. D. Pusch, 27–54. Washington, D.C.: National Association for Foreign Student Affairs. (ERIC Document Reproduction Service ED 208 790).
Patterson, T. D. 1990. The global manager. *World*, 24:11–17.
Pedersen, P. B. 1984. Levels of intercultural communication using the rehearsal demonstration model. *Journal of Non-white Concerns in Personnel and Guidance*, 12:57–68.
Pelto, P. J. 1968. The difference between "tight" and "loose" societies. *Transaction*, 5:37–40.
Perez, R., Johnson, L., and Proctor, D. 1980. *Institutionalizing a successful Teacher Corps inservice program: A model for building ownership*. Paper presented at the Annual Conference of the National Council of States on Inservice Education, San Diego, CA. (ERIC Document Reproduction Service ED 199 239).
Perry, D. G., and Bussey, K. 1984. *Social development*. Englewood Cliffs, NJ: Prentice-Hall.
Peters, M. E. 1990. *A functional analysis of the missionary orientation process of the board of international ministries of the American Baptist Churches, USA*. Unpublished doctoral dissertation, Eastern Baptist Theological Seminary.
Petrie, R. D. 1987. Group enactment procedures: Theory and application. *Journal for Specialists in Group Work*, 12:26–30.

Pettigrew, L. E. 1974. Competency-based teacher education: Teacher training for multicultural education. In *Multicultural education through competency-based teacher education*, edited by W. A. Hunter, 72–94. Washington, DC: American Association of Colleges for Teacher Education.

Pettigrew, T. F. 1971. *Racially separate or together?* New York: McGraw-Hill.

Phillips, D. Z. 1984. The devil's disguises: Philosophy of religion, "objectivity" and "cultural divergence." In *Objectivity and cultural divergence*, edited by S. C. Brown, 61–78. Cambridge, England: University Press.

Phillips, W. 1985. Your church can train and send missionaries. *Evangelical Missions Quarterly*, 21:196–201.

Pierson, P. E. 1986. School of mission: Fuller Theological Seminary. *Theological Education*, 22:74–78.

———. 1987. Non-Western missions: The great new fact of our time. In *New frontiers in mission*, edited by P. Sookhdeo, 9–15, Grand Rapids, MI: Baker Book House.

———. 1989. Missions and community development: A historical perspective. In *Christian relief and development: Developing workers for effective ministry*, edited by E. J. Elliston, 7–22. Dallas, TX: Word Publishing.

Ponterotto, J. C. 1988. Racial consciousness development among white counselor trainees: A stage model. *Journal of Multicultural Counseling and Development*, 16:146–156.

Ponterotto, J. G., and Benesch, K. F. 1988. An organizational framework for understanding the role of culture in counseling. *Journal of Counseling and Development*, 66:237–241.

Ponterotto, J. G., and Casas, J. M. 1987. In search of multicultural competence within counselor education programs. *Journal of Counseling and Development*, 65:430–434.

Popham, P. 1991. Miss poop scoops, love taxis. Management Today, May, 106–107.

Popkewitz, T. 1975. *Teacher education as a process of socialization*. Washington, DC: Office of Education. (ERIC Document Reproduction ED 185 011).

Price-Williams, D. 1972. Cross-cultural studies. In *Intercultural communication: A reader*, edited by L. A. Samovar and R. E. Porter, 35–49. Belmont, CA: Wadsworth Publishing.

Pusch, M. D. ed.. 1979. *Multicultural education: A cross-cultural training approach*. LaGrange Park, IL: Intercultural Network.

Pusch, M. D., Patico, A., Renwick, G. W., and Saltzman, C. 1981. Cross-cultural training. In *Learning across cultures*, edited by G. Althen, 72–102. Washington, D.C.: National Association of Foreign Student Advisors.

Pusch, M. D., Seelye, H. N., and Wasilewski, J. H. 1981. Training for multicultural education competencies. In *Multicultural education: A cross-cultural training approach*, edited by M. D. Pusch, 86–105. Chicago: Intercultural Press.

Pytowska, E. 1990. The teacher as cultural researcher. *Momentum*, 21:40–42.

Quarles, C. L. 1987. Kidnapped! A "successful hostage" will emerge alive. *Evangelical Missions Quarterly*, 23:342–249.

Queen, S., and Habenstein, R. W. 1974. *The family in various cultures*, 4th Ed. Philadelphia: Lippincott.

Quig, R. 1874. *Giant-Land: Being the complete history of the adventures of Tim Pippin*. London: James Henderson.

Quine, W. 1961. *From a logical point of view.* New York: Harper and Row.
Radin, P. 1987. *The method and theory of ethnology: An essay in criticism.* Boston, MA: Bergin and Garvey Publishers.
Randolph, L. B. 1988. Racism on college campuses. *Ebony,* 44: 126–128.
Ravitch, D. 1983. *The troubled crusade: American education, 1945–1980.* New York: Basic Books.
———. 1992. A culture in common. *Educational Leadership,* 49:8–11.
Reich, M. 1981. *Racial inequality: A political-economic analysis.* Princeton, NJ: Princeton University Press.
Reinicke, M. J. 1986. *Cultural adjustment of international students in the U.S.: A reevaluation using reformulated learned helplessness.* Los Angeles, CA: Biola University. (ERIC Document Reproduction Service No. ED 274 939).
Reusswig, J. M. 1981. *Immersion. A method in staff development?* Paper presented at the Annual Meeting of the American Association of School Administrators, Atlanta, GA, February 13–16. (ERIC Document Reproduction ED 204 850).
Reyburn, W. D. 1956. Problems of the participant role in a Bulu village. *Practical Anthropology,* 3:105–113.
Rhinesmith, S. H. 1985. *Bring home the world: A management guide for community leaders of international exchange programs.* New York: Walker.
Riesman, D., Glazer, N., and Denney, R. 1955. *The lonely crowd: A study of the changing American culture.* New York: Doubleday.
Rinehart, A. D., and Leight, R. L. 1980. The teaching internship: An opportunity missed. *Clearing House,* 54:278–281.
Rivers, W. M. 1988. Curriculum, student objectives, and the training of foreign language teachers. *Babel,* 23:4–10.
Rodgers, J. R. 1984. Managing the multinational firm: Finding the right expatriate for the job. In *Anthropology and international business,* edited by H. Serrie, 17–31. Williamsburg, VA: College of William and Mary, Department of Anthropology. (ERIC Document Reproduction ED 271 368).
Rokeach, M. 1960. *The open and closed mind.* New York: Basic Books.
———. 1973. *The nature of human values.* New York: Free Press.
Rollins, B. C., and Thomas, D. L. 1979. Parental support, power, and control techniques in the socialization of children. In *Contemporary theories about the family, Vol. 1,* edited by W. R. Burr, R. Hill, F. I. Nye, and I. L. Reiss, 317–364. New York: Free Press.
Rommen, E. 1985. Planting in tandem for church growth. *Evangelical Missions Quarterly,* 21:54–62.
Ronen, S. 1986. *Comparative and multicultural management.* New York: John Wiley and Sons.
Rose, P. Q. 1976. The senior Fulbright-Hays program in East Asia and the Pacific. *International Educational and Cultural Exchange,* 12:19–23.
Rosenberg, J. 1991. Out of the office, onto the shop floor. *Editor and Publisher,* 124:30–32, 51.
Rosenblum, S., and Jastrzab, J. 1980. *The role of the principal in change: The Peace Corps example.* Washington, DC: Department of Education. (ERIC Document Reproduction Service ED 197 501).

Rowland, S. 1985. Training local villagers to provide health care. *Evangelical Missions Quarterly*, 21:44–50.

Rozema, H. J. 1982. *The interplay between racism and sexism: Using assertiveness training techniques to reduce racism.* Paper presented at the Annual Meeting of the International Communication Association, Boston: May 2–5. (ERIC Reproduction Service ED 218 695).

Ruben, B. D. 1976. Assessing communication competency for intercultural adaptation. *Group and Organization Studies*, 1:334–354.

———. 1989. The study of cross-cultural competence: Traditions and contemporary issues. *International Journal of Intercultural Relations*, 13:229–240.

Ruben, B. D., Askling, L. R., and Kealey, D. J. 1979. Cross-cultural effectiveness. In *Overview of intercultural education, training, and research, Vol. 1. Theory*, edited by D. S. Hoopes, P. B. Pedersen and G. Renwick, 89–101. Washington, DC: Society for Intercultural Education, Training, and Research.

Ruben, B. D., and Kealey, D. J. 1979. Behavioral assessment of communication competency and the prediction of cross-cultural adaptation. *International Journal of Intercultural Relations*, 3:15–47.

Rubin, B. L. 1991. Europeans value diversity. *HR [Human Resource] Magazine*, 36:38–41.

Russell, R. W., 1978. Environmental stresses and the quality of life. *Australian Psychologist*, 13:143–159.

Sabnani, H. B., Ponterotto, J. G., Borodovsky, L. G. 1991. White racial identity and cross-cultural counselor training: A stage model. *Counseling Psychologist*, 19:76–102.

Salas, J. R. 1984. An analysis of international trainer programs conducted by multinational corporations in selected Midwestern states. (Doctoral dissertation, Southern Illinois University). *Dissertation Abstracts International*, 46:05A.

Samarin, W. J. 1959. Christian education among non-Christian peoples. *Practical Anthropology*, 6:29–42.

Sarbaugh, L. E. 1988. A taxonomic approach to intercultural communication. In *Theories in intercultural communication*, edited by Y. Y. Kim and W. B.Gudykunst, 22–40. Newbury Park, CA: Sage Publications.

Scherer, M. 1992. School snapshot: Focus on African-American culture. *Educational Leadership*, 49:17–19.

Schipper, G. 1988. Non-Western missionaries: Our newest challenge. *Evangelical Missions Quarterly*, 24:198–202.

Schleier, C. 1980. Foreign affairs. *Across the Board*, 28:47–50.

Schneider, M. J., and Jordan, W. 1981. Perception of the communicative performance of Americans and Chinese in intercultural dyads. *International Journal of Intercultural Relations*, 5:175–191.

Schneller, R. 1989. Intercultural and intrapersonal processes and factors of misunderstanding: Implications for cross-cultural training. *International Journal of Intercultural Relations*, 13:465–484.

Schofield, J. W. 1986. Black-white contact in desegregated schools. In *Contact and conflict in intergroup encounters*, edited by M. Hewstone and R. Brown, 79–92. New York: Basil Blackwell.

References

Schroeder, G., and Hainsworth, J. C. 1977. *A responsive inservice graduate education model.* Washington, DC: Office of Education. (ERIC Document Reproduction Service ED 180 961).

Schuller, D. S. 1986. Globalization in theological education: Summary and analysis of survey data. *Theological Education*, 22:19–56.

Seabrook, R., and Valdes, B. 1988. *So you were a language major: Corporate interviewing and training in foreign languages and cross-cultural skills.* In Proceedings of the Seventh Annual Eastern Michigan University Conference on Language for Business and the Professions, April, 1988. (ERIC Document Reproduction Service ED 304 889).

Sellitz, C., Christ, J. R., Havel, J., and Cook, S. W. 1963. *Attitudes and social relations of foreign students in the United States.* Minneapolis: University of Minnesota Press.

Semien, L. J. 1990. Opening the utility door for women and minorities. *Public Utilities Fortnightly*, 126:29–31.

Serrie, H. 1984. Cross-cultural interaction: Some general considerations for innocents abroad. *Studies in Third World Societies*, 28:53–58.

Sewell, W. H., and Davidson, O. M. 1961. *Scandinavian students on an American campus.* Minneapolis: University of Minnesota Press.

Shafer, S. M. 1983. Australian approaches to multicultural education. *Journal of Multilingual and Multicultural Development*, 4:415–435.

Shenk, W. R. 1980. The changing role of the missionary: From civilization to contextualization. In *Missions, evangelism, and church growth*, edited by C. N. Kraus, 33–58. Scottdale, PA: Herald Press.

Sherif, M. 1970. *Group conflict and co-operation: Their social psychology.* London: Routledge & Kegan Paul.

Shriver, D. W., Jr. 1986. The globalization of theological education: Setting the task. *Theological Education*, 22:7–18.

Sieveking, N., Anchor, K., and Marston, R. C. 1981. Selecting and preparing expatriate employees. *Personnel Journal*, 60:197–202.

Simpson, G. E., and Yinger, J. M. 1987. *Racial and cultural minorities.* New York: Plenum Press.

Sims, W. E. 1983. Preparing teachers for multicultural classrooms. *Momentum*, 14:42–44.

Singer, E. A. 1980. *What is cultural congruence, and why are they saying such terrible things about it? Occasional Paper No.120.* East Lansing, MI: Michigan State University. (ERIC Document Reproduction Service ED 292 914).

Skinner, K. A. 1988. Internationalism and the early years of the Japanese Peace Corps. *International Journal of Intercultural Relations*, 12:317–326.

Sleeter, C. E. 1989. Doing multicultural education across the grade levels and subject areas: A case study of Wisconsin. *Teaching and Teacher Education*, 5:189–203.

––––––. 1992. *Keepers of the American Dream: A study of staff development and multicultural education.* London: Falmer Press.

Smalley, W. A. 1953. A programme for missionary language learning. *International Review of Missions*, 42:82–88.

Smalley, W. 1963. Culture shock, language shock, and the shock of self-discovery. *Practical Anthropology*, 10:49–56.
Smith, A. 1991. Not such splendid isolation. *Industrial Society Magazine*, 1–12.
Smith, L. D. 1986. Oral history in mission evaluation. *Missiology: An International Review*, 14:71–81.
Smith, M. L. 1984. Culture in international business: Selecting employees for expatriate assignments. In *Anthropology and international business: Studies in third World Societies*, edited by H. Serrie, 1–12. College of William and Mary: Department of Anthropology. (ERIC Document Reproduction Service ED 271 368).
Smolicz, J. J. 1984. Minority languages and the core values of culture: Changing policies and ethnic response in Australia. *Journal of Multilingual and Multicultural Development*, 5:23–41.
Snyder, H. M. 1973. Cross-cultural training—Why? *Peace Corps Program and Training Journal*, 1:7–8.
Spaulding, S., and Flack, M. J. 1976. *The world's students in the United States*. New York: Praeger.
Spears, J. D., Oliver, J. P., and Maes, S. C. 1990. *Accommodating change and diversity: Multicultural practices in rural schools*. Manhatten:Kansas State University, Rural Clearinghouse for Lifelong Education and Development.
Spicer, E. 1976. Beyond analysis and explanation. *Human Organization*, 35: 335–343.
Spradley, J., and Phillips, M. 1972. Culture and stress: A quantitative analysis. *American Anthropologist*, 74:518–529
Stack, S. 1981. The effect of immigration on suicide: A cross-national analysis. *Basic and Applied Psychology*, 2:205–218.
Stafford, T. 1992. Campus Christians and the new thought police. *Christianity Today*, February 10, p. 15–20.
Stampp, K. 1965. *The peculiar institution: Slavery in the antebellum South*. New York: Knopf.
Stanojevic, P. S. B. 1989. *Coming back home: Making the most of international experiences*. Toronto: George Brown College. (ERIC Document Reproduction Service ED 318 517).
Starosta, W. J. 1990. Thinking through intercultural training assumptions: In the aftermath. *International Journal of Intercultural Relations*, 14:1–16.
Stein, M. I. 1966. *Volunteers for peace*. New York: Wiley & Sons.
Stening, B. 1977. Problems in cross-cultural contact: A literature review. *International Journal of Intercultural Relations*, 3:269–313.
Stephan, W. G. 1987. The contact hypothesis in intergroup relations. In *Group processes and intergroup relations*, edited by C. Hendrick, 13–40. Newbury Park, CA: Sage Publications.
———. 1991. School desegregation: Short-term and long-term effects. In *Opening doors: Perspectives on race relations in contemporary America*, edited by H. J. Knopke, R. J. Norrell, and R. W. Rogers, 100–118. Tuscaloosa: University of Alabama Press.
Stephan, W. G., and Stephan, C. W. 1985. Intergroup anxiety. *Journal of Social Issues*, 41:157–176.

Stephens, T. M. 1980. *The SBA [Small Business Administration] technical manual.* Columbus, OH: Cedars.

Stewart, E. C. P. 1966. The simulation of cultural difference. *Journal of Communication*, 16:291–304.

———. 1972. American advisors overseas. In *Intercultural communication: A reader*, edited by L.A. Samovar and R. E. Porter, 279–284. Belmont, CA: Wadsworth Publishing Company.

———. 1986. The survival stage of intercultural communication. *Language Research Bulletin*, 1:109–121.

Stipe, C. E. 1956. Anthropology in the Bible institute and Bible college curriculum. *Practical Anthropology*, 3:19–30.

Stocking, G. W., Jr. 1968. *Race, culture, and evolution: Essays in the history of anthropology.* New York: Free Press.

Stolovitch, H. D., and Lane, M. 1989. Multicultural training: Designing for affective results. *Performance and Instruction*, 28:10–15.

Stone, M. 1989. What really happened in Bensonhurst. *New York*, 22:48–56.

Storti, C. 1989. *The art of crossing cultures.* Yarmouth, ME: Intercultural Press.

Stuntz, H. C. 1949. What should a missionary know? *International Review of Missions*, 38:89–94.

Sullivan, A. R. 1974. Cultural competence and confidence: A quest for effective teaching in a pluralistic society. In *Multicultural education through competency-based teacher education*, edited by W. A. Hunter, 56–71. Washington, DC: American Association of Colleges for Teacher Education.

Sung, B. L. 1985. Bicultural conflicts in Chinese immigrant children. *Journal of Comparative Family Studies*, 16:255–269.

Sussman, N. M. 1986. Re-entry research and training: Methods and implications. *International Journal of Intercultural Relations*, 19:235–254.

Szapocznik, J., Santisteban, D., Kurtines, W., Perez-Vidal, A., and Hervic, O. 1983. Bicultural effectiveness training: A treatment intervention for enhancing intercultural adjustment in Cuban American families. *Hispanic Journal of Behavioral Sciences*, 6:317–344.

Tabachnick, B. R. 1980. Intern-teacher roles: Illusion, disillusion, reality. *Journal of Education*, 162:122–137.

Taber, C. R. 1984. The training of missionaries. In *Missions and theological education in world perspective*, edited by H. M. Conn and S. F. Rowen, 321–332, Farmington, MI: Association of Urbanus.

Tafoya, T. 1981. *What you say after hello: Pre-service orientation for native programs.* Seattle, WA: Northwest Institute for Native Education. (ERIC Document Reproduction Service ED 207 734).

Tajfel, H. 1970. Experiments in intergroup discrimination. *Scientific American*, 223:96–102.

Tallman, J. R. 1984. The demands of change. *Evangelical Missions Quarterly*, 20:276–278.

Tanney, F. 1982. Counseling psychology in the marketplace. *Counseling Psychologist*, 10:21–29.

Taylor, S. E. 1983) Adjustment to threatening events: A theory of cognitive adaptation. *American Psychologist*, 1161–1173.

References

Thompson, C. P., and English, J. T. 1964. Premature return of Peace Corps volunteers. *Public Health Reports*, 79:1065–1073.
Time Staff. 1986. Cleveland's neighborly way. 127:39.
Tiny cuts and constant pressure. 1988. Spring. *Life*, Spring special issue, 53.
Torbiorn, I. 1982. *Living abroad: Personal adjustment and personnel policy in overseas settings*. Chichester, England: John Wiley.
Torney-Purta, J. 1985. A model for using intercultural counselling insights and skills to enhance teachers' intercultural experience. In *Intercultural counselling and assessment: Global perspectives*, edited by R. J. Samuda and A. Wolfgang, 383–394. Lewistown, NY: C. J. Hogrefe.
Trautmann, F. 1978. Training sessions for witness and service. *International Review of Missions*, 67:67–73.
Travers, P. D., and Rebore, R. W. 1987. *Foundations of education: Becoming a teacher*. Englewood Cliffs, NJ: Prentice-Hall.
Triandis, H. C. 1977. Theoretical framework for evaluation of cross-cultural training effectiveness. *International Journal of Intercultural Relations*, 1:19–45.
Triandis, H. C., and Brislin, R. 1984. Cross-cultural psychology. *American Psychologist*, 39:1006–1016.
Triandis, H. C., Brislin, R., and Hui, C. H. 1988. Cross-cultural training across the individualism-collectivism divide. *International Journal of Intercultural Relations*, 12:269–289.
Trueba, H. T. 1988. Instructional effectiveness: English-only for speakers of other languages. *Education and Urban Society*, 20:341–362.
Tucker, M. F. 1974. *Screening and selection for overseas assignment: Assessment and recommendations to the U.S. Navy*. Denver, CO: Center for Research and Education.
Tung, R. L. 1981. Selection and training of personnel for overseas assignments. *Columbia Journal of World Business*, 16:68–78.
_____. 1987. Expatriate assignments: Enhancing success and minimizing failure. *Academy of Management Executive*, 1:117–126.
Turner, H. W. 1985. Yavatmal College for leadership training. *Missiology: An International Review*, 13:111–112.
Turner, S. 1980. *Sociological explanations as translations*. New York: Cambridge University Press.
Tylor, E. B. 1958. *Primitive culture*. New York: Harper Torchbooks. Original work published 1871)
Uehara, A. 1986. The nature of American student reentry adjustment and perceptions of the sojourn experience. *International Journal of Intercultural Relations*, 10:415–438.
U.S.A. Research, Incorporated, Staff. (1984). *A Nation at Risk*. Report of the National Commission on Excellence in Education. Portland, OR: U.S.A. Research.
U.S. Department of Commerce, Bureau of the Census. 1987. *Current Population Reports*. (Series P-20). Washington, DC: U.S. Government Printing Office.
U.S. Department of Commerce, Bureau of the Census. 1990. *Statistical Abstract of the United States*. 110th Ed. Washington, DC: U.S. Government Printing Office.
Useem, J., Useem, R., and Donoghue, J. 1963. Men in the middle of the third-culture. *Human Organization*, 22:169–179.

Verstraelen, F. J. 1985. World and mission: Towards a common missiology. *Mission Studies*, 2:34–47.
Vohra, S., Rodolfa, E., De La Cruz, A., Vincent, C., and Bee-Gates, D. 1991. A cross-cultural training format for peer counselors. *Journal of College Student Development*, 3:82–84.
Volard, S. V., Francis, D. M., and Wagner, F. W. III. 1988. Underperforming U.S. expatriate managers: A study of problems and solutions. *Practising Manager*, 9:37–40.
Wagel, W. H. 1990. On the horizon: HR [Human Resources] in the 1990s. *Personnel*, 67:10–16.
Wagner, R. F., and Lutz, C. P. 1985. Planting the church in an alien culture: How can Lutheran identity be maintained? In *Church roots: Stories of nine immigrant groups that became the American Lutheran Church*, edited by C. P. Lutz, 82–100, Minneapolis, MN: Augsburg Publishing House.
Wainwright, L. 1987. The unending nightmare of racism. *Life*, 10:13.
Wallace, G. 1980. *Training for international development: A summary of faculty and foreign student interviews*. Washington, D.C.: Agency for International Development. (ERIC Document Reproduction Service ED 206 428).
Walls, A. F. 1981. "The best thinking of the best heathen": Humane learning and the missionary movement. In *Religion and humanism*, edited by K. Robbins, 341–354. Oxford, England: Basil Blackwell.
Walsh, J. 1973. *Intercultural education in the community of man*. Honolulu: University of Hawaii Press.
Waltman, J. L. 1987. *Culture shock as a barrier to intercultural business communication*. Conference Proceedings of the Languages and Communication for World Business and the Professions. (ERIC Document Reproduction Service No. ED 293 365).
Wapner, S. 1981. Transactions of persons-in-environments: Some critical transitions. *Journal of Environmental Psychology*, 1:223–239.
Ward, T. 1987. Educational preparation of missionaries—A look ahead. *Evangelical Mission Quarterly*, 22:398–404.
Warner, T. M. 1986. Teaching power encounter. *Evangelical Missions Quarterly*, 22:66–71.
Warren, R. P. 1950. *World enough and time*. New York: Random House.
Warwick, D. P. 1980. The politics and ethics of cross-cultural research. In *Handbook of cross-cultural psychology perspectives, Vol. 1*, edited by H. C. Triandis and W. W. Lambert, 319–371. Boston: Allyn and Bacon.
Wax, R. A. 1976. Oglala Sioux dropouts and their problems with educators. In *Schooling in the cultural context: Anthropological studies in education*, edited by J. I. Roberts and S. K. Akinsanya, 216–226. New York: David McKay.
Webb, J. R. 1989. Planning ministry in a j-curve generation. In *Christian relief and development: Developing workers for effective ministry*, edited by E. J. Elliston, 37–48. Dallas, TX: Word Publishing.
Weber, W. A. 1975. Program conceptualization and design. In *Programmatic issues in teacher education: The Texas Teacher Corps experience*, edited by R. D. Olivarez, 1–12. Washington, DC: Office of Education. (ERIC Document Reproduction Service ED 186 392).

Weeks, W., Pedersen, P. B., and Brislin, R. W. 1977. *A manual of structured experiences for cross-cultural learning.* Washington, DC: Society for Intercultural Education, Training, and Research.

Weick, K. E. 1979. *The social psychology of organizing.* Reading, MA: Addison-Wesley.

Weissman, D., and Furnham, D. 1987. The expectations and experiences of a sojourning temporary resident abroad: A preliminary study. *Human Relations,* 40:313-326.

Wendt, J. R. 1984. DIE [Description, Interpretation, Evaluation]: A way to improve communication. *Communication Education,* 33:397-401.

Westwood, M. J., and Borgen, W. A. 1988. A culturally embedded model for effective intercultural education. *International Journal for the Advancement of Counseling,* 11:115-125.

Westwood, M. J., Lawrence, W. S., and Paul, D. Preparing for re-entry: A program for the sojourning student. *International Journal for the Advancement of Counseling,* 9:221-230.

Wexley, K. N. 1984. Personnel training. *Annual Review of Psychology,* 35: 519-551.

Weyler, R. 1992. *Blood of the land: The government and corporate war against first nations.* Philadelphia, PA: New Society Publishers.

Wigglesworth, D. C. 1983. When 'yes' means 'no': The importance of perception in cross-cultural training. *Training and Development Journal,* 37:58-59.

Wight, A. R. 1970. *Experiential cross-cultural training.* Estes Park, CO: Center for Research and Education.

Wight, A. R., and Hammons, M. A. 1970. *Guidelines for Peace Corps cross-cultural training: Office of training support, Peace Corps. Washington, D.C.: No. PC-25-1710.* Estes Park, CO: Center for Research and Education.

Wiley, J. 1987. The "shock of unrecognition" as a problem in participant-observation. *Qualitative Sociology,* 10:78-83.

Wiley, N. 1967. The ethnic mobility trap and stratification theory. *Social Problems,* 12:147-59.

Williams, S. 1981. *The cultural training semester: A model field-based program in multicultural education for non-urban universities.* Paper presented at the Annual Conference on Minority Studies, Las Cruces, NM, April. (ERIC Document Reproduction Service ED 204 039).

Wilson, A. H. 1983. Cross-cultural experiential learning for teachers. *Theory into Practice,* 21:184-191.

Wilson, W. J. 1978. *The declining significance of race: Blacks and changing American institutions.* Chicago: University of Chicago Press.

Wilson, L., and Green, J. W. 1983. An experiential approach to cultural awareness in child welfare. *Child Welfare,* 62:303-311.

Wilson, T. C. 1985. Urbanism and tolerance: A test of some hypotheses drawn from Wirth and Stouffer. *American Sociological Review,* 50:117-123.

Winter, R. 1984. Four frontiers in missiology. *Evangelical Missions Quarterly,* 20:400-402.

Wirth, L. 1945. The problem of minority groups. In *The science of man in the world crisis,* edited by R. Linton, 347-72. New York: Columbia University Press.

Wolcott, H. F. 1987. The anthropology of learning. In *Education and cultural process: Anthropological approaches,* edited by G.D. Spindler, 26-52. Prospect Heights, IL: Waveland Press, Inc.

Wong-Rieger, D. 1984. Testing a model of emotional and coping responses to problems in adaptation: Foreign students at a Canadian university. *International Journal of Intercultural Relations*, 8:153–184.

Wortman, C. B. 1984. Social support and the cancer patient: Conceptual and methodological issues. *Cancer*, 53:2339–2360.

Wright, W. J. 1992. The endangered black male child. *Educational Leadership*, 49:14–16.

Yao, E. L. 1985. *Implementation of multicultural education in Texas public schools*. Paper presented at the Annual Meeting of the American Educational Research Association, Chicago, March 31–April 4. (ERIC Document Reproduction Service ED 264 99).

Yinger, J.M. 1976. Ethnicity in complex societies. In *The uses of controversy in sociology*, edited by L.A. Coser and O.N. Larsen, 197–216. New York: Free Press.

York, D. E. 1992. *Cross-cultural training for teachers and the culturally diverse urban school: Evidence from an ethnographic case study*. In press.

———. 1993. *Fragile bonds: An ethnographic study of a white female teacher assaulted in a culturally diverse urban school*. Manuscript submitted for publication.

Yoshikawa, M. J. 1988. Cross-cultural adaptation and perceptual development. In *Cross-cultural adaptation: Current approaches*, edited by Y. Y. Kim and W. B. Gudykunst, 140–148. Newbury Park, CA: Sage Publications.

Zimbardo, P. G. 1969. The human choice: individuation, reason, and order versus deindividuation, impulse, and chaos. *Nebraska Symposium on Motivation*, 17:237–307.

Zuckerman, M. 1978. Sensation-seeking and psychopathology. In *Psychopathic behaviour*, edited by R. Hare and D. Schalling, 217–234. New York: Wiley.

Zurcher, L. A. 1977. *The mutable self: a concept for social change*. Beverly Hills, CA: Sage Publications.

INDEX

Acculturation process, 28
Adaptation, cultural; models of, 34
Adjustment indicators, 68
Adler, Mortimer, 34, 51, 53–54, 61, 123, 134
Age of candidates for cross-cultural work, 118–119
Alien Presence Model, 94–95, 104
Alienation, Deviance, Assimilation (ADA) model, 44
American Field Service (AFS), 108
Assimilation: defined, 16; difference in training, 72; theories of, 14–15
Attribution cross-cultural training, 102, 103
Awareness cross-cultural. *See* Cultural awareness training

Banks, James, 8, 16, 23, 33–34, 62–64, 66, 87, 106, 114–17
Bay Area Bilingual Education League (BABEL), 87, 126–127
Befus, Christine, 47–48, 54
Berman, Judith, 7, 83–84, 87, 116, 123–124, 135
"Blackouts," 89
Bochner, Stephen, 22–23, 27, 31, 33–34, 36, 39, 46, 54, 71, 122
Bogardus Social Distance Scale, 36; Law and Lane study, 5, 135

Brislin, Richard, 23, 29, 44–45, 63, 65–67, 71–72, 95, 97, 102, 104, 115
"Brownouts," 89

Candidates: characteristics of, 65, 118–19; personality traits, 65–66, 82, 109–110, 122; selection, 64–65; 81–82, 91, 107–112
Cardozo Project, 82
Changes in culture, 72
Cognitive-behavioral cross-cultural training, 102, 104-105
Cognitive dissonance, 43
Collusion theory, 43
Commercial shock, 46
Componential analysis, 28
Consultants, cross-cultural. *See also* Trainers, cross-cultural
Contact hypothesis, 39–42; Allport's conditions of contact, 40; Amir's conditions of contact, 41–42, Cook's conditions of contact, 40–41; criticism of, 42
Contrast American training, 104
Cross-cultural contact: consequences of, 33–35, theories of, 31
Cross-cultural training: of expats, 88–93 (*see also* Expat training); goals of, 63–64; of medical/mental health workers, 96–99 (*see also* Medical/

mental health workers); of military personnel, 93–96 (*see also* Military personnel cross-cultural training); of missionaries, 72–80 (*see also* Missionary training); outcomes of, 124–129; of Peace Corps volunteers, 80–82 (*see also* Peace Corps); philosophical basis of, 71–72; political dimensions of, 124–125; similarities of domestic and international, 22–24; stages of, 59–61; of Teachers Corps, 82–84 (*see also* Teacher Corps); of teachers, 85–89 (*see also* Teacher training, cross-cultural). *See also* Training programs, cross-cultural
Cultural adjustment models, 52–54
Cultural assimilator, 103. *See also* Attribution cross-cultural training
Cultural awareness training, 102, 104
Cultural change, ethics of, 62–63, 132–133
Cultural comparison, 32
Cultural myths in the workplace, 138–139
Cultural relativism, 27–28
Cultural universals, 32
Culture: defined, 29–30; as research construct, 30
Culture encapsulation, 51
Culture fatigue, 46
Culture shock: among extroverts, 49–50; among married people, 50; among students, 49; defined, 45; remedies, 53–55; symptoms, 46–47, 119
Culture theory, 26–27; of Boas, 27; of Tylor, 26

Deculturalization, 43
Demographics, matching organization to population, 92–93
Diplomatic Corps training, 57–58

Ethnic conflict: Marxist theory, 17; oppositional social identity, 19; outcome of modernization, 18; psychoanalytic theory, 18; psychological theory, 19; social psychology phenomena, 18; split-labor market theory, 18

Ethnic groups, characteristics of, 15
Ethnology, qualitative: characteristics, xiv–xv; defined, xiii; types of, xv
Expat training, 89–93, 105; amount of training, 89–90, 113, 119; comparison to other cross-cultural workers, 93; cost of untrained employees, 90; defined, 89; effects of expat assignment, 90, 114; level of foreign competition, 89; models of company response, 93
Experiential cross-cultural training, 103, 105–106

Failure rates: costs of failure, 10; among cross-cultural workers, 10; of missionaries, 74
Field training, 105–107, 117–118

Glazer, Nathan, 7–8, 14, 32, 60
Goals of cross-cultural training, 63–64
"Godfather," 92, 93
Goodlad, John, 133–134
Grant, Carl, 66, 83, 85, 116, 125
"Guardian angel," 92, 93
Gudykunst, William, 44, 68, 95, 102, 123, 128

Hall, Edward, 10, 32, 92, 98, 112, 128
Hatch, Elwin, 26–29
Hilliard, Asa, 62–63, 110
Holmes Group, 64, 135
Host environment, importance of, 121–123

Immigration, rates and countries of origin, 6
Information-oriented cross-cultural training, 102, 103, 116–117
Ingroup/outgroup distinctions, 22–23, 108
Interactive cross-cultural training, 103, 105
Intercultural communication, 43–44
International Executive Service Corps (IESC), 119
Interpretivist paradigm: defined, xiv; findings, xv
Involuntary immigrant groups, 14
Irvine, Jacqueline, 5, 27, 124

Index

J-curve model of cultural adjustment, 52
Jenkins, Mercilee, 87, 105, 114

Kahl's Achievement Orientation Scale, 35
Kamehameha Early Education Program (KEEP), 85, 113
Klineberg, Otto, 22, 25, 27, 31, 42, 112
Knowledge-based training. *See* Information-oriented cross-cultural training

Landis, Daniel, 44, 71–72, 102
Langer 22 Mental Health Index, 35
Language diversity, 7–8
Language shock, 46
Language training, 66
Learned helplessness, 48
LeCompte, Margaret, 10, 61, 102, 136
Length of training, 115–116
Lines-of-argument synthesis, xv
Location of training, 116–118

Mahan, James, 88, 106, 113–14, 117, 122, 126–27
Marginalization, 21
Medical/mental health workers, 96–99; changes in personal style of service provider, 97; comparison to other cross-cultural workers, 99; evaluating training results, 98–99, 128; peer counselors in higher education, 99; types of programs, 96–97; unintended outcomes of training, 98
Methods of training, 102–107; attribution training, 102, 103; cognitive-behavioral training, 102, 104–105; cultural awareness training, 102, 104; experiential training, 103, 105–106; information-oriented training, 102, 103; interactive training, 103, 105; mixed methods, 106
Militancy, 16
Military personnel cross-cultural training, 93–96; Alien Presence Model, 94–95; comparison to other cross-cultural workers, 96; history of training, 93–94; political aspects of training, 94, 115–116; results of training, 95, 115–116, 128

Miller's Scale Battery of International Patterns and Norms, 35
Minority groups, responses of dominant groups, 16
Minority leadership rates: in business, 9; in military, 9; in scholarship, 8; in sports, 3; in teaching, 8–9
Minority Mentorship Program (MMP), 88, 124–25
Minority population, growth of, 5–6
Minority sector, as sociological phenomena, 15–16
Missionary training, 72–80; demographic characteristics, 74; history of, 72–73, 117; medical missions, 73; seminary training, 73–74
Mixed methods of training. *See* Methods of training

Neal and Seeman's Powerless Scale, 35

Ogbu, John, 14, 19, 21, 31, 42–43
Oppositional social identity, 43
Organizational change: credentials, 137; employee participation, 137–138; initial steps, 139–140; links to professional organizations, 137; task orientation, 136; types of change, 141–142; work perspectives, 137
Outcomes of training, differences between blacks and whites, 98, 108

Peace Corps, 80–82; description of training, 81, 116–117, 118; evaluation of training, 124; inception, 59
Pluralism, 16
Police force with minorities, 2
Professors, as cross-cultural trainers, 119–121
Psychosocial shock, 46

Racial violence: at educational institutions, 4; police force, 2; street incidents, 3
Ravitch, Diane, 62–63, 133
Reciprocal translation synthesis, xv
Refutational synthesis, xv
Re-entry: shock, 50–51, 123; styles of response, 123

Remigration, 50
Research criteria for included studies, xvi
Reusswig, James, 7, 87, 126
Reverse culture shock, 50
Risk, professional, 114
Role shock, 46
Roman Catholic church missionaries, 79–80

Secession, cultural, 16
Selection of candidates to match host environment, 122
Selective diffusion, 28
Self-awareness training. See Cultural awareness training
Self-discovery shock, 46
Self-selection for cross-cultural work, 111
Shock, culture. See Culture shock
Short Term Abroad (STA), 75–76
Simulation games, cultural, 105
Situational variables. See Host environment
Sleeter, Christine, 87, 104, 114, 127, 135, 140
Social/family support for cross-cultural workers, 65, 91, 108–109, 122
Society for Intercultural Education, Training, and Research (SIETAR), 119
Sociometry Scales of Spontaneous Choice and Sociometric Preference, 36
Southern Baptist Conference missionaries, 78
Stages of cross-cultural training: adaptation, 59; interactional etiquette, 60–61; technology transfer, 59
Stephan, Walter, 8–9, 40–41, 85
Stereotypes. See Cultural myths in the workplace
Stranger status, 22
Street violence and minorities, 3

Teacher Corps, 82–84; Corps Members Training Institute (CMTI), 83; differences with Peace Corps, 84; effects of training, 83–84, 122, 125; goals of, 83, 84; inception, 82; internal difficulties, 84
Teacher training cross-cultural, 85–89; differences with other cross-cultural programs, 88–89; history of, 132–136; Kamehameha Early Education Program (KEEP), 85; Minority Membership Program (MMP), 88, 124; outcomes of training, 124–127, 135–136; state and local programs, 85–86, 114, 117–118; university-designed programs, 86–88
Trainers, cross-cultural, 119–121
Training methods, mixed, 95
Training programs, cross-cultural: content of, 66; core characteristics, 66–67; developmental model, 67; evaluation of, 67, 82, 124–125; goals of, 115–116; length of training, 113; location of training, 116–118; stages of training, 140–141; unintended outcomes, 68–69, 98, 104, 108, 120, 124. See also Cross-cultural training
Triandis, Harry, 32, 44–45, 66, 102–3
Transition shock, 46

U-curve of cultural adjustment, 52
Unintended outcomes of training, 68–69, 98, 104, 108, 120, 124

Violence in cross-cultural environments, 114
Volunteering to work in cross-cultural environments: medical/mental health professionals, 97; missionaries, 72–80; Peace Corps, 80–82; Teacher Corps, 82–84

W-curve model of cultural adjustment, 52
Workforce, demographic changes in, 6–7
Work responsibilities for cross-cultural employees, 91–92

York, Darlene, 2, 114, 117, 124; SALAMANDER model 142–144

About the Author

DARLENE ELEANOR YORK is currently a Visiting Assistant Professor at Emory University in Atlanta. She has taught at the University of Georgia and at Agnes Scott College. She is the author of several articles in professional journals and in periodicals. Dr. York speaks at conferences nationwide and is a consultant in cross-cultural training programs.

ISBN 0-89789-375-1

HARDCOVER BAR CODE